Effects of Globalization on 1 Development

THE WORLD COUNCIL OF COMPARATIVE EDUCATION SOCIETIES

Series Editors:

Suzanne Majhanovich, *University of Western Ontario, Canada*
Allan Pitman, *University of Western Ontario, Canada*

Scope:

The WCCES is an international organization of comparative education societies worldwide and is an NGO in consultative partnership with UNESCO. The WCCES was created in 1970 to advance the field of comparative education. Members usually meet every three years for a World Congress in which scholars, researchers, and administrators interact with colleagues and counterparts from around the globe on international issues of education.

The WCCES also promotes research in various countries. Foci include theory and methods in comparative education, gender discourses in education, teacher education, education for peace and justice, education in post-conflict countries, language of instruction issues, Education for All. Such topics are usually represented in thematic groups organized for the World Congresses. Besides organizing the World Congresses, the WCCES has a section in CERCular, the newsletter of the Comparative Education Research Centre at the University of Hong Kong, to keep individual societies and their members abreast of activities around the world.

The WCCES comprehensive website is http://www.wcces.com

As a result of these efforts under the auspices of the global organization, WCCES and its member societies have become better organized and identified in terms of research and other scholarly activities. They are also more effective in viewing problems and applying skills from different perspectives, and in disseminating information. A major objective is advancement of education for international understanding in the interests of peace, intercultural cooperation, observance of human rights and mutual respect among peoples.

The WCCES Series was established to provide for the broader dissemination of discourses between scholars in its member societies. Representing as it does Societies and their members from all continents, the organization provides a special forum for the discussion of issues of interest and concern among comparativists and those working in international education. The first series of volumes was produced from the proceedings of the World Council of Comparative Education Societies XIII World Congress, which met in Sarajevo, Bosnia and Herzegovina, 3–7 September, 2007 with the theme of Living Together: Education and Intercultural Dialogue.

The first series included the following titles:

Volume 1: Tatto, M. & Mincu, M. (Eds.), Reforming Teaching and Learning
Volume 2: Geo-JaJa, M. A. & Majhanovich, S. (Eds.), Education, Language and Economics: Growing National and Global Dilemmas
Volume 3: Pampanini, G., Adly, F. & Napier, D. (Eds.), Interculturalism, Society and Education
Volume 4: Masemann, V., Majhanovich, S., Truong, N., & Janigan, K. (Eds.), A Tribute to David N. Wilson: Clamoring for a Better World

The second series of volumes has been developed from the proceedings of the World Council of Comparative Education Societies XIV World Congress, which met in Istanbul, Turkey, 14–18 June, 2010 with the theme of Bordering, Re-Bordering and new Possibilities in Education and Society. This series includes the following titles:

Volume 1: Napier, D.B. & Majhanovich, S. (Eds.) Education, Dominance and Identity
Volume 2: Biseth, H. & Holmarsdottir, H. (Eds.) Human Rights in the Field of Comparative Education
Volume 3: Ginsburg, M. (Ed.) Preparation, Practice & and Politics of Teachers
Volume 4: Majhanovich, S. & Geo-JaJa, M.A. (Eds.) Economics, Aid and Education
Volume 5: Napier, D. B. (Ed.), Qualities of Education in a Globalised World

The third series of volumes has been developed from the proceedings of the World Council of Comparative Education Societies XV World Congress which met in Buenos Aires, Argentina, June 24-28, 2013 with the theme of New Times, New Voices. This series includes the volumes listed below:

Volume 1: Gross, Z. & Davies L. (Eds.) The Contested Role of Education in Conflict and Fragility
Volume 2: DePalma, R., Brook Napier, D. & Dze Ngwa, W. (Eds.) Revitalizing Minority Voices: Language Issues in the New Millennium
Volume 3: Majhanovich, S. & Malet, R. (Eds.) Building Democracy through Education on Diversity
Volume 4: Olson, J., Biseth, H. & Ruiz, G. (Eds.) Educational Internationalisation: Academic Voices and Public Policy
Volume 5: Astiz, M. F. & Akiba, M. (Eds.) The Global and the Local: Diverse Perspectives in Comparative Education
Volume 6: Geo-JaJa, M. A. & Majhanovich, S. (Eds.) Effects of Globalization on Education Systems and Development: Debates and Issues
Volume 7: Acosta, F. & Nogueira, S. (Eds.) Rethinking Public Education Systems in the 21st Century Scenario: New and Renovated Challenges, New and Renovated Policies and Practices

Effects of Globalization on Education Systems and Development

Debates and Issues

Edited by

MacLeans A. Geo-JaJa
Brigham Young University, USA

and

Suzanne Majhanovich
University of Western Ontario, Canada

SENSE PUBLISHERS
ROTTERDAM/BOSTON/TAIPEI

A C.I.P. record for this book is available from the Library of Congress.

ISBN: 978-94-6300-727-6 (paperback)
ISBN: 978-94-6300-728-3 (hardback)
ISBN: 978-94-6300-729-0 (e-book)

Published by: Sense Publishers,
P.O. Box 21858,
3001 AW Rotterdam,
The Netherlands
https://www.sensepublishers.com/

All chapters in this book have undergone peer review.

Cover image by Navjot Kaur

Printed on acid-free paper

All Rights Reserved © 2016 Sense Publishers

No part of this work may be reproduced, stored in a retrieval system, or transmitted in any form or by any means, electronic, mechanical, photocopying, microfilming, recording or otherwise, without written permission from the Publisher, with the exception of any material supplied specifically for the purpose of being entered and executed on a computer system, for exclusive use by the purchaser of the work.

TABLE OF CONTENTS

Introduction: Educational Development and Education Systems in a Globalized World ... ix
   Suzanne Majhanovich

Part I: Issues of Development in a Globalized World

1. From Right to Education to Rights in Education: A Dialogical Roadmap for Autonomy Development ... 3
   Xinyi Wu and Macleans A. Geo-JaJa

2. Employment, Democratic Citizenship and Education: Considering Alternatives to Commodification in South Africa ... 23
   Salim Vally and Enver Motala

3. The Problem of Underdevelopment and Perspectives on Transformative Development: The Case of Pakistan ... 37
   Nazia Bano

4. Policy Transfer for Educational Development: Complex Processes of Borrowing and Lending in Brazil and the Philippines ... 59
   Xavier Rambla

Part II: The Problematic Effects of Globalization on Education

5. How Higher Education Systems in Asia-Pacific Respond to the Challenges Posed by Globalization ... 79
   Nicholas Sun-Keung Pang

6. The Tortuous Path of Educational Decentralization in Mexico ... 93
   Carlos Ornelas

7. Privatization and Marketing of Higher Education in Mexico: Contributions to a Debate ... 109
   Angélica Buendía Espinosa

8. Education, Knowledge and the Righting of Wrongs ... 131
   Vanessa de Oliveira Andreotti

List of Contributors ... 143

SUZANNE MAJHANOVICH

INTRODUCTION

*Educational Development and Education Systems
in a Globalized World*

Globalization has had a profound effect on education systems worldwide. The developing world in particular which looks to the education of its youth as the pathway to prosperity and development has experienced both benefits and disadvantages in the internationalization of education brought about by modern globalization. As Altbach and Knight define globalization, it involves "the economic, political, and societal forces pushing 21st century higher education toward greater international involvement". They also note that, "globalization may be unalterable, but internationalization involves many choices" (2007, pp. 290–291). In the long-term, it might contribute to the expansion of educational development but demonstrably leads to unwittingly undermining education's impact on development of manpower, by-passing and overlooking human rights in education and the idea of development with security. This is central to the post-2015 education and development agenda. In this volume educational policy changes in aid-recipient countries are explored as well as and education choices and frameworks for better understanding of the agenda-setting processes that have evolved under globalization. The authors question the motivation of reforms in post-colonial states arguing that progress (or the lack thereof) in schools cannot be divorced from the burden of human capital theory's non-conceptualization of human rights in education. This means that education aid from international agencies has in fact hampered the ability of nations to constructively serve the economic, social and political project of nation building.

Tsui and Tollefson (2006) have pointed out how globalization entails interconnectivity, information transmission and the construct of national identity that is starkly different from that which existed before globalization. The speed of knowledge transmission through information technology and the facility of setting up higher education courses through e-learning with curricula based on Western/Northern models can benefit countries of the developing South but can also lead to growing disparity and inequality. When developing nations enter into agreements with bilateral and multilateral organizations for the provision of educational services citizens become subject to the high cost of education in order to gain access to the "quality" education they need in the hopes of stimulating economic development in their impoverished countries. In short as noted by Altbach and Knight (2007), "globalization, creating a new kind of poverty trap, tends to concentrate wealth, knowledge and power in those already possessing these elements" (p. 291). Bourdieu (2001) warned of the hegemonic aspects of globalization when he noted:

> "Globalization" serves as a password, a watchword while in effect, it is the legitimatory mask of a policy aiming to universalize particular interests, and the particular tradition of the economically and politically dominant powers, above all the United States, and to extend to the entire world the economic and cultural model that favours these powers most, while simultaneously presenting it as a norm, a requirement. (p. 84)

As I have mentioned before (Majhanovich, 2013), the dominant powers do not necessarily represent the government of the US *per se*, but rather the power represented by transnational corporations, and by organizations such as the World Bank, the International Monetary Fund and the World Trade Organization that promote neoliberal initiatives under a discourse of market fundamentalism espousing limited government involvement, privatization, deregulation and decentralization (Majhanovich, 2013, p. 81). This approach to education in limiting access denies people the opportunity to participate fully and meaningfully in economic, social and political change. The devastation of educational systems in developing nations as a result of neoliberalism was noted by UNESCO (2014). Despite the importance of political and cultural factors in globalization, it would seem that economic considerations ought to be the focus in any discussion of the phenomenon. One cannot avoid mentioning market forces, the influence of international corporations and financial institutions when trying to gauge the effects of globalization (see Capella, 2000; Carnoy, 1999; Morrow & Torres, 2000; among many others on definitions of globalization).

When we study implications of education and development, some of the issues that need to be considered include, according to Lewin (1994), recession, debt and structural adjustment (see also Abdi, 2012; Majhanovich, 2013; Geo-JaJa & Mangum, 2001) population growth and demographic change, urbanisation, displaced populations and refugees, scientific and technological change, the education of girls and women, among others. Other important factors include human rights, enlarging people's choices, and right to development (Geo-JaJa, 2016; Ellerman, 2009; Sen, 1999); human development and human capability. Although development is something nations and societies strive for, it cannot be seen as a universal "good" as right to development must receive high priority in any approach. Implications and negative effects must be recognized, studied and countered if we are to see a more socially just world with less inequality and disparity. For instance, scholars have cautioned that new reforms have alienated and/or divided large segments of the population of aid-recipient countries despite the desire for education aid to result in a more inclusive and global-localized education system (see Babaci-Wilhite et al., 2012; Ki-Zerbo et al., 2006).

INTRODUCTION

The chapters in this volume represent a series of case studies and reflective essays that address issues of development in a globalized world on the one hand and problematic effects of globalization on education systems on the other. Several of the chapters have been developed from presentations given at the XV World Congress of Comparative Education Societies with the overriding theme of "New Times, New Voices" which took place in Buenos Aires in June of 2013. The topic of development and higher education was addressed in several of the twelve thematic groups of the Congress but for this volume we have drawn mainly on papers from the group on internationalization as well as on presentations from the group dealing with voices from the south. Other chapters represent research carried out subsequent to the congress or papers that were proposed for the congress but which were not presented because the authors were unable to attend. In all we have attempted to bring together a coherent set of chapters that shed new light on education, economics, and globalization, issues so important for comparative education in our globalized world.

The first four chapters address various concerns about development. Xinyi Wu and Macleans A. Geo-JaJa in their chapter "From Right to Education to Rights in Education: A Dialogical Roadmap for Autonomy Development" argue that too often we have felt that ensuring the right to education to children around the world, that is seeing that they have access to schooling, is enough. In fact, simple right to education in the African context has often resulted in children attending classes with a curriculum that is alien to their reality and compromises their functionality in society and that inculcate the values of the developed north. Inferred, also is that the education they receive creates a new kind of poverty trap, when graduates remain either unemployed or cannot find meaningful work in local labor markets. They also experience devaluation of the local culture that is so important to the identity of the people. They contend that were rights in education to be part of the education program, students would learn about "human rights, social justice, citizenship, diversity, values and perceptions, teamwork, learning in a global context that support wider social equity and sustainable development." They note that the provision of development aid is a complex issue that will not always benefit the recipients since aid is not usually given without conditions and the donors expect to get something in return for their "generosity". When aid involves educational programs, it usually will involve reforms or conditionalities such as the sale to the recipient country of materials that have been developed in the North and which may have little relevance in the local context., The result is education and capability poverty, that is, deprivation of opportunities, choice and entitlement for the students (see also Freire, 1973; United Nations, 2005). They do not see development aid as an uncomplicated benefit as it can lead to dependency of the recipients whereas, they argue that autonomy of the recipients should be the goal and that any aid given should be sustainable so that everything will not just collapse after the project funded from the West or North has terminated. Essentially they see that development aid has typically been provided under the approach of neoliberalism that puts the market foremost to the detriment of local needs and people. They provide the example of China's approach to development aid in Africa where rather than top down provision of aid, the development of mutual benefit in partnerships is seen as the goal. In this model, the goal is to "promote the achievement of independent development while avoiding interfering with recipient countries' internal domestic politics". To conclude, they put forward the notion that in future rights in education should be taken into account in donor development aid to include collaboration and empowerment of the recipients in a way that will actually promote local capacities and significantly influence education and reduce capability poverty.

The second chapter in this section, "Employment, Democratic Citizenship and Education: Considering Alternatives to Commodification in South Africa" by Salim Vally and Enver Motala complements the first chapter in its call for alternative approaches to education, work and democratic citizenship from the usual rhetoric linking education to economic growth and employment which has resulted in marginalization of so many, particularly those in remote, rural areas.

The authors echo Bourdieu's (2001) warning about how current manifestations of globalization which favour those with existing power and exploit the disadvantaged are presented as the norm with no possible alternatives. Moreover, they argue that development of forms of work based on capitalist labour markets have also been seen as the only possibility whereas they maintain that the knowledge and skills gained from education cannot be viewed instrumentally only, but should entail traditions of praxis based on social justice and democratic citizenship. They question current conceptions of "relevant work" noting that those not engaged in work defined in a particular way, may be denied the benefits of citizenship even though their activities are needed to sustain communities. As alternatives to paid jobs contributing to building the economy, they list promising endeavours referred to as "livelihoods at the margins" such as "small 'independent' and self-sustaining initiatives which relate to household and communities developing autonomous ... economies ... likely to be driven by women in communities characterised by absent-men seeking employment in the formal economy". The advantage of these alternative forms of work according to Vally and Motala is that they produce goods that are needed and useful and contribute to sustaining the community, although the alternative initiatives are largely independent of conventional market mechanisms. Included in their alternative valued forms of labour are community service jobs in health and education, childcare and care of the aged as well as infrastructure construction. They underline the enhanced role of education to move beyond merely preparing workers for the global workplace as presumed by human capital theory scholars, but rather extol an education that is, as proposed by Freire (1973), emancipatory with critical attention paid to the actual nature of the workplace and where students will not be afraid to question the power hierarchy. They remind us how important it is to embrace alternative approaches found in progressive education such as adult and lifelong, non-formal and participatory learning, and imagine forms of livelihood outside current market conceptions to counter the neoliberal influence in defining social, political, cultural, environmental, and educational systems. They also call for further research "to examine the form, content, methodologies, and praxis related to the idea of socially useful work as intrinsic to the relationship between education and training, work and society". The transformative possibilities of such a conception of alternative education and work can only lead to a more socially just and equitable society. Indeed, the recognition of education as a public good argues strongly that markets do not play a strong role in equity and social justice considerations.

The third chapter in this section echoes the call of the other two for an alternative approach to development to meet the real needs of local populations. In "The Problem of Underdevelopment and Perspectives on Transformative Development: The Case of Pakistan", Nazia Bano presents a convincing case study of possibilities of transformative development in a traditional community in Baluchistan, Pakistan. As the authors of the first two chapters pointed out, Bano notes that the kind of development aid based on Northern values and expectations that Baluchistan has received in the past has not translated into any positive development. On the contrary, Pakistan's rank in the Human Development Index, particularly in the rural, traditional areas has declined in recent years, and they have been unable to meet the right to education goals in primary education as dropout rates have risen. Moreover, many of the youths have become radicalized, and victims of the fundamentalist ideology. Clearly, an alternative is needed in the provision of education aid.

Bano details the work of a local NGO, the Institute for Development Studies and Practices (IDSP) and its starkly different approach to development tailored to the needs of the local Baluchistan population. The IDSP is very critical of mainstream Western concepts of development as being: limited, sold as universal truths when they clearly are not; irrelevant to the local context and inapplicable to Pakistani rural communities; imposed in a top-down manner without consultation with the people they propose to assist; and insufficient, promoting only symbolic, not concrete aspects of development. As Vally and Motala contended in their chapter, development education must go beyond the instrumental to prepare critically conscious citizens. In the IDSP "development" entails intellectual development, humanist values, and development relevant to local needs, context, agenda and priorities. IDSP stakeholders were critical of development projects that ignored the local context by forcing communities to purchase equipment from the West or from Islamabad, the capital city of Pakistan rather than using local resources. Such projects that ignored the local context tended to actually destabilize the local economy rather than assisting it to develop. The courses offered by the IDSP in their Academic Development Program (ADP) include components to promote self-development, professional development and institution building with the goal that learners will exit the program with the goal of planning for others in their family, community or the marginalized groups in the community.

Some outcomes that graduates tried to introduce to their community once they returned home included efforts to ensure gender balance in the family and at work, being prepared to object to exploitation and oppression, and resisting nepotism and

xiii

corruption. This type of emancipatory action was carried out at the micro level (or personal level) and graduates reported considerable success in making these small changes that would help their traditional society become more tolerant and inclusive. At the meso level stakeholders reported on educational initiatives they had undertaken including a non-formal education project for out-of-school children; development of new education policies; development of a textbook for out-of-school children among others. Although not all of these changes were sustainable, the important part was that they targeted children, youth and women who had either never attended school or had withdrawn before completion; they tried non-traditional teaching approaches suitable to the context in which they were working and tried to make the teaching relevant to the reality of the students. Their approach constituted more of a grassroots initiative based on the needs of the region after consultation with them rather than the more typical top-down imposed development where Western curriculum and approaches are used, often with little success. An interesting initiative involved the revival of traditional practices in which the stakeholders undertook the rehabilitation of a traditional underground water management system called Karazes. The former IDSP student with a local team cleaned the wells of the Karazes with the result that in an area that had been suffering drought for many years was once again able to access flowing water to irrigate their crops and provide drinking water for local people. Another project used a traditional mud-construction method to construct buildings in the Community Development University. These two projects used local resources, knowledge and local people to carry them out rather than importing "expertise" from elsewhere, and so were deemed successes. Other projects attempted at the meso level are not operational today or are still in their infancy but, show the kind of alternative development approaches that can benefit local communities. Bano mentions two projects undertaken at the macro level involving the establishment of a College for Youth Activism and Development and a Citizen Community Board. Both of these initiatives have legal status but it is not clear whether they are still functioning. Thus Bano concludes that the program offered by the IDSP results in enlarging opportunities and positive transformation but were most effective on the personal (micro) level. Progress in the wider society has been painfully slow and fraught with opposition. Still the graduates pursue their dreams to work for social justice and improve their society.

The final chapter in this section, "Policy Transfer for Educational Development: Complex Processes of Borrowing and Lending in Brazil and the Philippines" by Xavier Rambla, looks at how the Education for All policy has played out in Brazil and the Philippines. As both countries are emergent, intermediate economies on the global landscape, they make good cases for comparison. Rambla focuses on educational policy transfer as it relates to the two countries noting that although both countries have undergone democratization in recent years, their relative standings on the Human Development Index have declined in the past decades. Interestingly, although the Philippines originally placed ahead of Brazil on the Index, in recent years, Brazil has overtaken it making more progress. Rambla notes that while Brazil has both collaborated and clashed with international agencies such as UNESCO and the World Bank in its efforts to improve its educational standards, the Philippines basically adopted educational reforms dictated by the World Bank and Asian Development Bank accepting the conditions laid down in order to benefit from the financial support of these agencies. One has to ask if this acceptance of such policies has contributed to the lower success rates in the Philippines in meeting EFA goals. Rambla's study looks for a correlation between external influences on education policy as opposed to local transformations as they played out in the two countries.

His analysis of the situation in Brazil shows that rather than depending solely on the support from agencies like the World Bank, the government has rather involved other layers of government at the federal and sub-national levels (along with international agencies) in its policy planning for educational governance. In Brazil, institutional responsibility is distributed among local, regional and Federal authorities and features elements such as cash transfers to regions conditional on school attendance which has improved school attendance. When local entities have voice and actively participate in policy making, benefits to education accrue. This compares to the message in previous chapters dealing with Africa and Pakistan that call for acknowledging the voices from the grass roots and acting on their needs to rein in the ongoing expanded control of the international community.

In the Philippines the picture is bleaker. Despite plans to improve schools, expand early childhood education, promote alternative learning systems and attend to professional development of teachers, results have not been promising with ongoing problems with early childhood education, gender disparities and lack of provision of training in life-skills evident in many areas. In trying to assess what has gone wrong, Rambla notes the influence of private corporations on school management and the evidence that economic elites enjoy access to most of the resources leaving the rest severely disadvantaged. He also comments that the Philippines has been far too willing to follow the dictates of the World Bank's belt tightening structural adjustment which impoverished countless developing nations around the world. Although the Philippines is now considered a middle-income country with fewer economic commitments to Western countries, still he questions why the Philippines would still be willing to collaborate with agencies such as the World Bank on such important issues as educational development while Brazil has not been as prepared to subject itself to World Bank policies. Could that explain the difference in progress between the two countries? In any case as Rambla remarks, with regard to EFA policies, it is obvious that perhaps countries paid too much attention to enrolment in compulsory education while overlooking possible solutions to problems of early childhood education, literacy, life-skills, gender parity and marginalization of certain minority groups. By ignoring these very real issues of education, they undermined their chances of realizing education for all. Since Brazil resisted a centralized approach to policy making, it was able to take some of the serious considerations beyond simple tabulation of enrolment into account and address some of the issues that are obvious at the local level, but easily ignored in macro policy making.

The way development aid is delivered to emerging economies and under what conditions can have an enormous effect on the education system it is meant to support. The authors of the four chapters in this section have been very critical of education development aid based on the construct of neoliberalism and the agenda of the aid-givers and international development organizations. They argue that this type of aid is imposed top down with expectations of returns for the donors and little consideration for the local context and the needs of the people in the developing countries. Typical projects organized under Western norms have poor outcomes and are often deemed irrelevant by the local country. The conditions placed upon the countries in order to receive the aid ultimately do more harm than good to the economy and education system. Hence Wu and Geo-JaJa argue that right to education as a goal of the EFA policy is not enough but that what is needed is rights in education or attention to social justice, human rights and local needs for economic development. Vally and Motala likewise decry top down approaches to education development that tend to ignore the reality of rural isolated regions and also contend that working in the global economy is not the only valid form of work but that alternative forms of work, perhaps involving volunteerism, barter and goals to develop products more in tune with the needs of the local area are preferable. They too call for education that will prepare critical thinkers aware of social justice and human rights. Bano provides a case study of the kind of projects that can really make a difference in an isolated traditional Pakistani province. The preparation for such projects also includes conscientization of the learners to make them aware of inequities in society and how to work to overcome them to create a more just but also sustainable society. Rambla in comparing how Brazil and the Philippines have fared on the Human Index after interventions of development aid concludes that Brazil has done better because in its policy planning it included all sections of government from the central governing body down to local authorities and has been at times at odds with the dictates of international aid donors such as the World Bank. The Philippines on the other hand has proven less successful in meeting EFA goals, possibly because it implemented the World Bank program which focused more on numbers of children in schools but ignored local conditions of inequality, disparity and gender equality. In other words the Philippines was concerned only with right to education but neglected the crucial issues of rights in education as Wu and Geo-JaJa expressed it. In the second part of this volume, chapters deal with the way globalization has affected educational systems with a concluding chapter on ways to "Right the Wrongs" that globalization has wrought.

The first chapter, "How Higher Education Systems in Asia-Pacific Respond to the Challenges Posed by Globalization", Nicholas Sun-keung Pang lays out the pluses and minuses of globalization with respect to the development of higher education in six areas of Asia; namely, mainland China, Hong Kong, Taiwan, South Korea, Japan, Singapore and Vietnam. In so doing he underlines just how problematic modern globalization has been in the region. Globalization has challenged traditional cultures with regard to educational governance and pushed these regions to adopt

INTRODUCTION

the neo-liberal agenda for education that entails a business oriented approach with focus on the market, competition, efficiency, managerialism and accountability.

To begin with, Pang offers a comprehensive overview of just what globalization means in the 21st Century, noting that it is not a new concept since humanity has always sought trade contacts, has shared ideas and inventions and seen migrations of people and goods. However, with the modern technological infrastructure and possibilities of instant communication worldwide, transfers can take place much more quickly. The economic features of modern globalization cannot be overlooked nor can the power and growth of transnational corporations. He cites Capling et al. (1998) who characterize modern globalization in economic terms driven by market forces of transnational corporations, international financial institutions and regional banks.

Globalization has brought massive change to education systems in Asia (and elsewhere). Countries look to higher education institutions to produce human resources and manpower that can advance their economic interests in an intensely competitive environment and be productive workers in the global marketplace. In order to situate themselves to serve the global markets, higher education institutions have undergone restructuring to make them reflect a greater business orientation. In addition a hugely profitable market in education has developed.

Pang details how in Asia higher education systems have been restructured to reflect greater influence of the market. Although the central governments still wield much influence in higher education, still there has been a move toward privatization and corporatization of public universities. Programs offered by foreign universities are welcomed. Pang regrets that under the new system the goal of universities will be less the pursuit of wisdom and truth and more crass market values. He is concerned that ethics, social justice and critical studies will fall by the wayside in the new push for practical, instrumental skill building.

He indicates that in China the restructuring has seen higher education become more diversified and decentralized. With a goal of improving international competition, China has focused attention on building high-quality universities that can compete worldwide and has particularly focused on ten top-ranked universities to deliver the kind of programs and graduates needed to succeed in the global market. Hong Kong has concentrated on expanding its higher education system and increasing the number of university enrolments. In this way it hopes to produce a highly educated workforce that can compete in the knowledge economy. Taiwan, likewise aims to improve the quality of their universities and raise their competitiveness globally. They have also pursued internationalization in their universities, hoping to attract more international students. In South Korea, the goal has been on the cultivation of human resources, and raising the competitive edge of their universities. They have introduced an evaluation system to enhance quality. In Japan the focus is on science and technology to boost its global competitiveness. They have also developed policies to encourage lifelong learning and possibilities for professionals to upgrade their skills in graduate education programs. Singapore, a country with no natural resources relies on its population to ensure its success in the global economic market; it encourages people to embrace lifelong learning so that they can continually prepare themselves to face the challenges of a rapidly changing and competitive globalized world. Pang notes that Vietnam's open door policy and international cooperative activities in education are because of globalization and Vietnam's desire to be a player on the international stage. Hence, Vietnam, like the other Asian entities described above expects its higher education institutions to provide high quality human resources, skilled workers able to compete in the global market. As such it has expanded and diversified its post-secondary education and has focused on training in the skills necessary for the nation's economic development.

For Asia-Pacific countries, globalization has forced them to choose between tradition and modern economic values. As Pang notes, "the traditional ethics and values of hierarchical relationships, collectivism, trust, empathy, compassion, grace and honesty in educational governance and management have changed into the so-called "new" values of contract, market, choice, competition, efficiency, flexibility, productivity and accountability". He contends that the restructuring of education to bring it into line with the goals of the market knowledge economy has not usually resulted in increased equality in educational access and services. On the question of whether globalization is a "good thing" Pang seems to come down on the sceptical side but still calls for further research into relations between the global and local; the debate as to whether globalization is leading to infusion of Western norms and culture around the world or whether it has led to more contact among different cultures; and finally an examination of the material effects of globalization. The chapter masterfully succeeds in laying out the problematic effect of globalization on higher education in the Asian region.

Carlos Ornelas provides a "voice from the South" in his chapter "The Tortuous Path of Educational Decentralization in Mexico". As has been noted above, in our globalized world, decentralization of educational systems has been viewed as a way to bring education into line with the neoliberal, business agenda of the global market. Ornelas outlines how in Mexico educational authorities have tried to grapple with the issue producing policies that have fluctuated between more and less devolution of administration of education to the States or to the Central Government. In the early 1990's Mexico began its decentralization strategy with the goal of increasing the quality of education, making the system more equitable and enhancing respect due to the teaching body. When the transfer came, the States gained control of financial resources to pay teachers and administrators as well as assumed responsibility to handle labor relations and manage school buildings and other assets related to education. However, the current Peña Nieto administration is seeking to reverse the decentralization policy and retake control of education through amendments to the Constitution. Ornelas characterized the first policy shift as doomed from the start but is equally sceptical about how successful the return to centralization of education will be. He contends that the 1992 'federalization of education' did not really bring about decentralization but rather represented a continuation of central bureaucracy.

He also notes that the infrastructure of the education system has two authoritative structures a formal and informal one and although it is the formal structure that establishes the legal layout of the system, legislators use the formal laws to make changes to the informal system which is the actual way education is governed. The Federal Department of Public Education (SEP) and the National Teachers' Union (SNTE) are two very powerful entities that were not disempowered by the policies of decentralization. In fact, as is so often the case when decentralization is undertaken the real power still resides at the centre while the regional authorities are left with the difficult and often costly decisions to keep the system running usually without sufficient funding from the central government. So the regional authorities will get the blame when problems arise, but actually have no power or leeway to address them properly. The extremely powerful Teachers' Union had the right to negotiate with the various states and the governors found themselves unable to challenge the union nor to actually take control of the educational system. Despite the attempt by the central government to alleviate financial difficulties of the Mexican States through the Fund for Basic and Normal Education (FAEB), inequalities persisted with the provision of funds to various States. When Peña Nieto became President, he proclaimed his intention to resolve the corruption problems in the education system where the SNTE instead of fighting for its members actually forced teachers to pay for their initial post and pay again if they wished for a transfer or a promotion. Nepotism abounded in the system with senior teachers passing on their position to relatives or selling them to the highest bidder when they retired. The SNTE had also been able to negotiate very beneficial contracts for teachers beyond the reasonable by, for example, arranging for teachers to be paid for more than twice the number of days worked. Ornelas also mentions the influence wielded by Elba Esther Gordillo Morales, leader of the SNTE. She had been able to coerce several Presidents to accept her demands because her union members would vote as a bloc in any election thus influencing the outcome. She was ultimately indicted by Mexican authorities for embezzlement and organized crime in 2013. After her arrest and imprisonment members of the union in several states organized civil disobedience actions including strikes, and seizing highways and public offices. This forced the government to make a deal with the teachers in that they would accept the reform (recentralization) but would receive some special benefits in return. Ornelas is not optimistic for the success of the move back to centralism in education in Mexico and foresees that the new legislation will be as fraught with corruption as the previous decentralization movement.

The third chapter of this section, "Privatization and Marketing of Higher Education in Mexico. Contributions to the Debate" by Angélica Buendía Espinosa, provides a nice companion piece to the previous chapter in that it too focuses on education in Mexico in the globalized world, but this time on effects of privatization of Higher Education institutions. Buendía notes that although unlike many nations in Asia and in Eastern Europe as well as in the Latin American countries of Brazil, Colombia, Peru and Venezuela where over half of university students attend private institutions, that is not yet the case in Mexico although privatization of tertiary education has been growing. She provides a historical evolution of the place of the private sector in Mexico with regard to education and identifies emergence (1935–1959); expansion and deregulation (1960–2000) subdivided into sub-sections of (1960–1980 and 1982–2000); a market stage (2000–2006) and uncontrolled stabilization since 2007. Over that period enrolment in higher education increased enormously and the private institutions became more popular although to date the majority of university students attend public institutions. While in 1970, 86.2% of students were in public institutions compared to only 13.5% in private universities, by 2014 public institutions accounted for 68.55% of students as compared to 31.45% in private higher education facilities. In the earliest stage of privatization a major reason for founding private universities such as the Instituto Tecnológico de Estudios Superiores de Monterrey (ITESM) was to prepare professionals for economy and business without any religious orientation. Buendía lists the private universities founded over the time period noting that many such as ITESM and other technologically oriented schools looked to such institutes as MIT and Southern California Institute of Technology as models and hoped that graduates of these prestige schools would help Mexico to compete in the international setting. Her chapter shows a clear development of growing neoliberal policies in the public sector granting favoured status to the private sectors. Once the GATT (General Agreement on Tariffs and Trade) was signed, even though educational matters were in general not included, Mexico embraced the notion of keeping the higher educational sector open to foreign investment particularly in the area of cross border trade in services for general, scientific and medical concerns. So although the state still has nominal control, there is an ongoing concentrated rate of privatization in higher education.

One of the problems of the encroachment of privatization in higher education has been regulation of quality. There is a great diversity of quality in the programs of the private institutions and it has been noted how easy it is to set up a college with little interference as to the kind of curriculum or quality of staff offering the programs. Following market notions "charge what the market will bear" the tuitions can vary greatly even among campuses of the same university in different states depending on what students can realistically pay. The elite institutions typically charge the highest tuitions (as high as 1,200,000 pesos per year) with those of questionable quality the lowest (circa 1,000 to 96,000 pesos per year). In addition the private institutions tend to offer limited programs in such areas as administration, law, accounting, finance and computer science, leaving the more traditional programs in education and humanities to the public universities. The private sector tends to avoid the more expensive areas of study such as natural and hard sciences of which only 1.89% are served by the private sector. Privatization in Mexico has no doubt followed Milton Friedman's neoliberal notions that the market should regulate education to produce higher levels of quality and greater "client" satisfaction. However, Buendía notes that marketization of higher education in Mexico has not proven to be "a triumph of the free market economy".

INTRODUCTION

Buendía provides a very helpful Market Model of Private Higher Education in Mexico (Table 5) in which she outlines the market conditions of institutional status, competition, price, information, registration and quality in relation to how these conditions play out in Mexico. Although the Federal Department of Education (SEP) since 2012 has attempted to implement quality assessment of private higher education institutions, so far many of the lower category private institutions have not signed on for assessment. In the balance, she does not consider the privatization of higher education on the market model a success in Mexico. The elite institutions are, to be sure, very good but are inaccessible to most of the population because of their high tuitions, so disparity in access remains a problem. A possible solution would be a mechanism for regulation of the institutions considering both academic and economic factors. The economic implications of globalization in the 21st century have far-reaching effects on higher education as Buendía's chapter so aptly demonstrates.

Globalization as it plays out in the modern world can provide solutions or create problems in educational systems as nations try to grapple with the economic order and strive to sustain their place in this very competitive environment. The neoliberal tenet of the sanctity of the market as the deciding factor in all decisions of nation building has caused immense challenges in the developing world as it has maintained the formalization of the customary – development dichotomy. The authors of the chapters so far in the volume have highlighted problems of development in several developing areas of the world, and suggested alternative approaches to counter the grand narrative of what development should mean. Faced with the necessity to prepare workers to compete in the global market, several nations, as outlined in the second part of the volume have undergone drastic restructuring of their education systems but apparently have failed to overcome the constants of inequality, disparity, social injustice and corruption.

The final chapter in this book presents something of a departure from the others in that it acknowledges the wrongs of our society, some brought about by the type of education we are offering, and by the type of society neoliberal globalization presents as the norm. Vanessa de Oliveira Andreotti in "Education, Knowledge and the Righting of Wrongs" offers a philosophical piece as her attempt to address the issues of injustice and offer possible recourses. Her piece raises more questions than it provides answers, but it invites us to consider assumptions about the state of the world and how to improve matters. The author uses metaphors and narratives to illustrate how colonized our thinking may be through social, cultural and historical conditioning, and urges hyper reflexivity—we must take nothing for granted and be ever be mindful of the "ethical imperative to relate to the Other, before will" (Spivak, 2004; see also; Ki-Zerbo et al., 2006 in this regard). In this way we will be better placed to confront hegemony, ethnocentrism, ahistoricism, depoliticization, paternalism, and deficit theorization of difference without unknowingly being a party to them. Responses to these wrongs or breaking asunder of the colonial histories would involve a cultural revolution, de-emphasizing of universality, and formulation of new ways of creating capital for development. She concludes with a series of "what if" questions, which if realized could make our world a kinder, gentler place and she asks us to consider "what knowledge would be enough, what education would be appropriate, and what possibilities would be opened then?" This call for thoughtful action mirrors the message some of the chapters in this volume have tried to articulate.

In summary, the chapters in this volume try to come to grips with complicated issues involving education and development cooperation in the modern globalized world. and ask important questions such as what type of development actually benefits emerging nations?; how do we best acknowledge and meet the educational needs of traditional and isolated populations?; how successful has policy borrowing been in improving educational systems?; what challenges has globalization brought to higher education?; what have been the effects on education of such neoliberal policies as decentralization, deregulation and privatization?; how can we right the many social wrongs of education aid in our globalized world? The questions merit much reflection and the chapters in this volume provide a beginning to the journey of addressing them.

REFERENCES

Abdi, A. (2013). Intensive globalization of African education. Re-interrogating the relevance of structural adjustment programs (SAPs). In Y. Hébert & A. Abdi (Eds.), *Critical perspectives on international education*. Rotterdam, The Netherlands: Sense Publishers.

Altbach, P., & Knight, J. (2007). The internationalization of higher education: Motivations and realities. *Journal of Studies in International Education, 11*(3/4), 290–305.

Babaci-Wilhite, Z., Geo-JaJa, M. A., & Shizhou, L. (2012). Education and language: A human right for sustainable development in Africa. *International Review of Education, 58*(5), 619–647.

Bourdieu, P. (2001). *Contre-feux 2: Pour un movement social européen* (p. 84). Paris: Raisons d'agir.

Capella, J. R. (2000). Globalization, a fading citizenship. In N. C. Burbules & C. A. Torres (Eds.), *Globalization and education: Critical perspectives* (pp. 227–251). London: Routledge.

Capling, A., Considine, M., & Crozier, M. (1998). *Australian politics in the gobal era*. Melbourne: Addison-Wesley.

Carnoy, M. (1999). *Globalilzation and educational reform, what planners need to know*. Paris: UNESCO, International Institute for Educational Planning.

Ellerman, D. (2009). *Helping people help themselves: From the World Bank to an alternative philosophy of development assistance*. Ann Arbor, MI: University of Michigan Press.

Freire, P. (1973). *Pedagogy of freedom: Ethics, democracy, and civic courage, Critical perspectives series*. Lanham, MD: Rowman & Littlefield Publishers.

Geo-JaJa, M. A. (2016). Human Rights undermined and development denied: Neoliberalism and the imperialism of development aid. Presentation at WCCES Congress, August, 2016, Beijing, PRC.

Geo-JaJa, M. A., & Mangum, G. (2001). Structural adjustment as an inadvertent enemy of human development in Africa. *Journal of Black Studies, 32*(1), 30–50.

Ki-Zerbo, J., Kane, C. H., Archibald, J., Lizop, E., & Rahnema, M. (2006). Education as an instrument of cultural defoliation. A Multi-voice response. In M. Rahnema & V. Bartree (Eds.), *The post-development reader* (pp. 153–160). London: Zed Books.

Lewin, K. (1994). Education and development. The issues and the evidence. *Oxford Studies in Comparative Education, 3*(2).

Majhanovich, S. (2013). How the English language contributes to sustaining the neoliberal agenda: Another take on the strange non-demise of neoliberalism. In S. Majhanovich & M. A. Geo-JaJa (Eds.), *Economics, aid and education. Implications for development.* Rotterdam, The Netherlands: Sense Publishers.

Morrow, R. A., & Torres, C. A. (2000). The state, globalization and education policy. In N. C. Burbules & C. A. Torres (Eds.), *Globalization and education: Critical perspectives* (pp. 27–56). London: Routledge.

Sen, A. (1999). *Development as freedom.* Oxford: Oxford University Press and Anchor Books.

Spivak, G. (2004). Righting wrongs. *The South Atlantic Quarterly, 103*(2/3), 523–581.

Tsui, A. B. M., & Tollefson, J. W. (2006). Language policy and the construction of national culture identity. In A. B. M. Tsui & J. W. Tollefson (Eds.), *Language policy, culture and identity in Asian contexts.* Mahwah, NJ: Lawrence Erlbaum Assoc.

UNESCO. (2014). *Global citizenship education: Preparing learners for the challenges of the 21st century.* Paris: UNESCO.

United Nations. (2005, May). *In larger freedom: Towards development, security and human rights for all.* Report of the United Nations Secretary General at the conferences and summits in the economic, social and related fields.

Suzanne Majhanovich
Faculty of Education
The University of Western Ontario

PART I

ISSUES OF DEVELOPMENT IN A GLOBALIZED WORLD

XINYI WU AND MACLEANS A. GEO-JAJA

1. FROM RIGHT TO EDUCATION TO RIGHTS IN EDUCATION

A Dialogical Roadmap for Autonomy Development

INTRODUCTION: BACKGROUND AND SCOPE

We live in One World. What we do affects others and what others do affects us, as never before. To recognize that we are all members of a world community and that we all have responsibilities to each other is not romantic rhetoric but modern economic and social reality. (DEFS, 2005, p. 5)

Understanding development aid is complex and always a two-edged sword, because the donors and recipients often hold different motives and interests based on their ideological backgrounds and schools of thought and are driven by economic, political, social, and cultural considerations. Previously, the money-centric conceptualization had been the norm to guide development aid. Even when rights in education is advocated, aid is predominately allocated for meeting the need for right to education – the purpose of increasing access to and quantity of education. The core puzzle of quality education remains unsolved, and the effectiveness of development continues to be criticized.

Unlike right to education, rights in education goes beyond the numbers game as it is extended to basic social, economic, and cultural needs of learners and nations. It defines schooling curricula upward to include the following concepts in a learner's experience: human rights, social justice, citizenship, diversity, values and perceptions, teamwork, learning in a global context, and sustainable development. However, the highly politicized right to education is currently given priority that often generates functional incompleteness of a national economy; whereas, rights in education programs that erode external power to intervene in local needs is shelved. Thus, it is vital and necessary to critically examine histories, converse with numerous ineffectual reforms in depth, and scrutinize contemporaneous issues of colonialization in education so that lessons from these past experiences could further inform existing elaboration of rights in education for autonomy-sustaining social progress. In this vein, a human-centered approach expressed in rights in education is central and critical to societal development.

The money-centric conceptualization originates from the Cold-War and Post-Cold War era when nations were seeking options to recover from the war. Although development was once thought to be effective to a larger end in that it provided nations with more options, its drawback of being a market model was criticized, as it was depriving recipients' capabilities and destroying significant values. This market-driven system has shaped globalization and competitiveness of schools and promoted Western values, especially capitalist values, the extent of which is characterized by the new international anti-dialogical development cooperation order. Some argue that development would be an inherently marginalizing/ disempowering factor unless donors could advance moral commitment to principles of human rights and recognize the beauty of interdependence within development cooperation for effective development. Such a debate continues with evidence that shows the persistent deprivation of recipients' values and steadily falling emphasis on aid recipients' core needs, which were the results of decisions made for aid allocation for development during the war on terror (Fleck & Kilby, 2010; Bearce & Tirone, 2010; Berthemelemy, 2006; Brown, 2009).

Debate on Development Approach

The early debates led to a shift in attention to theoretical critiques of the money-centric and disempowering nature of development. According to Ellerman (2009) and Dichter (2003), autonomy-respecting development considered an alternative theory of development is a bill of rights that respects culture and the needs of people. It is informed by the consideration that aid-donors should exercise less control over development cooperation so that people's desires can be expressed most effectively, which could grant the local responsibilities to organize activities and be empowered to carry out sustainable development with donors maintaining a less active role. In broader terms, capacity-building and right to development in aid-giving enable aid recipients to help people help themselves. If they are missing in development aid, it would cause people to be unable to help themselves and result in right to development being overridden, which is the fundamental conundrum of development cooperation. Similarly, Sen (2001) has also called for "development as freedom" that is instrumentally significant for helping nations achieve desirable socioeconomic capabilities by adapting new strategies and better development alternatives. The freedom of the local allows them to develop according to their priorities and recast the donor-driven agenda to localized development, through which countries can value their own education and their intrinsic role for expanding people's capabilities (Dreze & Sen, 2002). The rationale for rethinking the social engineering approach for autonomy-respecting development is due to: (1) the illusiveness of sustaining or promoting micro-successes in development cooperation; and (2) conflict of values and need, as well as the genuine uncertainty of motive and mission – Donors propose what recipients want to hear, but do what they want to do. According to Ellerman (2004), traditional Eurocentric notions of aid not only override help (social engineering) where the helper imposes goals or strategies on the doer, but also undercut (charitable) help where the doer is kept needy and incapacitated and cannot support or enhance the self-reliant capacities and take ownership of the development aid process (Dichter, 2003). Although many theoretical discussions have proposed a human rights based approach, a value-neutral mechanistic solution still practically dominates development aid cooperation (Sen, 2000). On the one hand, aid quantity has increased significantly; but the problem is that recipients continue to be excluded and marginalized through "development aid without the soul of recipients" (p. 21). Countries are not only denied opportunities to achieve valued growth, human rights are undermined thus depriving them the capacity and freedom to create systems of change. In Africa, Kenya, Nigeria, Tanzania, Ghana, and Zimbabwe, to name a few, dehumanization and the case of exclusion are set in motion on the altar of a retrogressive ideology embedded in development aid, particularly in education aid (Sen, 2000; Giroux, 2001).

Mason (2009) and Nordtveit (2010) further articulate a comprehensive understanding of exclusion in development. Using complexity theory, they point out that effective aid should simultaneously target philosophical, social, and political aspects of underdevelopment. It is just like in the context of education, quality education for freedom must enable people to understand their past, their present reality as well as to see connections between their own lives and wider political structures; otherwise these people will never participate in 'true' development. Therefore, bridge-building aid cannot only be motivated by directing actions based on donors' situated rights as rights bearers, but must take into consideration ethics and moral dimensions that have been lacking in development assistance to deepen understanding of the combining elements that hinder people from improving their lives. It is essential to respect universal rights, heterogeneous recipients and cultural protection, and moral commitment to responsibility and reliability, just as the standards of honesty and integrity that are a descriptive and analytical construct need to be unpacked to understand donors' true motivation (OECD, 2006). Furthermore, exclusion in development is also manifested in form of ties to former colonies or strategic factors that are based on international political interests (Bandyopadhyay & Vermann, 2013; Alesina & Dollar, 2000; Dreher et al., 2009). For instance, in the U.N. voting pattern, a developing nation that votes to support war on terrorism would receive increased aid allocation from developed countries in the name of liberalizing for greater democracy. In other words, some countries may be excluded from development if they consider their past and present realities rather than vote for war on terrorism. However, despite of these articulations, they fail to deal with human agency and cultural rights. Sen (1989), however, elaborates on human agency on the basis of freedom and argues that economic opportunity should be contextualized on normative norms rather than on economic indicators. This means that development should aim at achieving interconnected freedoms and enlarging opportunities, including political and social freedoms and protecting entitlements. This grass roots movement is a bottom-up dialogical developmental approach.

As far as educational development is concerned, criticisms have concentrated on the purpose and ethics of aid. Aid is criticized as donor-centric and an instrument that leads to vulnerability and dependency of recipients rather than fostering education pluralism and language security that could strengthen cultural identity for community development. Being a battleground for claimed goodness and consequential deprivation, aid could also be argued as a platform for greater dialogues between helpers (donors) and doers (beneficiaries) in development aid cooperation. To helpers, development aid is intended to improve well-being and change the quality of life and meet needs and aspirations at the local level; however, for doers, helpers have often failed humanity by providing pre-packaged solutions backed by sets of macroeconomic conditionalities rather than focusing on the multidimensionalities of poverty and deprivation experienced by doers and their capabilities within the aid construct (Unterhalter, 2005; Flores-Crespo & Nebel, 2005).

The previous theoretical work and empirical evidence demonstrate that both the material and non-material life of the masses cannot be actualized if the mechanisms for optimizing societal capacity are lacking in ways by which intelligent, creative, and knowledgeable interventions, by way of education, were impossibly executed to create a desired mode of livelihood. Neoliberal capitalism's standardized and rationality-bounded market-model with its disempowering effects makes it difficult to integrate human rights into development, as it deemphasizes economic inclusion and cultural rights. This explains the assertion that effective development needs to integrate human rights into development and to focus on the enhancement of capabilities and freedom that people of a nation enjoy. When people exercise human rights to design economic and social arrangements, they are also able to secure social benefits and freedom.

What Is Needed in a New Roadmap?

Development Aid's new roadmap needs to move beyond the money-centric conceptualization of education, and offer humanity sustainable and inclusive development. Specifically, aid conceptualized in the new roadmap would cultivate education to the extent of which would provide people with choices, to promote social reengineering, and to eventually capture the importance of both intrinsic worth and instrumental goals of education. While no roadmap is perfect and each varies in its effectiveness, this chapter attempts to capture the essences for understanding the relationship between socioeconomic conditions and cultural values in development and discuss what is taught and how it is done in school with respect to individual children's needs. More importantly, with school systems that discourage collaboration and creativity, but with the goal to train people instead of inspiring them – exactly the opposite what humanity needs – this chapter calls for decolonialization of the mind, an economic and poverty war waged by paternalistic education and ethical dimension in aid. It also recognizes the lack of a learner-centered approach to schooling in the past that has led to people's inability to understand and exercise agency in education. We firmly believe that education for all is a basic human right and together nations can break the vicious cycles of poverty. We also deem that understanding current development tensions and working collaboratively will save children from vulnerability and consumption of education for exploitation.

Colonialization of the mind and the consequences of lacking a learner-centered approach to education is further elaborated by Illich (1997) who characterizes development as planned poverty because schooling provided by development can lead to feelings of inferiority, especially when people are more educated before they drop-out. Thus, schooling does not actually lead to learning. Instead of alleviating poverty, schooling reinforces social inequities and causes some to be consigned to the bottom of the poverty industry. In short, the mentality of schooling in this type of factory discourages collaboration and creativity, let alone for people to help themselves transform national development. Therefore, granting right to education is a passive and insufficient approach to education for development, because it is against ensuring that people will take positive actions and transform paternalistic education into actual capabilities for dignity and optimum development. As we wonder why education does not teach values and encourage participation and self-reflection and why it is an ethical duty to show tolerance in order to learn from different knowledge in the world, this chapter will propose a roadmap to fill in these gaps. It will start with an overview of discontinuities and concerns with discussions of dominant discourses associated with current development aid cooperation, including neoliberalism, universalism, linguistic factors, and dependency. Then, it will introduce a rights-capability approach for development with our critiques. It will be followed by a proposed roadmap that folds right to education into rights in education as a dialogical framework. A dialogical framework is the mechanism that argues that people who are actually affected within a local context must be given the opportunity to define their problems for themselves and propose their solutions, because they might pursue a development path far different from both donors and people in other communities.

DISCONTINUITIES AND CONCERNS OF AID COOPERATION

Kofi Annan (UN, 2005) captures the three thematic pillars of development – security, development, and human rights in the quote below:

> We will not enjoy development without security, we will not enjoy security without development, and we will not enjoy either without respect for human rights. Unless all these causes are advanced, none will succeed. (United Nations, 2005, pp. 5–6)

These three pillars of development do not and cannot stand in isolation but are very much intertwined. They reflexively show why human rights is fundamental to both security and development. They also inform a rights-based approach as essential to achieving self-determination. More importantly, a rights-based approach reinforces concrete steps required to reduce selective applications and arbitrary integration currently dominated in aid development. The world must move from an era of externally applying pre-set carrots and sticks to internally empowering people. Similarly, Sen (2000) states that human rights should be brought into development aid to manifest realities of an interconnected global thinking rather than by a science of exclusion. In this vein, human rights and capabilities, rather than wisdoms from the developed North and gratefully acknowledged superior culture, become an intricate critical part of development cooperation (Sen, 2000).

However, post-Cold War development is filled with discontinuities and has not reflected the above claim but weakened capability development that sees individuals as fundamental cells of societies. Although right to education has been advocated for years and thought to be effective in alleviating poverty, the results are disappointing. Nation states have not been able to protect societies against the negative influences of neoliberal capitalism (Jepma, 1997). Universalism, as a primary orientation of development, ignores local values and complexities. Linguistically, social voices of local people are hardly heard, and people use pre-made frameworks to learn to serve the global market and are integrated into the world economy. More problematically, the tension of control still exists between donors and recipients in the way donors legitimize aid based on considerations of political strategic allies and market partners. In the next section, we discuss each aspect to provide our critiques on the current roadmap and suggest a new development cooperation that substantiates the centrality of people's views, preferences, and experiences, and give real weight alongside external interests.

Neoliberalism

Neoliberalism is one of the key and dominant ideologies that guides development cooperation. It includes anti-dialogical actions that align very well with globalization and market-based practices. Because it believes that a global free market is both the means and ends of development, nations are expected to develop to be a part of the global market driven by developed countries. Therefore, people in the developing nations are seen as commodities that are required to learn universal skills and knowledge predetermined by donors so that they can compete in the global market. Education, under this framework, loses its very fundamental ability to alleviate pervasive poverty (Alesina & Dollar, 2000; Jepma, 1997), even with a high flow of aid; this market-driven framework cannot lead to autonomous development (Kanbur, 2000). Furthermore, neoliberalism has led to fragmentation of national sovereignty, with the result that the assurance of human rights, security and voices are not fulfilled. According to Alesina and Dollar (2000), even if recipients are given opportunities to participate in development, not everything can be left to the market. The increasing "post-materialism" in aid is creating a divergence between what donors want to provide and what aid-recipients hope to achieve, which often results in no guarantee of basic human security.

Universalism

Teaching universal knowledge has been dominant in post-Cold War education aid; even with the growing control of the local, the prevailing orientation of education is still in the direction of universality rather than a synthesis of local and universal values. In the act of controlling skills and life, education becomes an instrument of cultural defoliation and plays a role of conquering nations and alienating cultural values. This practice is driven by the methodological orientation of metrics-based learning objectives. According to Giroux (2007), education is largely defined by corporate demands that aim to provide universal skills and knowledge to compete in the global market and to maintain global economic superiority and military power. In this sense, education excellence is no longer a matter of quality, diversity, and equity central to the notion of schooling as a public good, but rather is reduced to a private good that ignores culture, freedom, and social justice. Influenced by universalism, education lacks pedagogy to cultivate valued and ethical local people; such cultivation is actually needed for aid receiving countries, not only for collective resistance to unbalanced relations, but also for addressing crises and challenges to reconstructing development roadmaps.

As aid continues to expand, it is never far from fostering uniformity of cultural and knowledge systems and creating static dichotomies. This universalized and one-size-fits-all approach hinders voices of recipients from being heard and takes no consideration of chronic and transient un-development and underdevelopment. Moreover, even if aid receiving countries are allowed to develop with traditional knowledge and material resources, local values and culture are seen as barbaric for development. Therefore, a new roadmap needs to guide development practices to shift and change its ideology, its partners, its aims, its processes, its imperative systems and procedures (World Bank, 2013).

Linguistic Factors

People in aid receiving nations are currently experiencing lack of linguistic power to speak their own histories and cultures and to challenge the ground on which knowledge is constructed in their schooling, because development aid donors often provide universal learning methods for the local without even consulting the local's needs. This portrays a situation in which local cultures and values are likely to be erased by a politicized world that prioritizes global concerns over local needs. Without voices heard in development aid programs, the local would be pushed into participation in global competitions at the expense of losing their own desired way of living. In many cases, development initiatives are written by and for donors, and methods of operations are decided by Eurocentric beliefs. For example, in the wake of the 9/11 and other terrorist attacks in Europe, an increasing number of OECD donors devoted increasing efforts to the global war on terror rather than aligning their aid policies with development aid standards set by the OECD. Thus, the context and content of aid from OECD donors are troubling, as these aid policies have led to human rights needs being excluded or being assigned low priority in development assistance.

Considering that aid receiving countries lack linguistic power in development, the new roadmap requires setting principles on the basis of cultural pluralism or epistemic relativism, integrating diversity rather than universality in knowledge production, and recognizing and respecting various perspectives and languages. Guided by this framework, people and nations would be the bearers of their own development, and no single practice can transcend and be appropriate everywhere. Education will be merely a form of second colonialism if teachers ingrain in learners the belief that his/her liberation is succumbing to universal standardization.

Dependency

The universalization of knowledge in creating linguistic and development inequality also leads to dependency among unequal power relations. Dependency positions certain knowledge and culture above other forms and creates the dichotomy between success and failure, developed and developing countries, and modern and barbaric culture. Ngugi (1986) points out that aid donors often make explicit colonization of consciousness by way of consciously elevating their own languages and deliberately devaluing receiving nations' cultures, religions, histories, and education systems. In this practice, aid donors are also able to regulate the international flow of people by gatekeeping aid recipients and influencing global relations through aid (Pennycook, 1994; Kuziemko & Werker, 2006; Dreher, Sturm, & Vreeland, 2009). Given the above suppositions, developing countries, therefore, operate in a subordinate or dependent position. Moreover, aid-givers establish a dependent partnership, because they generate a degree of control through aid. This control can be used for a variety of reasons dictated by the Global North, and it may create an unreciprocated relationship leading to interventions in the recipient's fiscal, monetary and development policies.

Addressing the problem of linguistic and cultural hegemony needs a rights in education and autonomy approach that would respect development aid, and pluralism of education is the key. However, those theories rooted in the decolonization of the consciousness of recipients are often identified with languages of aid givers, their cultures and peoples (Tsuda, 1986). The ideological and linguistic gatekeeping deprives people of rights in education, a transmitter of culture for social integration and a reflector of historical development of freedom for humane societies (UNESCO, 2006). Therefore, if education and linguistic povertization or disempowering economicism are the drivers of development aid, aid would be in vain.

The complex relationship between what happens at the global level and at the local level is at the complex core of the development aid outcome. On the one hand, previous studies abound with results showing that development aid has "moral vision", and it has a holistic roadmap promoting capabilities that inspired education pluralism; on the other hand, the majority of these messianic do-gooders and modern reincarnations of the colonial conceit of yore ignore significant local heritage and customs, as they put economic and political conditions in place that strain doers' abilities to adjust to insecurity and actualize right to pedagogy. When socioeconomic transformation is needed and requested by the local in the diverse and dynamic context, education has to determine its functionality to connect knowledge with overcoming disempowering economicism and language hegemony. Therefore, education aid must resist the universality provision with its twin ideologies of anti-dialogical action and marketization. Clearly, post-Cold War politics of aid universalism threatens the State's ability to act and intervene in education for autonomy development. In the absence of a new shared understanding found in many Human Rights Declarations, such aid has become a driver for a multitude of global interactions, ranging from the expansion of global capitalism, the intensification of economic exclusion, and is the creator of asymmetrical relationships. We draw the conclusion that the efforts of aid to create a more inclusive and equitable world have ebbed the stronger influence of donors' interests as compared to global responsibilities that require the pursuit of credible, affordable, acceptable and adaptable policies, and such efforts cannot be traded for economic progress (Stiglitz, 2002). We clearly posit that developing countries failed to restructure the postcolonial state and replace colonial education; rather, they have preserved the legacy of colonialism, which is the concentration on right to education that is vulnerable to exogenous terms and conditionalities.

DECONSTRUCTION OF ESSENTIALIZATION OF DEVELOPMENT AID

Above, we have criticized the old roadmap with neoliberalism as its guiding principle and proposed some suggestions for a new roadmap that is culturally pluralistic, linguistically diverse, and free of dependency. Right to education is primarily based on this old roadmap, and it is insufficient to alleviate poverty and promote sustainable development. In the following, we review a rights-capability approach and provide our explanations and critiques on how this broadly advocated framework would better serve receiving nations' interests in development, though it may have its limitations in current applications.

A rights-capability approach is developed and further elaborated by Sen (1989) and Nussbaum (2000) that gives more emphasis to the intrinsic value of education as an entitlement and as an opportunity for people to develop capabilities through education so that they are able to live a life of their own choice. With culturally rich articulations, this approach is distinctive from the human capital paradigm that uses quantitative measurements to determine types of educational programs, its delivery methods, curricular, and assessment criteria (Hanushek, 2013; Glewwe et al., 2013; Easterly, 2001), and it regards individuals' freedom and flourishing as essential components in education delivery. In addition, Sen (1996) also argues that a rights-capability approach is the solution to bridging the development choice gap and empowerment parity between donors and recipients because right to education has often not been achieved in that aid recipients ignore their own education path and development value in hopes of a single optimal roadmap. Kanbur (2008) argues that neoliberal capitalisms consider humans as agentic individuals rather than societal duty bearers, making it difficult to fulfill the substantive freedom of people to enjoy valued life (Kanbur & Summer, 2012). He also cautions that discriminatory practices are already ingrained in development by peer pressures and entitlement provided to individuals, which affects opportunities available for people and creates inequality by assigned roles in the market. Therefore, the capability approach is so critical in redirecting development to ultimately satisfy individual needs rather than market needs, and it provides a framework to help further understand entitlement to resources and promotion and protection of human rights.

To be more specific, the rights-capability also criticizes epistemologies influenced by dominant political ideologies. Nyamnjoh (2011), in his conceptualization of knowledge relevance in Africa, states that local knowledge containing local identities, values and functionalities has become a ground for political conditionalities for dependency. For example, colonists and neo-colonists have used education as a method of imposing dominant ideas, which leads to a common heritage of oppression (Abdi, 2006). Indigenous education systems are also being replaced by irrelevant, limited and purposefully imposed languages and related structures of learning by donors as political considerations to attach dominant political ideologies to the local social welfare system (Babaci-Wilhite, 2012). These political conditionalities neither reflect local people's best interests, nor do they contribute to foster promotion of culture of education and capacity-building development. In this sense, local knowledge production is critical because it is directly tied to how local people would perceive, behave, and value themselves as individuals as well as participants in communities. Anything less would betray societal causes and be associated with human rights sacrifices. As a result, decision-making would only bring false hopes. In fact, right to education is just the beginning, and rights in education is the means and ends to development. Therefore, quality schooling becomes especially important, as it is essential to knowledge production.

However, investments in delocalization of schooling and ban of local languages in schools are ubiquitous and stymie creativity and freedom. Such a construct overlooks the fundamental aim of supporting human development and encapsulating multiple dimensions of justice. The rights-capability approach is informative, as it also argues that the construction of authority and subjectivity in education should be governed by ideologies inscribed in the process of freedom. In particular, it accords respect for human rights and responsibility and grants different possibilities for people to construct their relationships to themselves, others, and the larger reality. What meanings are considered the most important, what experiences are deemed the most legitimate, and what obligations are committed for enlarging people's choices should not be determined by donors. In this case, schooling, particularly the classroom, has to be an environment that configures practices of dialogues, struggles, and contestations to challenge pedagogies emphasizing passive consumption of knowledge and skills. This preeminence of the rights-capability approach, a welcome methodological framework, which embraces pluralism, is validated by the former Director General of UNESCO, Amadou-Mahtar M'bow, who argues that aid should not be:

> Reduced to imitation of donor societies, ... Aid must be endogenous, thought out by people themselves, springing out from the soil on which they live and attuned to their aspirations, the conditions of their environment, the resources at their disposal and particular genius of their culture. (Sifuna, 2001, p. 32)

Although these authors point out the importance of roadmaps going beyond instrumental goals and provide ample thoughtful conceptualizations of freedom and process to freedom for pushing forward development aid, unfortunately, the ethics of the market place and its moral low ground in development aid continue to be clearly biased against the ethics of cultivating cultural pluralism and connecting local realities into practice.

Therefore, we argue that universality and indivisibility of human rights are all inherent to the dignity of people and sovereignty of a nation. Right to education lacks the essential component of connecting education to scientific, economic, political, and valued realities of the local because it is after all a neoliberalism-driven approach. Alternatively, rights in education articulated in the rights-capability approach with its root in the culture and history of the local recognizes the complexity and forms of social arrangements, and it conceptualizes the values of each individual's substantive freedom, rights, agency, identity, and empowerment. However, this broadened approach also alerts us to ways in which background conditions can limit life experiences that guide an understanding of human functionings. With experiences heavily influenced by universalism and neoliberalism, some individuals may want a life similar to what dominant ideologies claim to bring. Although the nature of the intrinsic good of education distinguishes schooling from intertwined achieved functionings, it also respects individual freedom to choose their own lives.

RIGHTS IN EDUCATION FOR DIALOGICAL DEVELOPMENT

Within the context of the previous sections, we would like to provide a brief account of our conceptualization, understanding and definition of education. There are two aspects to understand education: the skills and knowledge for employment and functionality in daily life. The first aspect reflects the condition in right to education, through which people build their credentials for competition in labor markets. The latter aspect speaks of the essence of rights in education that is positioned for vibrant relationships with unfixed sets of meanings, and people not only commit to the workforce, but also strive to expand capacities to acquire communal responsibilities to actively participate in societies. While right to education becomes the global norm with its importance to provide people with equal access to educational resources, rights in education further facilitates people with opportunities and conditions to exercise reflexivity and social responsibilities. Along with right to promote equity, rights in education respects diversity and quality, which enables expansion of enlarging opportunities and social inclusion and provides people with an educational experience imbued with critical and investigative inquiry for sustainable development.

However, right to education is currently the discourse many international organizations follow, and many educational practices are mainly based on legitimatization of right to education. Though these practices are important, they are also likely to promote questionable education archetypes that only value universal skills and knowledge. Rights in education, on the other hand, are overlooked with basic indigenous methods of quality learning being replaced by quantity measures in education targets, such as enrollment rates and literacy rates, etc. This missing link in customizing education has resulted in knowledge-based competition and internationalization of education that only facilitate fragmentation of a nation's sovereignty and dilution of its responsibility to social transformation, such as in forms of drastic reduction of social budgets and whole-sale privatization of education in some African countries.

Therefore, both aspects are essential to a new roadmap that aims to preserve local culture and values and foster and strengthen individual capabilities to live a life of their choice, within which principles of rights in education should guide practices of right to education. In other words, learning should be conditioned on the premise to include all inalienable rights in that learners' freedom to construct their own meaning of schooling is the basis to receiving educational resources provided by supranational organizations and bilateral donors. In this sense, students who remain in school would have their own learning options rather than learning what teachers want them to learn.

Since right to education has received much attention in the past, we want to focus on rights in education and provide more elaboration on how rights in education further encompass right to education in ways in which they are integrated to facilitate individuals' ability to achieve freedom.

Rights in Education

Rights in education is a discourse with its central focuses on localizing curricula and incorporating local pedagogic approaches to learning. Rather than by imitation and emulation, it promotes a process of acquiring knowledge and experience with freedom that can capture challenges of poverty and underdevelopment through observation and questioning. Therefore, rights in education empower rather than disempower children in ways in which they are able to exercise their agentic power to develop critical thinking and to challenge norms and bring about desired change. Rights in education are also manifested in quality classroom teaching, through which students have the freedom to produce contemporary knowledge on their own, as David Ellerman (2001) points out "Students must be given the maximum amount of choice or voice possible to develop according to their beliefs and locality so that the teacher can discover learners' idiosyncratic nature" (p. 2). In these authors' opinions, the complex problems and challenges faced by developing countries defy universalistic solutions, and they can be remedied by multi-centric ways of knowing/doing/being, such as claiming indigeneity in a diasporic context. Within such a relationship, if teachers only teach (disseminating knowledge) and provide motivation in one direction rather than the other, owned learning would not be sustained when teachers' incentives are removed.

Within this integrative discourse, a teacher's major task is to watch and learn about the ever-changing learners, as they learn to communicate across cultures based on reciprocity and networks of sharing. To a certain extent, learners' voices become an effective tool for building an environment of trust and love. However, because rights in education is not always in place, learners tend only to acquire information from a prescriptive curriculum thought out by a teacher likened to a robot and driven by extrinsic motivation. The results are that overt imposition of right to education infiltrates local people with teachings of universal skills and knowledge. Therefore, it is crucial to integrate right to education into rights in education and establish rights in education as the basis to guide right to education, which means that right to education must be provided in the context of rights in education framework.

From Anti-Dialogical to Dialogical Roadmap

As we previously discussed, right to education is still a dominant discourse in development aid; whereas, rights in education is often ignored. It seems either aspect of education, teaching universal skills and knowledge or functionality of daily life, can't fully satisfy approaches of international development aid for poverty alleviation. Rather, an integrative roadmap that includes equity, quality, and diversity in its conceptualization would provide a solution to the complexity and multidimensionality of poverty. In others words, education initiatives must consider elements of social, cultural, economic, political and religious perspectives, and these elements are the bases to validate international aid.

A roadmap acknowledging local values needs to understand the complex interconnectedness between culture, power, and knowledge, driven by the will to ensure that the poor achieve common humanity by reducing Eurocentrism in aid partnership. This roadmap foundation on dialogical action borrows the rights-capability approach elaborated by Sen (1989) and others who argue that development aid should be liberated from Eurocentric distortions and returned to culturally rich articulations. The result will be the transfer of development power to the local so that they could undertake true restructuring for ownership. For example, in the case of China and other emerging aid-giving nations like India, Brazil and others, aid is delivered in the context of the doctrine of mutual benefits – building regional friendships, partnerships and trust, as opposed to OECD Cold War ideological and political motivations (Chong & Gradstein, 2008; Babachi-Wilhite, 2012). Chaponnière (2009), Cheng, Oseph and Shi (2009), and Li (2007) also indicate that aid from China involves cooperation, and no longer focuses on the geo-strategic policy of spreading Communism with its aspects of humane internationalism.

In the meanwhile, by recognizing the limitations of anti-dialogical schooling policies with an imposed universal learning framework and questioning the visions of reality, it also finds values in right to education. The basic idea is very relevant in the education aid construct as it encourages reflections on the fulfillment of learning or development on the basis of respecting rights in education. In a nutshell, the foundation of this approach sits on objectives of achieving human rights through granting local socioeconomic and knowledge security. The battle is between including complex and diverse societal relations in education and delivering education as the scientific prestige of neoliberal capitalism social engineering scheme of the post-Cold War era. In addition, rather than seeing education as a goal of development as defined by the World Bank, this approach insists that rights in education is critical to achieving development and not its reward (Manzo, 2003). Therefore, although this articulated roadmap includes both right to education and rights in education, the understanding of rights in education is non-politicized and humanistic; especially rejecting any forms of violation of people's entitlements to quality education, however defined, and a nation's sovereignty attached to right to development.

To promote and protect people's entitlements and a nation's sovereignty, this roadmap emphasizes a broader normative framework. In formalizing some socially acceptable approximation to rights, it facilitates practices that advance equity, quality, dignity, well-being, as well as empowering people to actualize democratization of linguistic and education rights – rather than the opposite. To be more specific, protecting people's entitlements and strengthening their capabilities and empowering them to be functional calls for education pluralism as a counterstrategy against monolingualism and monoculturalism. This inclusive decentralization reform similar to autonomy-respecting help can only come from education much closer to the ground; where there is relative acceptability and adaptability between education and society. This process rules out an alienating decentralization reform with global agency for a retooled comprehensive autonomy–respecting education. Therefore, we argue to capture the goodness of humanity in all its diversity and particularity; the post-2015 international education agenda should be committed more to interpreting or regarding the world in terms of human values and histories than to the negative freedom of real knowledge.

Furthermore, with right to education infused into rights in education, people receive equal opportunities to quality education access and resources where science, technology, engineering, mathematics, and medicine are developed by citizens and for citizens (STEMM). In addition, achieving a nation's sovereignty calls for traditional knowledge being added in the curriculum as well as linking local practices to the global. Anything which contrasts this framework culminates in an inequitable distribution of education and comes with enormous human cost – excluding social normative construction of realities that are meaningful for the means-ends- relationship. In this sense, non-marketization of education is the crucial gatekeeper for social and economic progress, as it guides universal STEMM to serve the nation and its people.

In summary, this comprehensive roadmap serves to creating a balance of economic, cultural, and linguistic power as it mitigates breaking up communities into virtually powerless units. It puts rights in education at the center of development by critically integrating right to education into a diversity-and-quality-based normative dialogical framework. This construct regards education as an integral part of society to build capabilities that will produce social equity and promote a range of human rights objectives for all citizens. For development actors and all development organizations in the 21st century, they must remake themselves to be relevant to the development agendas and needs of developing countries.

China's Aid Policy

We have mentioned that China and other emerging aid giving nations have taken a different approach than the OECD to deliver aid to developing countries for mutual benefits. We want to further the discussion to demonstrate how China's aid policy exemplifies our proposed dialogical framework, though future assessment is required to ensure its agendas.

The foreign aid arena has traditionally been dominated by OECD countries. Non-traditional donors, such as China, have only emerged over the past three decades. However, the increasing importance of non-traditional donors indicates that the economic and political stronghold of the Global North in emerging countries has gradually been weakened. China, as a non-OECD country, takes an altruistic and more realistic approach to deliver aid that is seen as a useful policy instrument for ownership control in development cooperation.

Unlike traditional donors, China, currently as the largest contributor of aid to developing countries, couches its relationship with these countries in terms of South-South cooperation. As Sun (2014a) and Power and Mohan (2011) point out, China produced an African Policy document that emphasized the ideational principles of partnership, equality between partners, mutual benefit, respect for sovereignty, high transferable lessons for both parties and enhancing the self-reliance of Chinese aid recipients (Beijing Declaration, 2012). It has the core purpose and responsibility of laying a solid foundation for promoting economic and social development, improving basic education and health care in recipient countries, as well as promoting the growth of China's investments (Sun, 2014b). This norm of self-help and its related concept of self-determination or ownership, taps into a recurring missing development framework that lacks meaningful participation into the anti-dialogical development aid practices, especially the Global North nonresponsive framed idea of development partnership.

Furthermore, China's aid approaches are sometimes characterized as opposed to the *Angola Model* that not only promotes selfish quests for business, but also damages a country's fragile efforts to build a sustainable future. It is suggested that aid from China is "virtuous" because it strengthens bilateral ties and contributes to a foundation for long-term economic and social development through soft loans for infrastructure projects and revenue creation. Between 2000 and 2013, this was actualized and effected in three main ways: the creation of a $5 billion fund made up of soft and commercial loans; an undertaking to double aid by 2009, and an agreement to build 30 hospitals and train 15,000 high level workers. Although the benefits of China aid in developing countries is significant, we should reassess the type of aid China provides, its composition, and its goal and nature so that the aid tied with countries' development agendas is imperative. In terms of moral or ethical balance, China's comprehensive and multi-dimensional agenda of aid is based on the principle of equality and mutual benefit without imposing conditionalities on recipient countries. It seeks to protect right holders' rights and defies dictating rights to policy (Wen, 2011). In a word, it intends to promote the achievement of independent development while avoiding interfering with recipient countries' internal domestic politics.

CONCLUSION

Development cooperation driven by money-centric ideology has failed to broaden human capabilities and empower communities. For the future needs of humanity, global partnerships for effective development cooperation and defending rights in education contribute to improved results and support for local ownership. Through attaching conditionalities to aid and providing universalized pre-made solutions to education development, donor countries have found ways to satisfy their interests in development cooperation. The authors observed that aid provision patterns reflect and reinforce donor concerns for their own national security and preponderance of economic imperialisms. These are driven by trade and investment concerns and tensions of dependency active within the essentially unmoderated market-based aid roadmap, which allows donors to write themselves into the past, present and future of recipients as masters and arbiters. For the twenty-first century development actors and all development organizations must remake themselves to be relevant to the development agendas and needs of developing countries.

A major obstacle for development lies on the absence of human rights, ideological pluralism, and cultural relativism. Currently, development assistance still focuses on right to education rather than promoting dialogical rights in education. The interconnectedness of normative elements in aid encompassed in rights in education recreates a communalism over individualism and a platform for dialogues between aid-givers and recipients. In other words, universalism must be integrated into pluralism; then locals are able to adapt universal education and schooling to their cultural values and practices. Right to education certainly needs to be folded into rights in education to achieve autonomy respecting development and building mutuality in aid partnership. To contribute to a genuine multifaceted choice option for recipients and the concerns of countries they serve, donors must consider the unsubstantiated concept of dualism in development in unapologetic terms. Joseph Stiglitz (1998) points out the true motivation of development cooperation as:

> ... Rather than empowering those who could serve as catalysts for change within these societies, it demonstrates their impotence. Rather than promoting the kind of open dialogue that is central to the democracy, it argues at best that such dialogue is unnecessary, at worst that it is counterproductive. (p. 16)

An effective development roadmap requires a new dialogical rights-capability approach that promotes sensitivity for cultural pluralism and gives space for introspection and tolerance towards creative appropriation. This evokes the observation that right to education provides a platform for dialogues between aid donors and receivers, while rights in education informed by rights-capability approach makes it possible for the voices of all agents to be incorporated into the public debate and frameworks of action (Morin & Hessel, 2011), and also ensures that the world is not perceived in modernity or tradition as preached by hegemonic certainties of neoliberalism. To sum up, to move beyond notions of romanticization of development and benevolent development aid, development aid strategies must shift toward collaboration and empowerment, rather than be based on a hierarchical relationship between the parties involved. Thus, any cooperation must recognize donors' positions in the local context informed by how their privileges and social behaviors impact local capacities, cultures, and communities.

REFERENCES

Abdi, A. A. (2006). Culture of education, social development, and globalization: Historical and current analyses of Africa. In A. A. Abdi, K. P. Puplampu, & G. J. S. Dei (Eds.), *African education and globalization: Critical perspectives* (pp. 13–30). Lanham, MD: Rowman & Littlefield Publishers.

Alesina, A., & Dollar, D. (2000). Who gives foreign aid to whom and why? *Journal of Economic Growth, 5*(1), 33–63.

Babaci-Wilhite, Z. (2012). A human rights-based approach to Zanzibar's language-in-education policy. *World Studies in Education, 13*(2), 17–33.

Bandyopadhyay, S., & Vermann, E. K. (2013). Donor motives for foreign aid. *Federal Reserve Bank of St. Louis Review, 95*(4), 327–336.

Bearce, D. H., & Tirone, D. C. (2010). Foreign aid effectiveness and the strategic goals of donor governments. *The Journal of Politics, 72*(3), 837–851.

Beijing Declaration. (2012). *Beijing declaration of the fifth ministerial conference of the forum on China-Africa cooperation.* Beijing, China: Voltaire Network.

Berthélemy, J. C. (2006). Bilateral donors' interest vs. recipients' development motives in aid allocation: do all donors behave the same? *Review of Development Economics, 10*(2), 179–194.

Brown, S. (2009). Donor responses to the 2008 Kenyan crisis: Finally getting it right? *Journal of Contemporary African Studies, 27*(3), 1–15.

Chaponniere, J. R. (2009). Chinese aid to Africa: Origins, forms and issues. In M. P. Van Dijk (Ed.), *The new presence of China in Africa* (pp. 55–82). Amsterdam: Amsterdam University Press.

Cheng, J., Oseph, Y. S., & Shi, H. (2009). China's African policy in the post-cold war era. *Journal of Contemporary Asia, 39*(1), 87–115.

Chong, A., & Gradstein, M. (2008). What determines foreign aid? The donor's perspective. *Journal of Development Economics, 87*(1), 1–13.

Department for Education and Skills. (2005). *Five year strategy for children and learners: Putting people at the heart of public services*. London, UK: The Stationery Office.
Dichter, T. W. (2003). *Despite god intentions: Why development assistance to the third world has failed*. Amherst, MA & Boston, MA: University of Massachusetts Press.
Dreher, A., Sturm, J. E., & Vreeland, J. R. (2009). Development aid and international politics: Does membership on the UN Security Council influence World Bank decisions? *Journal of Development Economics, 88*(1), 1–18.
Dreze, J., & Sen, A. K. (2002). *India: Development and participation*. New York, NY: Oxford University Press.
Easterly, W. (2001). *The elusive quest for growth: An economist's adventures and misadventures in the tropics*. Cambridge, MA: The MIT Press.
Ellerman, D. (2001). *Helping people help themselves: Toward a theory of autonomy-compatible help* (World Bank Policy Research Working Paper, 2693). Washington, DC: World Bank.
Ellerman, D. (2004). Autonomy-respecting assistance: Towards an alternative theory of development assistance. *Review of Social Economy, LXII*(2), 149–168.
Ellerman, D. (2009). *Helping people help themselves: From the World Bank to an alternative philosophy of development assistance*. Ann Arbor, MI: University of Michigan Press.
Fleck, R. K., & Kilby, C. (2010). Changing aid regimes? US foreign aid from the Cold War to the War on Terror. *Journal of Development Economics, 91*(2), 185–197.
Flores-Crespo, P., & Nebel, M. (2005, September). Identity, education and capabilities. In *fifth international conference on the capability approach* (pp. 11–14). Paris: UNESCO.
Giroux, H. A. (2001). *Theory and resistance in education: Towards a pedagogy for the opposition*. Westport, CT: Greenwood Publishing Group.
Giroux, H. A. (2007). Beyond neoliberal common sense: Cultural politics and public pedagogy in dark times. *JAC, 27*(1/2), 11–61.
Glewwe, P., Hanushek, E. A., Humpage, S. D., & Ravina, R. (2013). School resources and educational outcomes in developing countries: A review of the literature from 1990 to 2010. In P. Glewwe (Ed.), *Education policy in developing countries* (pp. 13–64). Chicago, IL: University of Chicago Press.
Hanushek, E. (2013). Economic growth in developing countries: The role of human capital. *Economics Education Review, 37*, 204–212.
Illich, I. (1997). Development as planned poverty. In M. Rahnema & V. Bawtree (Eds.), *The post development reader* (pp. 94–112). London: Zed Books.
Jepma, C. (1997). *On the effectiveness of development aid*. World Bank, unpublished.
Kanbur, R. (2000). Aid, conditionality and debt in Africa. In F. Tarp (Ed.), *Foreign aid and development: Lessons learnt and directions for the future* (pp. 318–328). London: Routledge.
Kanbur, R. (2008). Attacking poverty: What is the value of a human rights approach? In B. A. Andreassen, S. P. Marks, & A. K. Sengupta (Eds.), *Freedom from poverty as a human right: Economic perspectives* (pp. 13–18). Paris: UNESCO Publishing.
Kanbur, R., & Sumner, A. (2012). Poor countries or poor people? Development assistance and the new geography of global poverty. *Journal of International Development, 24*(6), 686–695.
Kuziemko, I., & Werker, E. (2006). How much is a seat on the Security Council worth? Foreign aid and bribery at the United Nations. *Journal of Political Economy, 114*(5), 905–930.
Li, A. (2007). China and Africa: Policy and challenge. *China Security, 3*(3), 69–93.
Manzo, K. (2003). Africa in the rise of rights-based development. *Geoforum, 34*(4), 437–456.
Mason, M. (2009). Making educational development and change sustainable: Insights from complexity theory. *International Journal of Educational Development, 29*(2), 117–124.
Morin, E., & Hessel, S. (2011). *La Via para el futuro de la humanidad*. Barcelona: Paidós.
Ngugi, T. (1986). *Decolonizing the mind: The politics of language in African literature*. London: J. Currey.
Nordtveit, B. (2010). Development as a complex process of change: Conception and analysis of projects, programs and policies. *International Journal of Educational Development, 30*(1), 110–117.
Nussbaum, M. (2000). Women's capabilities and social justice. *Journal of Human Development, 1*(2), 219–247.

Nyamnjoh, F. B. (2011). Relevant education for African development: Some epistemological considerations. In. L. Keita (Ed.), *Philosophy and African development: Theory and practice* (pp. 139–154). Dakar: CODESRIA.

OECD. (2006). *Aid effectiveness: 2006 survey on monitoring the Paris declaration overview of the results.* Paris: OECD. Retrieved from http://www.oecd.org/dac/effectiveness/39112140.pdf

Pennycook, A. (1994). *Cultural politics of English as an international language.* London: Longman.

Power, M., & Mohan, G. (2011). China and the geo-political imagination of African 'development'. In C. M. Dent (Ed.), *China and Africa development relations* (pp. 42–67). New York, NY: Routledge.

Sen, A. (1989). Development as capability expansion. *Journal of Development Planning, 19,* 41–58.

Sen, A. (1996). On the foundations of welfare economics: Utility, capability and practical reason. In F. Farina, F. Hahn, & S. Vannucci (Eds.), *Ethics, rationality and economic behaviour* (pp. 50–65). Oxford: Clarendon Press.

Sen, A. (2000). A decade of human development. *Journal of Human Development, 1*(1), 17–23.

Sen, A. (2001). *Development as freedom.* Oxford: Oxford University Press.

Sen, A. (2004). How does culture matter. In V. Rao & M. Walton (Eds.), *Culture and public action* (pp. 37–59). Stanford, CA: Stanford University Press.

Sifuna, D. N. (2001). African education in the twenty- first century: The challenge for change. *Journal of International Cooperation in Education, 4*(1), 21–38.

Stiglitz, J. E. (1998). *Towards a new paradigm for development.* United Nations Conference on Trade and Development, Geneva.

Stiglitz, J. E. (2002). *Development policies in a world of globalization.* New International Trends for Economic Development Seminar, BNDES, Rio de Janeiro, Brazil.

Sun, Y. (2014a). *Africa in China's foreign policy.* Washington, DC: Brookings.

Sun, Y. (2014b). *China's Aid to Africa: Monster or Messiah?* Washington, DC: Brookings.

Tsuda, Y. (1986). *Language inequality and distortion in intercultural communication: A critical theory approach.* Philadelphia, PA: John Benjamins Publishing.

UNESCO. (2006). *Literacy and life (EFA global monitoring report 2006).* Paris, France: UNESCO.

United Nations. (2005). *In larger freedom: Towards development, security and human rights for all: Report of the United Nations Secretary General.* The conferences and summits in the economic, social and related fields, United Nations, New York City, NY.

Unterhalter, E. (2005). *Education and the capability approach.* The 5th International Conference on the Capability Approach, UNESCO, Paris, France.

Wen, J. (2011). China did not exploit one single drop of oil or one single ton of minerals from Africa. Retrieved from http://www.china.com.cn/economic/txt/2011 09/15/content_23419056.htm

World Bank and Organization for Economic Co-operation and Development. (2013). *Integrating human rights into development: Donor approaches, experiences, and challenges* (2nd ed.). Washington, DC: World Bank.

Xinyi Wu
Center for Language Studies
Brigham Young University

MacLeans A. Geo-JaJa
McKay School of Education
Brigham Young University

SALIM VALLY AND ENVER MOTALA

2. EMPLOYMENT, DEMOCRATIC CITIZENSHIP AND EDUCATION

Considering Alternatives to Commodification in South Africa

Toward the end of 2011, four South African progressive research organisations with staff members steeped in the struggle against the erstwhile apartheid system's education policies formed a consortium called the Education Policy Consortium (EPC).[1] The EPC embarked on a five-year research project entitled 'Building a Progressive Network of Critical Research and Public Engagement: Towards a Democratic Post-Schooling Sector'. It was understood that research which has an orientation to the wider political economy examining the intersection of the labour market, education and training requires systematic analysis including its limits and possibilities in the context of national and global development. In effect our approach was to provide insights for longer term policies and strategies and institutional interventions to build an enduring platform both for the genuine transformation of the present system and for its sustainability over time. Our primary concern revolved around the pervasive problems of unemployment, inequality and poverty and its relationship to education and training in post-apartheid South Africa.

Members of the EPC contributed to a recent book on education, the economy and society (Vally & Motala, 2014) where we critique human capital theory and systematically challenge the simplistic claims related to the link between education, economic growth and employment. We refute the perspective that situates knowledge and skills in purely instrumental terms. We argue instead that the value and purpose of education is much broader – linked to a rich tradition of praxis based on social justice and democratic citizenship.

In this chapter we examine this alternative vision and discuss alternative approaches to work, democratic citizenship and education. There is an accumulated body of practical experience and conceptual thinking about what is entailed in the conception of a wide range of demonstrable alternatives to the conventional and dominant approaches defining the relationship between learning and work. In effect the approach we take is unconstrained by the idea that there can be no alternative to the prevailing forms of work based on the requirements of capitalist labour markets. Perspectives that are skeptical about these possibilities reside in the discourse of 'there can be no alternative'. We hope to show that the possibilities for reconstituting the relationship between education and training even within the present capitalist mode of production are hardly novel but have been deliberately muted by the authority of market based systems and their ideologies. We do not regard the power and reach of these systems as unassailable, permanent or as a 'natural' state of affairs immune from human agency. We understand that dystopia ridden social systems are considerably resistant to change and that a great deal of social agency is required for change to happen. The endurance of global corporate capital, despite its continuing cycles of 'boom and bust,' wreaks havoc on the lives of millions of human beings in societies everywhere. Yet this durability and the capacity for periodic regeneration continuously fails to resolve the deeper contradictions though it simultaneously provides the impetus for transforming such societies and their social relations at the same time.

Understanding the relationship between the global and local economy and its demands on education remains critical because of the powerful and pre-emptive grip these make on the very possibility of employment shaped by conceptions of 'relevant work' and an obeisance to the requirements of such work through education and training systems. Wage-labour, we now know, is increasingly becoming more and more characterized by the life of 'wagelessness' (Denning, 2010). It has the power of reconstructing the very conception of citizenship – since without work the benefits of citizenship seem to be out of reach for so many, through the globally exclusionary forms of gendered, racist and ecological ideas and practices that sustain them (Barchesi, 2011).

Denning's (2010) provocative approach is apt for much of the process by which 'wageless life' has emerged from the rich heritages of prior experience in rural based production in South Africa out of which the process of conquest created a class of migrant labour – hostage to the wage economy and dispossessed of the means of livelihood in the emerging edifice of the formal economy. In this sense unemployment was no less the effect of creating wage labour as the dominant norm of social life. It provided the historical and conceptual form by which employment appeared as the societal standard, obfuscating the reality of its origins in the process of dispossession. In this way we can conceptualize waged work, removed from its cyclical ebbs and flows (employment and unemployment), as 'wageless life' and as the historically specific form of life based on the emergent structures.

ALTERNATIVE AND SOCIALLY USEFUL FORMS OF WORK

If the phenomenon of unemployment is irreversible in and through extant social organization, we are obliged to examine forms of work that fall outside these conventional economic and normative categories and outside the framework of the prevailing consciousness. There is and has to be life outside these normative forms given the wide diversity of work that takes place in the interstices of capitalist production even though it is often wracked by contradictory forms. Work is integral to our collective being and needs to be wrested from the terrorizing grip of its present organization since:

Paid jobs are only part of the picture. People also work to find and keep jobs and homes; to nurture others; to build communities; to access services; and more. Migrants and refugees work to sustain transnational families and build new lives. People work to establish and transform identities, protect privileges, and resist the indignities of marginalization. They work to make change. Children work, in the informal economy, as well as at home, in school, and in their communities. Many people have long worked in shadow economies; some have begun to create new kinds of local economies. And new technologies are producing novel forms of work that are only beginning to be understood. (Eastern Sociological Society, 2013)

Despite the alienating characteristics of capitalist labour that places almost insurmountable limits on personal development and the realization of one's potential, there remain 'glimmers of possibility in the conditions that capital's use of labour dictates'. Not all is 'doom and gloom' despite the socio-psychological problems generated by an era of neoliberal ideas where even the mild concessions of capitalist forms of knowledge have been reneged on in the name of austerity as Harvey (2015) argues. For him the very development of technological change would require 'a flexible, adaptable and to some degree educated labour force' (Ibid, p. 126) and the possibility of forms of family and gender relations which supersede the limits imposed by capitalism.

The question we have to ask is about how we conceptualize the difference between the forms of work that, on the one hand, are largely responses to the crisis of personal and community lives – subsistence and sub-subsistence and other forms of work – from the potentially more direct challenges responding to the alienating characteristics of capitalist production.

A whole range of socially organised forms of work – both as alternatives to formal wage-labour and in response to its marginalising effects have developed in a variety of contexts to provide meaningful avenues for livelihoods and social life. The concept of livelihood, about which much more has been written refers to attributes of work and work relationships that transcend the idea of a means to make a living and implies, definitionally, 'ways of living' which recognise socio-economic life and political, historical, geographic and other contextual factors affecting the options available for producing a living, and includes 'those labours and responsibilities associated with reproducing life' through other kinds of work (Von Kotze, 2009: 20). In such an approach it would bear reference to social institutions such as the family and community, gender relations and geographic attributes, cash and in-kind incomes to take into account the 'wider spatial context' that is implicated in such an approach to conceptualizing livelihood (Staples, 2007). These refer to avenues of work sometimes described as 'livelihoods at the margins' and could include activities which range from individual to collective responses to the failure of the market in producing useful forms of employment, through the formation of common wealth trusts, production, consumption and distribution cooperatives, solidaristic economies, climate change jobs not subject to 'greenwashing', occupied factories and communes amongst other forms of socio-economic and livelihood organisation. Each of these forms has specific characteristics although they together represent alternatives to the dominant capitalist modes of economic organization based on alienating and exploitative social relationships and unequal power.

While each of these can be described in some detail, that is not possible or necessary here. Suffice it to say that they represent important differentiating characteristics relative to conventional forms of commodified work. They represent moreover the emergence of literally hundreds (if not thousands) of small 'independent' and self-sustaining initiatives which relate to household and communities developing autonomous (and sometimes solidaristic) economies. Many of these are likely to be driven by women in communities characterised by absent-men seeking employment in the formal economy. Each of these remains fragile and many are embryonic, *and* can fail. Their sustainability is the critical issue and it raises important historical and conjunctural questions for all of those immersed in the social 'mobilization' of alternatives. In South Africa at this time a few of these initiatives have taken on the role of engaging the state in a strong sense.

Orientations to the state are affected as much by the global agenda of 'struggle' as by local context and this means that there are diverse approaches to this issue relating to the nature of the state, its historical evolution, conceptions of 'civil society organizations', and the political economy of globalisation. Indeed, formulaic approaches to the state remain unhelpful in this regard since there are no simple or general guidelines save for the recognition of the need to transform a failed system of social relations in which work is implicated, as dehumanizing and exploitative, and to build an alternative that promises forms of organization that have democratic possibilities for social change. Democratic states and their resources are without doubt critical to any social re-organization and democracy in the state is stimulated or retarded by synchronous social processes. Waiting for the state to democratize itself has no historical precedent. There is no alternative but to struggle for such democratisation by creating the spaces for engaged and active citizens to play the crucial role to play in this regard. Alternative approaches to the 'fundamental structures of power' need to be explored more fully because of the growing recognition of the power of such alternatives not beholden to conventional forms of organizing based on production processes in the main.

It is also clear that these emergent organizations are yet to develop their orientation to the practical issues of relating education to work more fully – even though they are engaged in the daily socialisation of work in practice and the application and enhancement of knowledge for development. In this sense theorising the role of education is as yet somewhat rudimentary though strongly reliant on past conceptions of Freirean approaches to adult learning, curriculum and pedagogy – emerging even more purposefully in some of the work done by members of the EPC in South Africa. In a sense the rapidity or slowness of these processes represent a failure not of the communities – but of 'educated elites' whose role can be to initiate, facilitate and foster the process of wider understanding and consciousness together with communities – as engaged intellectuals and socially responsible citizens who have the advantage of years of 'scholarly' learning and reflection.

Some of the weakness of locally based organizations can be attributed in part to the indifference of elites to their democratic responsibilities and the 'boycott' of the processes of autonomous local democratic development. This is perhaps the biggest failure of the role of universities and the institutions of learning more generally and less of the public bureaucracy, whose conceptions are limited by the immediacy of the need to reproduce social roles uncritically. In this regard there is in academia for instance a staid view about the concept of 'voice,' which is critical of it. Its critique relates to epistemological questions – i.e. questions about whether the knowledge obtained through the process of engagement is 'authentic'. In fact, the accusation leveled at engaged intellectual work is that they are driven much more by 'romantic' ideas than by 'rational' or intellectually defensible modes of 'knowledge production'. In this way, (and whatever the merits of that argument) the problematic of the role of intellectuals (and academics) in society is reduced to a debate about how knowledge is organized and developed – abandoning any reference to the underlying purposes in society. Questions about the integrity of sources and the accuracy of interpretations – and especially about the role of intellectuals in this are extremely important although such questions should be subsumed under the larger question of the obligations of intellectuals as engaged citizens – engaged in the difficult and sometimes 'messy' realm of public reasoning, activism and being.

The alternatives referred to above represent much more than the technique of survival used by marginalised communities. They present to us possibilities based on the production of socially necessary and useful goods and services – outside the forms of commodification that is at the heart of capitalist production and democratic social control and accountability based on a mixture of community and personal systems of ownership having relative independence from conventional market mechanisms and generative of a broader solidaristic economy. These exemplify ways of avoiding traditional capitalist pricing mechanisms in favour of new ideas about pricing, exchange, distribution and social reserve in the absence of the possibility for large-scale national planning; possibilities for the development of a system of agro-ecology as a viable solution to the need for food sovereignty freed from the structural inequalities and the prevailing arrangements of power; community based work in health and education, childcare and the care of the frail and aged; cooperative forms of production for school and public sector institutions offering nutrition based on localized work and community solidaristic economies; examples of municipal works projects requiring infrastructure construction, water reticulation, housing and related services and a wide range of 'development' initiatives to meet local need and properly understood as public work.

> Public work is the ability to move beyond seeing civic opportunity to actually working with others to create things of lasting social value, the essence of a free and democratic society. I would argue that public work is the defining outcome we are aiming for when we talk about civic education and community-engagement efforts. (Weinberg, 2013)

AND WHAT OF LEARNING?

How these alternatives affect any orientation to the role, forms and purposes of education is a question which needs detailed exploration which is not possible here but it is possible to signal some of the implications for education and training systems. It should be clear that in the first place what these alternatives imply is a much broader view of the role of education than is contemplated by the dominant discourse which regards education as an instrument of the labour market or even as the foundations of a 'liberal' and democratic society. The important issue for us is that in addition to the broad and multifaceted purposes of education in enhancing ideas of social justice and citizenship, education should also orient itself to supporting the development of useful livelihoods and the production of socially necessary goods and services for the survival and growth of societies.

In this regard, Southern Africa has been the locus of a very important initiative that was overtaken by the rapid development of racial capitalism shutting out its potential as an alternative possibility for education. This alternative is worth re-examining as an approach to education and training under a set of relations not so intent on destroying social lives and marginalizing rural and urban poor communities. We refer here to Patrick van Rensburg's Report from Swaneng Hill which was an extremely useful experiment and practical example which could have far reaching consequences for the shape of the education and training system and has continued relevance even if conditions have changed quite considerably from the time of its writing (Van Rensburg, 1974).

The report describes in some detail the beginnings of the project, the many ideas that were developed towards the goal of relating education to productive work based on voluntaristic approaches as a 'real saving in costs', the relationship between education and social justice through access at a time when African governments were introducing policies for 'development,' and for education as a 'major tool of this modernisation' (Ibid, p. 19). It confirms the importance of recognizing the capabilities of students and teachers in the educational process as opposed to regarding their ideas and practices as marginal relative to the larger policy objective of modernisation; the creation of 'brigades' which formed the first significant structure for 'self-help; the inculcation of ideas of social justice through the curriculum 'amongst the educated minority,' making education 'less costly, less exclusive and available to greater numbers of people'; linking what was learnt with skills that were directly useful to projects that were socially relevant in the context of limited resources and which were reinforced by 'timetable discussions with the students about their society and the country's economy' (Ibid, p. 21).

The Report describes a 'development studies' course provided to students in some detail showing that it included sections of economic analysis, studies of pre-industrial societies and the agricultural revolution, the use of natural resources and the growth of innovation and scientific progress as well as the history of innovation preceding its appearance in Europe; politics and government and the role of ruling classes in 'the control of the surplus'; contrasting pre-industrial and industrial societies and the exploitation of women and children's labour in the processes of industrialisation, slavery and colonialism and the consequences of the process of industrialisation. Van Rensburg's approach to the curriculum was shaped by his view of the attributes brought to education by its learners and how these affected their ability to learn.

> Intelligence is clearly inherent and while initiative, the ability to discriminate and to reason, and original thought are bound up with it, all these qualities can be improved through education ...Young people can probably be trained in reliability, self-discipline, self-confidence and organising ability. Integrity, moral courage and enthusiasm can possibly be inculcated: so too, possibly compassion – and through it – dedication and commitment and tolerance: qualities which make leadership at all levels sounder, wiser and more humane. Certainly the ability to communicate with others can be improved by education. (Ibid, p. 64)

Van Rensburg's assessment of the limitations of the Swaneng school refer in particular to the influence of problematic social values- 'the dominant ethos of society,' at variance with those of the school and their effects on conceptions of pay, voluntary work, certification, reward systems and the like. In his view the school constituted a 'pressure group' for altering policy; it spoke to a 'sub-culture' which even though it did not provide lucrative jobs was accepted by 'a fairly large section of the population ... provided reasonable minimum wages can be earned through their agency,' while encouraging a new approach to employment and education (Ibid, p. 65).

After returning from exile to South Africa, van Rensburg developed and presented a course on 'Education with Production'(EwP) between 1992 to 1994 as part of a Bachelor of Education programme at the universities of Cape Town, Natal and the Western Cape; conducted a series of seminars on EwP with provincial education departments between 1995–1999 and initiated projects in Mpumalanga including the Betrams Development Brigade aimed at educating and training unemployed youth in constructing housing units and renovating derelict buildings (Van Rensburg, 2001). It's useful to quote van Rensburg at length about what he refers to as "unfinished business":

> A number of meetings have been held by FEP [Foundation for Education with Production] with MECs in Provinces to discuss projects related either to the EwP curriculum or Brigades, without progress. As FEP Director, I had a meeting with Heads of Departments of Education (HEDCOM), but it brought us no closer to follow-up action.

> Approaches to the Minister of Education, Prof Kader Asmal were answered, with what seemed like interest, but my request for a meeting with the Minister to discuss FEP projects was not accepted.

> The Heads of Curriculum of nine Provinces agreed at a meeting in September 1988, attended by me as Director of FEP, to a follow-up one-day workshop to discuss the EwP curriculum. Not only was the workshop never held, but FEP never received any reply by telephone or letter to its reminders that such a meeting had been scheduled and our enquiries as to when it might be held.[2]
>
> Perhaps the most serious omission, however, relates to the failure to pursue the recommendation of the 1998 Jobs Summit about the Brigades. Here, I can only repeat what I was told by a highly placed official in the National Department of Education who would be critical to pursuing the recommendation, (and who worked in trade union education in the struggle), namely that "Brigades have not succeeded anywhere." (Ibid, pp. 129–130)

A clearly frustrated van Rensburg laments:

> Whereas in the past, liberation movements in Southern Africa had radical visions of broad socio-economic and political policy, and of education systems that would promote and serve them, today the various governments they gave rise to have almost all settled for the prevailing neo-liberal realities of a global free market…Most South Africans have tunnel vision about formal education and the capacity of matriculation to secure jobs. Many of its jobless fall prey to a burgeoning education industry, and to the diploma disease…In the course of its struggles, the ANC had looked with interest at alternatives in education and health and medical provisions. It would have looked at the potential of alternative technologies, alternatives in agriculture and alternative energy, especially in rural development, but also in housing and job-creation initiatives in towns and cities… South Africa seems now to hold alternatives in contempt, seeing them as beneath its dignity as an advanced industrialised country. (Ibid, pp. 130–131)

We are enjoined by these compelling views to be more fully conscious about the challenges to the dominant forms of production, consumption and distribution and their consequences for educational interventions which seek to introduce new approaches to learning, social consciousness and its systemic development. Not recognising some of the intractable challenges of such interventions would be naive and could have adverse consequences for any attempt at supplanting the power of what we have at present – the ideas of human capital development underpinned by global neo-liberal dogma. Supplanting the extraordinarily resistant contradictions between capital and alienated labour is not adequate unless the 'other contradictions' relating to the 'money form' and the 'private capacity to appropriate social wealth' are also dealt with (Harvey, 2015), and unless one accepts a long-term orientation to building an alternative- 'brick by-unyielding brick'. This means that it should be clear *ab initio* that attempts to create such alternatives such as through co-operatives, worker control and even the more recent expressions of solidaristic economies are likely to meet with limited success

If the aim of these non-capitalistic forms of labour organization is still the production of exchange values, for example, and if the capacity for private persons to appropriate the social power of money remains unchecked, then the associated workers, the solidarity economies and the centrally planned production regimes ultimately either fail or become complicit in their own self-exploitation. The drive to establish the conditions for unalienated labour falls short. (Harvey, 2015, p. 66)

Hence the barriers that block any attempt to construct an alternative system should not be underestimated since innovations that are intended to counteract the power of conventional systems invariably face strong resistance. Moreover, questions about the scope of alternative interventions arise almost inevitably from the perspective of planners and bureaucrats dealing with large national systems. This question has also entered the vocabulary of some academics who seek to provide 'solutions' in place or providing analytically rigorous critique which might be of use to policy-makers and the answers they seek. Systemic transformation is not simply about large-scale planning or the wider and immediate replicability of particular interventions. It is much more about changes in the public consciousness, the ability to demonstrate the efficacy and social relevance of new approaches, their sustainability, the strategies that would be required to deal with resistance to change and the organisation of the public agency to engender and support the processes for change. This is dependent on the role of intellectuals for the critical evaluation of the strengths and weaknesses of what is proposed as an alternative, foregoing the attractions of linear 'solutions' and discussions about the resource and other requirements or the appropriate 'policy interventions'. In effect a long-term orientation is required for any fundamental reorganisation to succeed.

In this regard some issues augmenting the important propositions raised by van Rensburg need much more consideration than is possible here. Amongst these is the revitalization of civic education and civic learning as important to new conceptions of work and citizenship. It would imply the development of ideas about work as intrinsic to any conception of citizenship – develop the capabilities of "citizen teachers" or "citizen faculty members," and other similar socially conscious applications of work drawing on past experience; for example, exemplified in the work of the black consciousness movement and its activists and on the important experiences of 'education with production' in the Southern African region.

Furthermore, as Boyte (2013) has argued we need to develop the methodologies and practices of 'civic science' in which the role of 'citizen educators' is critical.

The fate of democracy is inextricably tied to the work of educators, as well as to the meaning of citizenship and the practices of civic education. If we are to create a citizen-centred democracy—with citizens capable of tackling the mounting challenges of our time—we must revisit conventional ideas. We will have to reinvent citizenship as public work, for the sake of ourselves as educators, as well as for our students and for the democracy itself. (p. 1)

The relationship between work and learning must be regarded as emancipatory for both work and learning and not largely – as we think it is presently conceived in many places, as 'change oriented workplace learning' where, the conception of learning is central to the relationship with work but does not problematize the nature of workplace itself and the social relations or the relations of power it reproduces. We have to take further the argument made by Cooper and Walters (2009) that

> power relations are key to understanding learning/work processes, and that the global political economy and policy contexts have shaped social relations and impacted on learning processes, knowledge hierarchies, and educational policies and practices (p. xx)

by examining both the forms of learning and those of work that are key to the 'global political economy,' *simultaneously*. This means that, for example, worker's education can't be simply about the present forms of work and the validation of prior learning or lifelong learning but has to be about new socially determined forms of work related to new conceptions of production and realisation outside the framework of exploitative and oppressive systems. There is a great deal of experience based on the work of the many Freireans in South Africa and their work over the years including the history of such pedagogical development through organizations like the South African Committee for Higher Education (SACHED) (Coleman, 1989) and others in the past. We simply have to recall these ideas and the strategies developed with them. These included a 'pedagogy of contingency' responding to context and new discovery, taking into account conditionality, chaos and uncertainty in dealing with the dynamics of changing social relations. This will inevitably imply a careful look at the best methodologies of enquiry for promoting what might be called 'public and participatory' methodologies so that the issues, context and modes of participation in the research process are planned fully beyond their present limits. We know that there are real possibilities in this direction in the organizations which have grown autonomously as a consequence of the present social and political crisis. And as we are finding out there are many such organizations in our communities.

An orientation to the concepts of *work and education* avoiding the danger of becoming categories of accommodation to the multiple forms of their commodification is therefore of great contemporary value. Implicit in our definitions and analysis of these concepts is the prior question of 'what social system'? For example, we do not seek more and wider recognition of women's work and a validation of women's contribution to society, without asking the question about what kind of society we are talking about. Nor are the challenges to workplace learning simply about 'empowering' workers, within the framework of existing 'labour relations.' Put another way, we are interested to know how the specific form of work ('women's work' or other) leads to social ends that do not reproduce the forms of social power prevalent – even if the alternatives contemplated in the forms of work and learning are in an embryonic form opening the wider social possibilities for contesting the hegemony of its present forms. It means making capitalist relationships more explicit in our approaches to concepts like lifelong learning, etc., without treating its production systems as inevitable and normative, and re-examining concepts about lifelong learning relative to work and its contradictory applications. This requires an elucidation of the theoretical reappraisal of the work/learning relationship as presently conceptualized against the 'materiality' of capitalist social relations, that are gendered and racialized, eliciting new forms of social organization – and therefore of work in a new relationship to the acquisition of knowledge, practical know how and wisdom.

THE IMPLICATIONS OF OUR CRITIQUE

As we have argued, the prevailing global economic system has an extraordinarily dominant role in shaping social, political, cultural, environmental, and educational systems – because global corporate profit-seeking organizations exercise such an overpowering influence and reach in shaping their planetary interests even while they seek to universalise these interests through 'manufacturing consent.' This is true even after the 'great collapse' of 2008 when the most powerful capitalist states stepped into the breach to support some of the largest corporations on the globe.

Several implications flow from the foregoing critique. Policy makers, academic analysts, social commentators and all those concerned with 'transformation' need to explore more fully the relationship between the alternative livelihood, socio-economic, citizenship-based and cultural and solidaristic activities in which especially the most marginalized sections of society are engaged *together with* the learning that takes place in the alternative activities of such communities. Such an exploration would provide a stronger theoretical, practical and organisational basis for an alternative, more robust and meaningful curriculum – not determined by the requirements of capitalist labour markets but by the requirements of a democratizing society, seeking support for the self-generative activities of such communities towards the development of a conscious and engaged citizenry.

Furthermore, the implications for academics and others interested in the process of knowledge development that new areas and programmes of research must be developed arising from the growth of alternative educational systems, processes and actions. Other areas include, new and appropriate criteria for educational assessment, practical arrangements for a wider range of educational settings, and volunteer-based advanced learning, using both conventional and non-conventional pedagogies. Careful attention needs to be given to participatory processes in which communities are directly involved in research, curriculum and pedagogical planning.

Our approach suggests that educational phenomena must be examined from the perspective of a range of academic disciplines because we recognize the complexity of such inter-related phenomena even though it is often the case that one or other domain of knowledge can have a stronger role than others for critical analysis. For instance – while looking at in-classroom practice it is obvious that factors relating to how teachers teach and learners learn, the curriculum, text, language and their related issues have a large role to play. But this role too is circumscribed by the conditions which provide the socio-linguistic context that impacts on how learning takes place. So too for instance we know that nutrition is critically important in making learning possible and that its absence inhibits the process of acquiring knowledge since social issues like the background of learners is implicated in the health and education of a learner. Yet there is a wider set of considerations to be taken into account even here since as we have observed the issue of language (and culture, tradition and practice in the home) are as central to the construction of the process of learning and the pedagogical strategies implied in this.

We are also obliged therefore to avoid linearity – simple causalities – and to pay regard to the relationship between the complex interplay of the sociological, political (policy and political choice-related), economic, linguistic, cultural, economic and ecological issues which need to be brought into a framing analysis to understand complex social phenomena more fully. This would imply an analysis of the assumptions, concepts and categories useful for analysis. Greater support for research that transcends disciplinary limitations is necessary to examine such alternative approaches and much more needs to be done beyond an examination of the efficacy of the Post-School legislation and its implementation on the institutional structures, governance and management of Technical Vocational Education and Training, and the curriculum and qualifications appropriate to post-schooling. While these latter have importance for informing policy and institutional practice such research should not be hamstrung by the limitations of formal education systems and formal labour markets to the exclusion of all else. Progressive research should strive to situate its enquiry within a framework of alternative approaches to power and agency, both as means and ends to a society freed from the limitations of wage-relations, market-based ideologies and the cultural consciousness these produce. Such research could deepen our understanding of work as it has evolved historically towards its present form in the ubiquitous formal labour markets characterized by 'brokered', 'underutilized,' 'wasted', 'underemployed', alienating, marginalized, and forms of work in their gendered and racist incarnations in both the North and South, 'centre' and 'periphery,' in global regimes of production.

We need to examine even more deeply the uses of concepts familiar to the world of progressive education, like adult learning, lifelong learning, continuous learning, access, non-formal learning, inclusion and exclusion, and participatory learning, in relation to alternative social forms of work organisation. Inherent to such an approach is a better understanding of socio-linguistic requirements of educational systems drawing on ethnographic accounts of the life of the most socially marginalized. The latter accounts are useful to understand better the lives, experiences, knowledge, aspirations, political and social traditions and the struggles of the communities of the rural and working classes. These ethnographies provide a depth of qualitative understanding not given to survey based research even if these are augmented by group based enquiry and other similar methods. The advantage we see in ethnographic work is derived from the possibility of acquiring historical and contextual 'evidence' beyond the data available through more conventional forms of enquiry.

Moreover, the alternatives we suggest relative to work and learning should be consistent with progressive ways of thinking about sustainable planetary ecology.

> The relentless privatization of nature and production ... leaves little option – if human beings are to continue to advance – other than the socialization of nature and production. Only in this way can the conditions of life and human existence be safeguarded. Since work constitutes the basis of the human relation to nature, the socialization of nature can only be fully realized if accompanied by the socialization of production. (Foster, 1994, p. 142)

This relationship between production and nature too requires a deeper understanding of the possibilities for new forms of work based on cooperative, collective, democratic and other genuinely alternative forms of socially useful learning.

Ultimately our research and the work we do should enable us to explore the fuller possibilities that exist for the production of strong and purposeful research and practical ideas based on integrative science, engaged scholarship and social consciousness based on a broader intellectual perspective for committed educational activism inspiring public and democratic agency. We suggest that it is necessary to examine the form, content, methodologies, and praxis related to the idea of socially useful work as intrinsic to the relationship between education and training, work and society. This should be done neither solely as a response to corporate power, nor simply as a reform of the legacies of the apartheid state, but as a transformative of social life, livelihoods, citizenship and rights, predicated on a fundamentally different organization of social power and on the agency of those in society most affected by the present arrangement of social relations in the labour market and its associated forms of education and training. Most of all it requires us to demonstrate the possibilities, efficacy and socially just implications of such transformative approaches bearing reference to local and other experiences in the quest for work and learning as useful for the realisation of humanistic values. We can only hope that this provokes us all to think about the intellectual challenges for producing a radical and alternate consciousness, culture and society.

NOTES

[1] The constituent organisations are the Centre for Education Policy Development; University of the Witwatersrand's Institute for Research into Education and Labour; University of Johannesburg's Centre for Education Rights and Transformation; University of Fort Hare's Nelson Mandela Institute and the Nelson Mandela Metropolitan University's Centre for Integrated Post-School Education and Training.

[2] Similarly, the Betrams Development Brigades has received no support, financial or technical, from either the Department of Education or of Labour, at either National or Provincial level. Visits were made by three persons from the Department of Education to the project, about which they were positive, but there was no follow-up action to any of the visits. An invitation to the Deputy Director General was refused.

REFERENCES

Barchesi, F. (2011). *Precarious liberation: Workers, the state, and contested social citizenship in post-apartheid South Africa.* New York, NY: SUNY Press.
Boyte, H. (2013). *Reinventing citizenship as public work.* Dayton, OH: Kettering Foundation.
Coleman, G. (1989). *A history of the South African Committee for Higher Education (SACHED) 1959–1987.* Durban: University of Natal.
Cooper, L., & Walters, S. (Eds.). (2009). *Learning/Work: Turning work and lifelong learning inside out* (pp. xx). Cape Town: HSRC Press.
Denning, M. (2010). Wageless life. *New Left Review,* (66), 79–97.
Eastern Sociological Society. (2013). Call for contributions: Invisible Work 2014 Conference.
Foster, J. B. (1994). *The vulnerable planet: A short economic history of the environment* (p. 142). New York, NY: Monthly Review Press.
Harvey, D. (2015). *Seventeen contradictions and the end of capitalism* (p. 126). Oxford: Oxford University Press.
Staples, J. (2007). *Livelihoods at the margins.* Walnut Creek, CA: Left Coast Press Inc.
Vally, S., & Motala, E. (2014). *Education, economy and society.* Pretoria: UNISA Press.
Van Rensburg, P. (1974). *Report from Swaneng Hill: Education and employment in an African country.* Uppsala, Sweden: Almqvist and Wiksell.

Salim Vally
Centre for Education Rights and Transformation
Faculty of Education
University of Johannesburg

Enver Motala
Nelson Mandela Institute
University of Fort Hare

NAZIA BANO

3. THE PROBLEM OF UNDERDEVELOPMENT AND PERSPECTIVES ON TRANSFORMATIVE DEVELOPMENT

The Case of Pakistan

The problem of underdevelopment of traditional/indigenous communities in Pakistan has created enormous socio-politico challenges at various levels. It is argued that on one hand religious fundamentalism has fostered extremist ideology (Cohen, 2009) in indigenous communities, and, on the other hand, the waves of Marxism have raised consciousness and expectations among the youth of these communities but have failed to solve development problems (Bakhteari, 1996). In the current chaotic scenario, youth and young adults are the centre of attention in two respects: (i) they are the victims of false and irrelevant ideologies prevalent in their tribal/traditional/ isolated society, and (ii) they are the hope for reshaping a better society in Pakistan. 'Change' is inevitable now at every level.

It is largely acknowledged by development economists that Pakistan has failed to translate its impressive economic growth into the improvement of human development indicators. Since the 90s, its rank in UNDP's Human Development Index has declined from 139 (Human Development Reports, UN, 1997) to 147 (Human Development Report, UN, 2015). In the spectrum of economic policy and planning development, investment in human capital was inevitable for attaining high economic growth that recommended building more schools in the areas where people do not have access to education services. Most of these areas are located in rural communities where the majority of the population resides. However, despite continuous national and international efforts Pakistan has not achieved either the target of 100% universalization of primary education nor has it been successful in controlling the dropout rate of children and youth in rural areas that is above 50% in all provinces of Pakistan (National Commission for Human Development, 2013).

According to local intellectuals and practitioners in the field of development education working in traditional communities, in the absence of relevant, useful education, proper guidance and leadership, local people even those who have completed their formal education are left isolated, facing the dilemma of identity crises as they do not feel connected with their local communities nor have they established their position or status in mainstream institutions. In this critical scenario, there are organizations and people who now question the basic ideas of 'development' and 'education'.

In 2004, I had an opportunity to engage with an NGO, the Institute for Development Studies and Practices (IDSP), that has been working in the most deprived province of Pakistan for more than 30 years. This organization mostly works with young male and female members of tribal communities in various districts of Balochistan. Being part of rural communities for a long time and knowing their realities, strengths, weaknesses, issues, culture, and people, IDSP firmly asserts that "every human being is equal and has the potential to create, develop, produce, generate, vitalize and revitalize processes, thoughts, and actions based on humility, humanism, trust, justice, truth, self, and mutual accountability and transparency" (IDSP, 2010, p. 1). IDSP strives "to relearn, regenerate, regain, and reclaim the indigenous values, practices, processes, and repressed knowledge based on local wisdom and knowledge" (IDSP, 2010, p. 1).

IDSP strongly voices the critique of mainstream notions and practices of development and it uses alternative approaches to educate and develop its targeted population. In order to empower youth of traditional society and to develop a cadre of effective thinkers, practitioners, and activists, it offers two types of non-formal development studies courses under its Academic Development Program (ADP). The two main courses are (i) a "Development Studies Course" for both men and women and (ii) a "Mainstreaming Gender and Development (MGD) Course" for women only. This program integrates community-development practices and critical theoretical perspectives. The theoretical framework of ADP courses was developed in the form of three core themes. The themes are: (i) the Colonial and imperialist basis of leading development practices, (ii) Critical pedagogy and radical education, (iii) Spirituality, culture, and social change. In this emancipatory educational program, students experienced self-actualization, gender-sensitization, decolonization, re-inhabitation, and praxis. Their transformative learning experiences in IDSP and their development practices have reshaped and transformed their perspectives, their personal lives, and their professional community development practices.

This chapter is based on a case study that was conducted in IDSP at Balochistan to examine the IDSP stakeholders' transformative notions of development and their emancipatory actions at micro, meso, and macro levels. I employed two critical theories to understand their transformative perceptions and practices: Boaventura de Sousa Santos's (1999) *Postmodern Critical Theory* and Jack Mezirow's (1978) *Transformative Learning Theory*. This chapter will share key elements and conditions that contributed to bring 'change' at the micro level in a traditional society that is dealing with the challenges of extremism, poverty, and the gravity of globalization.

In this case study twenty-one IDSP stakeholders including 4 administrators, 3 teachers, 8 male learners, and 6 female leaners participated. These participants were selected using purposive, convenience, and theoretical sampling techniques and following specific selection criteria designed for each group of stakeholders, administrators, teachers, and learners. Two primary qualitative-research research methods were used to collect data from the research participants: (i) document analysis and (ii) in-depth interviews with IDSP administrators, teachers, and students (Marshall & Rossman, 2006).

IDSP STAKEHOLDERS' CRITIQUE OF MAINSTREAM DEVELOPMENT NOTIONS AND PRACTICES

IDSP stakeholders explained the following problems they associate with the mainstream or Western notions of development. Such notions, they believe:

- are limited in perspective: they are fictitious, posing as universal truths when they are not;
- are irrelevant to local realities; they are not applicable in rural communities of Pakistan;
- are imposed, not evolved; people and systems were not prepared for globalization, certainly not for "instant globalization;" and
- promote mainstream symbolic aspects of development.

Transformation of IDSP Stakeholders' Perspectives on Notions of Development

IDSP stakeholders explained their perceived notions of development in a variety of ways. For example, they explained it in terms of implications for the personal level, local level, and global level. The IDSP Director explained it both in an ideological or philosophical form and in a practical or functional form.

When I asked, "what does it (development) mean to you? Or how do you define the word "development," most participating IDSP learners (students), responded that real development is "development of your intellect." However, most of the administrators relate the notion of development to humanism, humanist values, and humanity. Humanism and humanist values, in IDSP's ADP, are defined in terms of humans' unlimited potential for growth, human freedom and autonomy, of equity and equality, and of human responsibility both to self and others. Cranton and Taylor (2012) referred to these humanist values as humanist assumptions which, they claim, are "inherent in transformative learning theory" (p. 6).

In terms of development at the local level, all IDSP stakeholders put emphasis on pro-people and local-relevant development projects and programs. The IDSP Director and other administrators, in the light of their own community development practices, shared a philosophy of doing development education at the grass-roots level. Their alternative notions of "development" focus on:

- intellectual development,
- humanism, humanist values, and humanity, and
- development relevant to local realities – local needs, local context, local agenda, local priorities.

Development as intellectual development. "Intellectual development" was the most common response among all IDSP learners as their alternative notion of development. They emphasized development of critical and analytical minds in their society. While they were explaining this notion they were actually comparing it to materialistically symbolic pursuits and goals (construction of high rise buildings, promoting high socio-economic status for some in society) and the agenda of Westernization or modernization at the center of mainstream development. Instead, they emphasized human development, but not in the sense in which it is generally understood in the field of national development and development education. For example, human development is generally taken as synonymous with educated, healthy, responsible "human resources" for increasing already high economic growth rates. IDSP learners instead emphasized human intellectual development, not specifically for development of the country, but for the sake of the individuals' own enlightenment or liberation.

By the word "development" they refer to the following human capabilities: high level of intellect, critical thinking skills, combination of both intellect and personality development, conscience, thoughtfulness, wisdom, developing broader perspectives, adaptation of knowledge and skills, learning new things, cognitive development, emotional development, keeping one's mind positive, clear and clean thinking, ability to convert negative things into positive things, giving awareness, bringing change, better understanding, mental progress, and understanding of systems.

In the view of IDSP learners, the intellectual development of a person greatly reduces the probability that others will misguide you; one learner said you will not follow others blindly if you are developed in a real sense. In her view, the development of intellect greatly enhances one's potential power over one's destiny; she said "you will never develop until you stop [blindly] following others" (A Female Learner). IDSP learners believe in the power of a critical and analytical mind because it gives one strength to get control over one's own life. One female learner concluded "the power of mind is greater than the power of arms".

IDSP learners' advocacy for developing critical thinkers at grassroots levels is logically consistent with today's ugly reality in Pakistan where youth and people of traditional and tribal communities are being abused and destroyed by several political and religious extremist groups. In the views of IDSP stakeholders, people of such communities will be genuinely developed if they are given critical awareness and taught "hidden knowledge," if they are able to analyze every situation, ideology, action, happenings, and events, with a critical mind. However, "Hidden knowledge" refers here to knowledge that consists of critical perspectives and theories, alternative ideas and views, and literature focused on knowledge of particular relevance to marginalized people but not usually taught in mainstream institutions. According to IDSP stakeholders, with an analytical and critical mind people of their community can choose their own path and no external or internal group would easily be able to exploit them.

Development as humanism, humanist values, humanity. With regard to the concept and practices of development, IDSP stakeholders, particularly IDSP administrators, emphasized humanism, humanist values, and humanity. With respect to IDSP's own position on the concept of "development" one administrator said:

> There is a definition of development, but basically what really matters is how we look at it and what vision we have of it. Like if we say a society should be developed then what (things) will make it developed. Normally, in a typical way, the physical state and social conditions of that society should be better. For us (in IDSP) development should, most importantly, focus on human values or principles of humanity, for example the aspects of equality, justice, equal treatment; it should not promote discrimination and hatred. It should have (or portray) a human face. (A Male Administrator)

He added that, to preserve socio-economic stability, provision of basic needs is necessary (infrastructural development); however, what is essential in the "project of development" is the element of "humanist values." IDSP administrators and other stakeholders define the humanism or principles of humanity in the concept of development in following terms:

- It must acknowledge and respect diversity
- It must maintain peoples' dignity
- Everyone must be treated equally
- Everyone must be respected
- Everyone must be heard and given voice
- It should not promote discrimination and hatred
- It should be pro-people
- It should not contain exploiting factors

IDSP administrators urged promotion of these principles of humanity in programs and projects of development education. They stated that it is imperative for development practitioners to raise their voice for incorporating these human values in all kinds of development programs. One administrator said that human values must be central to the framework under which development programs are designed. In his view, human-related development projects and programs, such as poverty reduction programs sponsored and shaped by international organizations and state institutions of education are useless if they cannot address issues of inequality and discrimination in a society.

IDSP learners too stressed teaching basic principles of humanity in development education programs. In their views, "development" means to be aware as a human being grounded in humanism and having firm belief in the value of humanity as a whole. In their views, human beings can only be called developed if they learn to value other human beings and humanity and if they able to acknowledge or "understand what righteous actually is" (A Male Leraner). One learner said "To respect human values is actually the development. Otherwise, if the meaning of development is constructing high-rise building, roads, and bridges then Karachi should be the most developed place, but it is not" (A Male Learner).

In my view, the IDSP learners' interpretation of humanism specifically includes the principles of openness and acceptance of others. Their approach to understanding the issue of inequality was practical and related to existing social issues in our society. Their intention in defining development in terms of creating faculties of openness and acceptance within people is an effort to address people's rigid and hostile attitudes and perceptions toward "other" people because of their different religious background, ethnicity, sexual orientation, geographical location, socio-economic status, etc.

IDSP stakeholders urged that it is very important to highlight these human values in the concept of development and also in designing development projects; otherwise, anything encompassed in mainstream "Western" stereotypes of development will be considered as development by common people. They are not against building infrastructure and provision of basic human facilities for their communities. They acknowledge the importance of infrastructure, as well as technological, and communication development; however, their main focus is to give humanity, humanism, and humanist values the central place in the concept of development. In their view, "a society can function and grow only on the principles of humanity" (IDSP Administrator).

Development must be contextualized in local realities. IDSP stakeholders also define the term "development" by making references to development projects run by government, non-government/non-profit, and international development organizations in the province of Balochistan. Their concern and interest in community development projects and programs makes sense because hundreds of development programs in the fields of education, health care, women's development, child welfare, poverty reduction, rehabilitation, rural development, non-formal education, and so forth are currently operating in Balochistan. Besides some mega-projects of national and provincial governments (e.g., Balochistan Rural Support Program) and international development organizations (USAID, UNICEF, Concern, Save the Children, UNDP, CIDA) more than 1035 registered Non-profit Organizations are functioning in the development sector of Balochistan since 2000 (Social Policy and Development Centre, 2002).

The focus of IDSP stakeholders' conversations with respect to development programs in Balochistan consistently gravitated around one word, "localization." Within this rubric, they criticized the role of global institutions such as the United Nations and other international-development organizations and institutions in the development sector of Pakistan. They argued that, in Balochistan, global institutions bring their own specific agenda and they influence the practices of all stakeholders in the development projects they sponsor and control. One administrator explained this and said "if the UN decides to declare a decade as [dedicated to] prevention of HIV, immediately all NGOs and development interventions start working on HIV" (IDSP Administrator). According to IDSP stakeholders, global institutions' development agendas undermine local public issues by overwhelming and ignoring them. In their view, poverty, health, water resource management, women's education, religious extremism, and ethnic violence are the basic issues of Balochistan. They argued that, in the presence of such issues, one would expect to find development programs focused on environment, family planning, and charity schemes. Therefore, each aspect of any community development program, in the views of IDSP stakeholders, must be relevant to local realities. From conceptualization of each program to its design, planning, budgeting, implementation, monitoring, and evaluation, they like to see local peoples' involvement at every stage of the program.

In the view of IDSP stakeholders, improvement or development will occur only if it is relevant to local realities. It is important to understand here what they mean by local relevancy or local realities. They mean that local resources, local capacity, local wisdom, local needs, local issues, local culture, local knowledge systems, local interventions, local human resources, local agendas, local priorities, local development indicators, local economic conditions, and the local political situation shape and delimit the success of all development projects. They urged that International Development Organizations (IDOs) incorporate local issues and local needs in all development interventions in Balochistan.

IDSP stakeholders argued that communities will "develop" when local resources are used in the implementation process of projects. They reproached international development projects that come with conditions that ignore local realities. They shared some examples of projects in which officials were instructed to buy vehicles from the West. In a similar vein, in some flood relief projects project leaders were instructed to buy food items only from the Islamabad (Capital of Pakistan) and certain international food companies instead of local vendors. However, IDSP stakeholders insisted upon using local markets. In their views, such initiatives that leave out the local context and ignore local resources destabilize the local economy when they could play a significant role in boosting it.

IDSP stakeholders repeatedly highlighted the importance of local peoples' involvement in each phase and stage of community development programs. They believe in the capabilities of local people to pursue and execute any task of community development projects. In this regard, they criticized the extensive involvement of outsiders or foreigners in development of projects and programs. According to one IDSP teacher, non-local consultants denigrate local practices in their project evaluation reports and leave a negative impression of local people and their culture in these reports. In their view, this approach to development and associated methodologies only benefits those who are already privileged, although it certainly exploits those local people whose issues are used for initiating these projects. One IDSP teacher stated with anguish that "A project that involves and represents local people's views is still missing" (IDSP Teacher).

IDSP's Conceptual Framework of ADP for the Development of an Individual

The conceptual framework of ADP explains the phenomenon of development or transformation of an individual in IDSP. This framework has three main components: Self-development, professional development, and institutional building. These components are presented as components of a triangle in Figure 1.

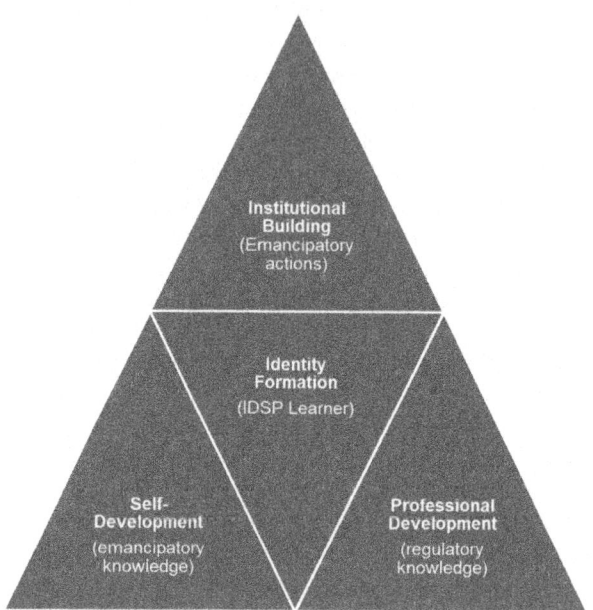

Figure 1. IDSP framework of ADP

The first component of the triangle is self-development. In ADP, self-identity is first developed through a process of self-actualization in which participants in the courses revisit assumptions and beliefs they have embraced over the years about their own personality and identity. They identify their weaknesses and strengths and assess their actual potential. Then, by learning about dynamics of different kinds of behaviour, their "new self" starts to develop. However, the journey of self-development is furthered by participation in gender discourse, religious discourse, and development discourse and by constant interaction with their own community during field assignments.

The second component of this triangle is professional development or professionalism. The IDSP Director said that professionalism starts when the self is developed. In ADP, participants have to learn several kinds of skills such as writing, presentation, computer use, planning and budgeting, and organization and management of field activities. In ADP, a discrete module on communication skills and types of behaviour (e.g., assertive, aggressive, and passive) is taught to all participants to develop their public communication skills with co-workers, community members, and governmental officials.

The apex of this triangle is institution-building. In ADP, individuals come with their own ideas and they test out their ideas and work on them. It is expected that at some point learners should be able to theorize, research, and integrate their practices by themselves. According to the Director of the IDSP, "these practices will create a fire and curiosity in them and they will be eager to know the impact of their work." In her view, that curiosity and eagerness should lead them towards institution-building. However, the institution-building she envisioned for her learners is quite atypical. She clarified:

> We want our learners to learn institution building but not typical institution-building; the institution building [that we want them to learn is one] in which you can house your own growing program and accommodate your own idea(s). And, for grooming your ideas, whatever the kind of capacity, whether you are doing it from your home or your car or sitting on a road or renting a room. There is no [necessary] condition; rather what is really important is the understanding of systems, how do systems work, what do I need to continue my idea; so that is the third point of triangulation, and then again it will connect with self and then you will reach professionalism. So that was the method we have created in our course for youth development.

Explaining the overarching cumulative phenomenon in this framework (i.e., the IDSP-learner identity formation) Dr. Bakhteari stated that the identity of an IDSP learner should be formed in a way that would not boost her or his own ego; rather it should be formed so as to orient the learner toward planning for "others." The emphasis is placed on "others." And who are the relevant "others?" They are family, community, and marginalized groups of the community. She explained that in this triangle "young people will build a mirror and they will develop themselves by looking into that mirror. So, they should make the mirror and carefully consider the reflection in that mirror; and, who is the mirror — their people, their community, that is the mirror."

IDSP's Ideology of Development Practices: A Journey of Moving from Micro to Macro & Macro to Micro

In the context of doing or practicing development in local communities of Balochistan, the IDSP Director and other participants shared their concerns regarding existing development practices. They particularly criticized the short duration of community development projects. In their views, such short-term projects leave a black hole at the ground level that causes new social problems in the communities. Focusing on this particular issue, the IDSP Director stated her own idea of community development practices.

According to her, the process of development has many dimensions. In her view, it is absolutely unethical and unprofessional for a development practitioner to complete one dimension and leave it without addressing other emerging dimensions. She said people who think they have completed their job after executing only one development project should not step into this field. She explained her own philosophy of doing development work in local communities. She envisions community development practice as a journey of constant movement from a micro level to several macro levels (see Figure 2). In her view, it does not matter if a development project is small or big; what really matters is identifying the emerging dimensions of development in the process of development. Her philosophy of development practices is presented below in her own words:

> I, after doing all this (PhD and building 2000 girls schools in Balochistan or breaking one of the myths about Balochistan) again want to return to the same unit. This is what I believe all the time – from point to macro and from macro to point (start from a point to reach to macro level and then again return to the point and go to macro). This has been the centre point of my life.

In her view, it is crucial for a development practitioner or group of development practitioners to come back to the point from which a development project started. She believes that a number of changes occur "on the ground" during a project creation and execution process; therefore, it becomes essential for the practitioners involved to take account of all the changes that have occurred and start addressing them.

Her vision of development practices is captured in Figure 2. In this figure, different colours indicate different dimensions of the development. To show the journey of

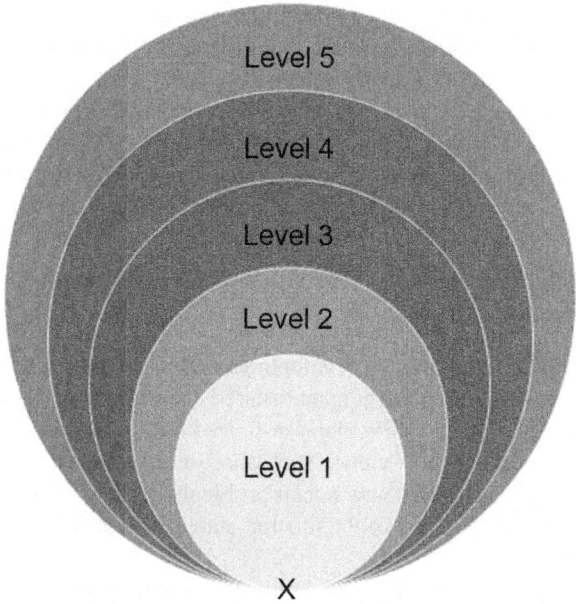

Figure 2. IDSP philosophy of development practices

the development process I use circles of different sizes. These sizes do not reflect the scope of the development project; instead they show the significance or strength of grasping the development process. Each circle indicates completion of one cycle addressing one dimension of development. For example, Level 1 indicates that a development project was initiated from a "Point X" and reached completion the apex of the Level-1 circle; however, the practitioner will come back to the same Point X and start addressing another dimension from the same point and take it to the macro level (i.e., the apex of level 2), but it again comes back to the Point X and continues its journey until a strong model of development will emerge.

EMANCIPATORY ACTIONS: SUCCESSES AND SHORTFALLS

Baumgartner (2001) believes that "action on… [a] new perspective is imperative;" for her, "not only seeing, but living… [a] new perspective is necessary" (p. 17). This chapter illuminates the influence of participants' participation in ADP on self-reported perceptions of their engagement in community development practices, the main thrust of the final research question of this study. In the following sections I will outline actions which participants took both individually and collectively at three levels in terms of scope: micro, meso, and macro. Actions taken individually to address personal, family, and societal issues are reported as "micro level." Actions taken (individually or collectively) to confront some community issues on a small scale are reported as "meso level." Actions taken either at a national level or which received national attention are reported as "macro level."

Emancipatory actions at the micro level. There are three major kinds of intentional micro-level actions reported by IDSP stakeholders. The first type of action they took was focused on ensuring gender balance at all levels, family, work, and community. The second important type of action they took was raising voice against exploitation and oppression. The third category of their emancipatory actions is related to serious societal problems such as corruption, nepotism, oppression and exploitation of marginalized groups. This third category of emancipatory action relates to ethical decisions that they took to prevent themselves from taking part in any activity that could lead them into corruption or force them to exploit others. They took these actions because they did not want to compromise their personal integrity based on the humanitarian principles which they learned in ADP courses. I explain the details of these three key actions below.

Ensuring gender balance at family level and work. The process of self-actualization and gender sensitization during the IDSP transformative learning process crystalized in learners' minds the injustice prevailing particularly at home and generally in society. After reframing their subjective and gendered identities, participants took bold steps to ensure gender balance in their families, work places, and community. They are trying to create gender balance in society by fighting against gender inequality through making appropriate personal choices, becoming involved in all family decisions, and sharing knowledge on gender issues with family and community members. A recent evaluation study conducted by IDSP in 2012 on its MGD graduates, *Explore and study the impact of Mainstreaming Gender and Development courses of IDSP since 2003–2010 on its graduate learners of Balochistan*, reports that, after completing the course, sixty-three percent of the IDSP female graduates have resumed their education. Bypassing the teaching profession which is considered the "most suitable" profession for females, forty-three percent of female IDSP graduates decided to choose community development work by joining non-government organizations and by establishing self-employed skill-development centres (Qambrani & Qambrani, 2012). Most of them, after the course, decided to join the higher-education institute, also an uncommon phenomenon in a traditional society.

Research findings of this study demonstrate that, after going through the gender sensitization phase in ADP courses, both male and female participants examined the role and status of female family members with a new understanding. They came to see clearly the male dominance in most family matters, particularly in the lack of voice and power of their mothers and other significant female family members in the family decision-making process. Female participants stated that during their studies at IDSP they shared their transformative knowledge, particularly on gender issues, with their parents. By transferring gender-sensitive knowledge they convinced their parents that they should be given freedom to make personal choices and be consulted on family decisions, particularly those related to their own lives. However, some female participants reported that becoming part of the family decision process involved long arguments with their parents. Sometimes they even had to face opposition from male relatives who have unwarranted and unnecessary influence over and interfere in the family matters. In most cases, these relatives opposed girls' education and career choices.

Male research participants also shared their efforts to promote gender balance in their own homes and in their work environment. Their statements on their intentional actions toward that end reveal that their vehemently-entrenched attitudes towards gender-specific (stereotypically male) roles have changed. They have come to understand that the social reality specific to gendered identities and subjectivities is not the natural order of things. They claimed that now they participate in home chores while earlier it was a matter of honor and ego not to do so. Some male learners who are married and have daughters shared courageous decisions they took to open the doors of new opportunities for their daughters. For example, one father allowed his teen-age daughter to travel to Quetta, Karachi, and Islamabad from his home town Sibi, to compete in an Intel computer-software project.

In a similar vein, male participants shared ways in which they have tried to create gender balance in their work places. They stated that in their organizations they have always tried to recruit local females and oppose hiring non-local females. They further reported that they had tried their best to provide local females a supportive working environment so they can become a source of inspiration for other local women. Most of the male learners are associated with the NGO sector; so, not surprisingly, they claimed that at every opportunity they encourage gender mainstreaming. They claimed that in all kinds of developmental activities they assured a fair representation of women. Contrary to female participants, male participants did not mention any challenges in reducing gender imbalance in work places. Instead they shared their efforts to introduce gender-sensitive policies and initiatives at work.

Female research participants claimed that consciously and unconsciously they have acted upon gender-relevant issues and events in their lives. However, despite continuous efforts, they face difficulties in fostering gender balance in the work place and at the community level. In their view, "people do not want to accept it [gender balance] ...and they take it as a joke" (A Female Learner). They explained that it was extremely hard for them to create gender balance outside the home boundaries. In their view, achieving gender balance in a traditional society is the most important but also the most difficult task. They said that, in their work places and in informal gatherings in their communities, they had always felt alone whenever they raised their voices on gender-sensitive issues or took a stand to defend their rights. They said that people in their offices and in their communities laugh at them and make fun of their views related to gender.

Raising one's voice against exploitation and oppression. One important outcome of emancipatory education in ADP courses is the IDSP stakeholders' capacity to challenge agents of hegemonic institutions, unscrupulous employers, and supporters of oppressive social structures. Findings of this research reveal that, in many public forums and meetings, participants had openly criticized and challenged those meta-narratives, habits, and ways of being that have been major sources of exploitation and oppression of vulnerable members of society.

In de Sousa Santos's Postmodern Critical Theory, the existence of a culture of silence in postcolonial societies is considered one of the main difficulties preventing reinvention of alternative knowledges. All IDSP stakeholders also confirmed the presence of a culture of obedience and conformity in their communities. They said that this culture had made the common rural and tribal people believe that everything is fine in their social systems. One learner said that "Somehow we are taught/given a message to be silent and to be quiet on events happening in the world or in a family or in our society or in our area. We are not allowed to question anything" (A Male Learner). They said that this culture of obedience and silence is reinforced so strongly that it is very hard for common people to challenge it. In the views of IDSP stakeholders, this hegemonic phenomenon has created a culture of fear within society so that people are afraid to speak up before powerful, authoritative, and dominant groups. According to one administrator, one basic task of ADP was to defeat that fear.

In this study, almost all research participants proclaim that they feel fearless when they present their critical views to powerful authorities and audiences. They said they know what they are saying is righteous and that is the reason they do not care about the consequences of their actions. Their shared stories suggest strongly that they never hesitated to speak up before anyone and in any forum whether it was a large coordination meeting at the district level or an informal gathering at the community level.

IDSP stakeholders claimed that they have broken the culture of silence of their traditional society. Because of this type of human agency, IDSP faculty believe the contribution of IDSP learners is quite different from that of other players in the development sector in Balochistan.

Resisting nepotism and corruption. Nepotism and corruption are two major social evils rooted in Pakistani societies. In the latest Transparency International Annual Report (2012), Pakistan is ranked the 34th most corrupt country among 176 countries of the World. The findings of this study show that, on several occasions, IDSP stakeholders took actions to stop nepotism at their work places. Many stakeholders, on an individual basis, refuse to become the part of organizations where exploitation and corruption are unavoidable. On ethical grounds, they have set their career choices accordingly and have declined many attractive job offers.

I heard a widely-shared maxim from many IDSP learners, "if you cannot stop the exploitation, oppression, and corruption, then, at least, try not to become part of those institutions where these social evils cannot be avoided." One IDSP learner said that his fellow course participants clearly understood what social construction and change really is and how it can be furthered in society. In his view, the essence of this discourse was that you should not be part of the establishment and the mainstream system because they are corrupt and promote inequality in the society.

IDSP stakeholders stated that over the years their critical thinking, knowledge of truth, and their working experiences have helped them in setting their priorities, working principles, and boundaries for development. They said that they are now in a position where they can refuse a 50,000-rupee or 100,000-rupee salary package if they feel that in that organization they would have to compromise their working principles.

Although most IDSP learners have joined non-mainstream institutions, they are still facing issues of nepotism and corruption in their organizations. Both male and female participants reported that they have frequently switched their jobs in the NGO sector. They cited a couple of reasons including the short-term duration of the projects, highly-structured policies and operational plans, non-negotiable frameworks, the presence of a culture of corruption and nepotism, and excessive use of resources on non-developmental activities. Some learners stated that they resigned from their jobs because they found themselves in an environment where it was very hard for them to avoid taking bribes or where they noticed that developmental activities were going against the interest of the local people and the actual purpose of the project.

IDSP faculty responding to my question regarding their expectations for IDSP students stated that the biggest challenge for their students is to challenge the standard practices of development. They said it is very difficult for them to do something which they dislike, which they believe is wrong, and which they know is not going to benefit the targeted audience. In the view of the IDSP Director "one of the biggest challenges for learners is to follow their perceptions and dreams and to put forward/apply/advance those ideas".

Their emancipatory action at the micro level has established a general perception of IDSP and its learners in the society of Balochistan, a perception that people from IDSP are not "normal," "common," and "ordinary" people. In the words of IDSP stakeholders they are defined as "different," "unusual," "radical," "difficult," "strange," "weird," "crazy," "insane," "revolutionary," and "exceptional" people by their friends, family members, and development practitioners. Participants reported that some of their friends and family and community members questioned their new identity and made fun of their revolutionary ideas. They disliked their critique on modernization, the formal schooling system, and globalization. In the development sector, according to participants, people either like them a lot or completely reject them as soon as they find out that they come from IDSP. On one hand, they are in high demand in the NGO sector of Balochistan and, on the other hand, they are facing several challenges in finding a stable position in this sector. One learner said that, "people of other NGOs think that people who have been associated with IDSP have a different psyche" (A Male Learner). He said there are several people in the NGO sector who do not like this "psyche" and consequently they avoid employing IDSP learners in their development projects.

At a micro level, IDSP stakeholders' individual reflective decisions and actions have brought significant positive changes. At the family level, they have been successful in creating a gender balance that has certainly changed the family dynamics in the favour of women. At the community level, their continuous resistance towards gender discrimination, oppression, exploitation, nepotism and, corruption has played a significant role in breaking the culture of silence of their society. The next section of this chapter will focus on those community-development initiatives that were undertaken on a small scale by IDSP and its stakeholders.

Emancipatory Actions at the Meso Level

During the discussion on alternative development practices, research participants shared details of some community initiatives that were either taken by them or by IDSP itself or other IDSP fellows who were not participants in this research. These initiatives are divided into five categories: educational services, social-service delivery, activism, creative writing and publishing, and revival of traditional practices.

During my field work, I gathered evidence of some of these actions, but, it was hard to collect evidence regarding those undertaken by non-participants in this study. The main purpose of explaining these actions here is to illustrate how emancipation of critical and alternative knowledge has influenced the developmental practices of IDSP Stakeholders.

Educational services. IDSP stakeholders reported five key educational initiatives: (i) development of eight district education policies; (ii) a short-term non-formal education project for out-of-school children in the Sibi district (an intervention of IDSP); (iii) development of a textbook for out-of-school children; (iv) initiation of a home school for children and women in Lasbella District; (v) building a tuition academy for children and youth of Khuzdar District. Among these five, the first two initiatives were taken at the institutional level in IDSP while three others were undertaken by IDSP learners.

There are certain features of these IDSP initiatives that distinguish them from other government and NGOs initiatives such as:

- IDSP and its learners targeted specifically children, youth, and women who either had never attended school or had withdrawn from formal schools;
- They used non-traditional teaching approaches and methods such as a mentoring approach;
- Their purpose in teaching was not limited to the development of literacy and numeracy skills but also extended to creating consciousness on certain social issues such as gender, economic activities, accountability, governance, and violence, and extremism;
- They tried to make teaching content relevant to the realities of their students;
- These initiatives were taken after examining the local needs of the area.

Social services

During the interviews, IDSP teachers and administrators shared information and perceptions on the contribution of IDSP and its learners in social-service delivery. They specifically mentioned the following five key self-initiatives in which their learners were intensively involved: (i) installation of a water purification plant in a desert area; (ii) establishment of IDSP campuses for women in five districts of Balochistan; (iii) training of newly selected women councillors; (iv) establishment of a skill-development centre for women; and (v) formation of a farmers' association in the district of Sindh.

Most of these initiatives were being undertaken by the IDSP and graduates who did not participate in this study. All of these initiatives operated at the local level. According to IDSP teachers, these initiatives are good examples of alternative development practices by IDSP and its learners as they emerged "on the ground" as a result of their students' interest in specific issues and needs of their local communities. In other words, these initiatives were not taken due to any national or international campaign in the field of community development.

Activism. Four participants in this study stated that they have been involved in "activism" since they have graduated from the IDSP. One female learner shared a case of honour killing in which she was secretly involved in saving the life of an intended woman victim. In a similar vein, one Baloch male learner stated that he, along with other course participants, protested in front of a Press Club against extra-judicial killing in Sindh province. The most interesting case of activism reported by study participants is one learner's efforts to launch a campaign on impacts of a dam on the local people of his area. This campaign was launched as a result of an IDSP learner's impact study on the Mirani Dam that was built in the region of Makran. In this study he found flaws in the design and construction of the dam that later ruined the lives of hundreds of local people. That specific learner has written about this disaster in a provincial newspaper, Daily Intekhab. His campaign received substantial coverage from the print media. In fact, he has taken on the issue at the policy level as well. With the victims of Mirani Dam, he launched an official complaint to the Governor and Chief Secretary of Balochistan. With the support of IDSP, he presented the case of the Mirani Dam project in reputable policy institutions, such as the Sustainable Development Policy Institute (SDPI), in Islamabad. With the support of a Senator, he got an opportunity to discuss the issue in a formal meeting of the Planning Commission of Pakistan. He also met with the Federal Minister of Power and Energy and requested him to help the victims of the Mirani Dam project. This campaign is still continuing.

Creative writing and publishing. Participation in ADP courses has created and sharpened learners' writing skills. There are many IDSP learners who have written in local newspapers, newsletters, IDSP's quarterly published journals Transformation and Aks ul amal (Reflective Actions), and in IDSP's other publications. An overview of their published articles and papers show that they pay attention to the issues of formal schooling, the health system, environment, food security, unemployment and extremism. They have also written on topics such as "modernity and human values," "democracy," the "role of media and schooling," "traditional values and practices," "imperialism," and "mother languages and globalization."

Revival of traditional practices. There were two examples of revival of traditional practices which most of the research participants cited during their conversation on alternative practices: (i) rehabilitation of Karezes (a traditional water management system) in Pishin district and (ii) IDSP's mud-construction Project (a traditional architecture method of construction).

Karezes are used for irrigating crops and for meeting drinking and domestic requirements. They are "defined as man-made underground water management systems" (Ullah, 2012, p. 5). One student of the IDSP DS course rehabilitated a five-hundred-year-old Karezes in his district that had been dysfunctional since 1997 due to a severe drought in Balochistan. During the course, he shared the problem of dysfunctional Karezes in his area and conducted a small study on this issue. Later, IDSP provided him with a fellowship to work on his idea. Under the supervision of an IDSP team and with the support and contribution of his community he initiated a cleaning of the wells of the Karezes. According to an IDSP report on the project, he hired fifteen labourers as well for this job, and, with the cleaning of the first few wells, water started to flow again in the Karazes. By the time all the wells were cleaned, sufficient water was available to irrigate crops and to fulfill the domestic needs of local people.

The second important traditional practice that research participants mentioned was the IDSP's mud-construction-projects initiative. In early 2000, IDSP intended to establish a Community Development University (CDU) in the city of Quetta. IDSP, following one of its core values of revival of traditional practices, decided to construct the main campus of CDU, Hannah Campus, by using traditional local practices. For this purpose, a preliminary base-line study was conducted to understand local construction structure and the life style of local people living in the neighbourhood of the campus. According to one IDSP administrator, IDSP and its team spent a year studying the area and the people of Hannah. In the process, according to him, they learned that local people use "mud structure." As a result, the final decision of IDSP was to build the Hanna campus with mud. This project is now under construction.

At the meso level, it is difficult to assess the significance of emancipatory actions. There seems little doubt that all of them were undertaken out of community spirit and with good intentions using a non-traditional approach. However, it is also a fact that most of them are not operational. In fact, the current status of some actions is unknown. Among seven operational projects only two, revival of Karazes and installation of a water purification plant, seem significant since they have benefitted local people. The impact of the other five action projects is hard to assess because some of them are in their infancy and others had no evidence of extended benefits.

This limited success at the meso level has created frustration among some IDSP stakeholders. According to one teacher, because of these frustrations IDSP learners have built a love-hate relationship with IDSP. During my field work, I also came to understand that IDSP learners think of themselves as "change agents" and that they are proud to be that; at the same time, however, they are frustrated because they are facing several challenges in bringing about "change." They shared with me their limitations in practicing their revolutionary and alternative ideas in the field. I noted moreover that whenever they face problems they expect IDSP to support and help them. However, the reality, as IDSP teachers and administrators pointed out, is that IDSP does not have sufficient resources to meet each learner's needs for support.

Emancipatory Action at the Macro Level

There are two specific initiatives of IDSP stakeholders that are pertinent to discussion here: (i) establishment of a College for Youth Activism and Development (CYAD) at the national level and (ii) establishment of Khawateen Ittehad Citizen Community Board (CCB) in the Lasbella District. Both initiatives were taken following a formal protocol; both initiatives have legal status as they are registered under the Social Welfare Act 1963; CYAD was established with the intention of reaching out to youth of troubled areas at the national level while the CCB was established at the district level but has received recognition at the national level.

College for youth activism and development (CYAD). The founder of CYAD is an IDSP administrator who established this organization in 2007. In his interview he explained key influences that led him to establish CYAD: (i) his working experience in IDSP led him to study the issues of terrorism, extremism and Talibanization in the region which have severely affected the youth of his Pashtoon community; (ii) his teaching experiences in IDSP helped him to understand the phenomenon of youth, particularly adolescence; (iii) he was exposed to some very hard realities in which he learned that people who are trained as suicide bombers were transformed without their own intention. He said that with the help of some local people in troubled areas of Pakhtoonkhwah he managed to meet a group of people who were being trained as suicide bombers.

According to him, all these experiences taught him that the things that encouraged youth to become extremists, even to the point of acting as suicide bombers were not based on sophisticated philosophies. He concluded that "it was the delicacy of their age, and some psychological, emotional, and political factors which encouraged them to choose that path" (IDSP Administrator). With this conclusion in hand, he felt the need for an institution or network of individuals who could transform these fragile youth and reintegrate them with the society. To convert this idea into reality, with the support of IDSP, he established an office of CYAD in Quetta with a plan to reach out to 300 youth in troubled areas of Pakistan. According to him, instead of 300, CYAD was able to engage 1500 youth in a period of one year. Now, its own head office is in Quetta; two sub-offices have been created, one in Loralai and the other one in Swat; and one liaison office in Islamabad.

CYAD provides diverse opportunities for training to youth to manage and avert their radicalization towards extremism, to develop their leadership skills, and to expand their role in local-level planning, decision-making processes, and community development. It uses generative approaches that focus on participants' interests, needs, realities, and aspirations. Taking inspiration from IDSP's ADP framework, it also aims to revitalize participants' sense of belonging with their self, family, community and the world. CYAD is similar to a virtual and distance-education institute as it engages its participants through various means: internship, volunteer work, workshops, training sessions, seminars, and student exchange programs. Its aim is to convey to youth effectively and efficiently the message of social reconstruction or positive transformation of their society—and engage them in it.

Khawateen Ittehad citizen community board. This particular initiative was the result of collective efforts by IDSP female learners in Lasbella District. A group of MGD course graduates who participated in the 2003 and 2005 courses decided to establish a local library for women of their area. This initiative was taken under a local government ordinance enacted in 2000 that encouraged local communities all over Pakistan to establish Citizen Community Boards (CCBs) to address their local issues.

These female IDSP learners, following all required procedures and legal formalities, formed the first women's CCB in their area. IDSP helped them in the process of project development as well as in the provision of space for the library. It was the only library in the area that was established and managed by the local women. Soon it received recognition at the national level from the Devolution Trust for Community Empowerment in Islamabad. According to one IDSP teacher who was intensively involved in MGD courses, there were some other CCBs as well which were formed by female graduates of IDSP; however, *Khawateen Ittehad* CCB received great attention from the print and electronic media because it emerged as the first women's CCB in the history of Pakistan. Despite all that recognition and attention, however, this library was closed in 2007. The main reasons for this failure were lack of resources to bear the operational cost of the library and dispersion of the group members who initially established it.

CONCLUSION

IDSP stakeholders' transformative notions of development and their emancipatory actions reveal that they believe in human-centred development. The point of reference of their conversations on development was humans or humanity, and not primarily the economy or democracy. Their approach towards development seem opposite to the popular theories and approaches of development. For example, in human capital theory the development of humans is considered essential for agriculture or economic development. In other words, they are used as an input in the production function of development. Their development in most cases is linked with the attainment of social efficiency and development of democratic society. These mainstream approaches of development made the individuals and humans the secondary positions while their primary and prime focus is institutions or economy or infrastructure. IDSP stakeholders are not entirely against physical or materialistic development or economic development; however, they relate these developments first and foremost with the development of human beings.

Also, human development in the IDSP program is not limited to provide only regulatory knowledge and a few skills. They emphasized the development of critical agency in humans. In their views, people of their community will be developed when they will be free of oppression, free from false pre-conceived ideas, fears of incompetence, feelings of denigration, confusion, and inferiority complexes. In their views, their people will be developed when their confidence in their own diverse cultural identity and their local culture and tradition will be restored. In their views, their people will be developed when they feel prepared in engaging with the global forces and powers without compromising on their own integrity. They believe, it is possible only by enhancing people's intellectual capabilities. IDSP learners were actually speaking from their own lived experiences. After the course, most of the participants, particularly learners, realized they had developed an enhanced capability for analytical and critical thinking which helped them both in their personal and professional lives.

I also personally observed that their critical-thinking ability and intellectual strength have brought sustainability in their personalities and within their inner selves. I believe that sustainable development, which has been the core agenda of most development education programs and projects, should give attention to the sustainability of people's individual development. From the experientially grounded views of IDSP stakeholders, it seems that *sustainability must start from the sustainability of one's self.*

In the light of their emancipatory actions. it is evident that IDSP stakeholders constructed and embraced alternative or new knowledge in ADP courses, knowledge intended to improve their lives and community-development practices. The findings of this research exhibit that, at a micro level, they have been successful in bringing positive changes in their personal and family lives. However, in the workplace and at the community level they face several challenges in putting their emancipatory perspectives into practice. Despite the fact that some of their community actions were recognized at both provincial and national levels, it is hard to claim they have brought any major and significant changes at the macro level.

Freire (1978), in fact, opposed a "mechanistic view of social changes;" he insists that "[e]ven if there is a serious changeover, such as revolution, the myths from the previous structure will carry over and continue to influence the new governmental structure" (p. 302). Instead, he emphasized that "cultural revolution" can occur when people "culturally attack culture" and they "do not let it become static, becoming a myth and mystifying" it (p. 302). IDSP stakeholders' actions against the culture of silence, culture of domination of men over women, culture of corruption and nepotism, and so forth, are also indicators of "cultural revolution" in a traditional society. Their actions show that IDSP and its stakeholders are following a promising and potentially effective approach towards transformation of their society; however, the speed and scope of this social transformation is undeniably quite slow.

REFERENCES

Bakhteari, Q. (1996). *Concept paper to establish Institute for Study and Practice of Development: Initial working paper*. Retrieved January, 2011, from http://www.idsp.org.pk/wp-content/uploads/2010/08/Concept-Paper-IDSP.pdf

Baumgartner, L. M. (2001). An update on transformational learning. *New Directions for Adult and Continuing Education, 89*(Spring), 15–24.

Cohen, J. (2009). Diverting the radicalization track. *Policy Review, 154*(April/May), 51–63.

Cranton, P., & Taylor, E. W. (2012). Transformative learning theory: Seeking a more unified theory. In P. Cranton & E. W. Taylor (Eds.), *The handbook of transformative learning [electronic resource]: Theory, research, and practice* (pp. 2–20). San Francisco, CA: Jossey-Bass higher and adult education series. Retrieved September 2, 2013, from http://lib.myilibrary.com/Open.aspx?id=365165

Institute for Development Studies and Practices (IDSP). (2010). *Our core values*. Quetta: IDSP. Retrieved January 10, 2010, from http://www.idsp.org.pk/?page_id=2

Marshall, C., & Rossman, G. B. (2006). *Designing qualitative research*. London: Sage.

Mezirow, J. (1978). Perspective transformation. *Adult Education, XXVIII*(2), 100–110.
National Commission for Human Development. (2013). *Let's join hands to promote quality education in Pakistan: Annual report 2013*. Retrieved March 3, 2016, from http://www.nchd.org.pk/ws/documents/Final%20PDF%20%20Annoal%20Reporrt%202013.pdf
Qambrani, F., & Qambrani, K. J. (2012). Explore and study the impacts of mainstreaming gender and development courses of IDSP since (2003–2010) on its graduate learners of Balochistan. Retrieved June, 2013, from http://www.scribd.com/doc/113583560/Impacts-analyses-study-of-Mainstreaming-Gender-and-Development-Courses-of-IDSP-since-2003-to-2010
Santos, B. D. S. (1999). On oppositional postmodernism. In R. Munck & D. O'Hearn (Eds.), *Critical development theory: Contributions to a new paradigm* (pp. 29–43). New York, NY: Zed Books.
Social Policy and Development Centre. (2002). *Dimensions of the non-profit sector in Pakistan*. Retrieved March 3, 2016, from http://www.spdc.org.pk/Data/Publication/PDF/WP1.pdf
The United Nations Development Programme. (1997). *Human development report, 1997*. Retrieved March 3, 2016, from http://hdr.undp.org/sites/default/files/reports/258/hdr_1997_en_complete_nostats.pdf
The United Nations Development Programme. (2015). *Human development report 2015: Work for human development*. Retrieved on March 3, 2016, from http://hdr.undp.org/sites/default/files/2015_human_development_report_1.pdf
Transparency International, The global coalition against corruption. (2012). *Transparency international annual report 2012*. Retrieved March, 2014, from Transparency International website: http://www.transparency.org/annualreport/2012; http://issuu.com/transparencyinternational/docs/annual_report_2012/25?e=2496456/4242764
Ullah, F. (2012). Rehabilitation of Karez. In S. Shah (Ed.), *Successful stories of practice based development courses for youth in community development and partnership building* (pp. 2–7). Quetta: Institute for Development Studies and Practices. Retrieved August, 2013, from http://www.scribd.com/doc/102619964/Success-Stories-of-IDSP-Learners

Nazia Bano
The University of Western Ontario

XAVIER RAMBLA

4. POLICY TRANSFER FOR EDUCATIONAL DEVELOPMENT

Complex Processes of Borrowing and Lending in Brazil and the Philippines[1]

INTRODUCTION

This chapter presents a comparative analysis of Education for All plans in Brazil and the Philippines. These two countries share a number of commonalities not least due to their current status as emergent, intermediate economies in the global world. However, the official indicators of educational development show disparate trends in the middle term, with Brazil overcoming the Philippines in the last decades. The analysis draws on two different strands of literature in order to make sense of these trends. On the one hand, it uses historical neo-institutionalist accounts of the 'developmental state' to account for the endogenous social transformations that both of them have experienced. On the other hand, the chapter draws on the literature on education policy transfer in order to spell out the clues of external influence in each case. The findings discuss some significant correlations between patterns of state development and the reception of the global educational agenda.

Nowadays, policy-making normally entails international transfer somehow, even in allegedly 'national' areas such as education. At the same time as new issues such as climate change, finance, migration or the use of big data enter the diplomatic agenda, the initiative Education for All, a worldwide programme designed over fifteen years ago came to the fore to extend schooling and learning to everybody, to be assessed in a global summit in 2015. The current widespread pessimism on the achievements of this initiative is a poignant reminder of our need to rethink the institutional underpinnings, the prevailing procedures of planning and implementing, and the methods of evaluating policies in order to envisage new and more effective projects. Simultaneously, development banks are making some of their loans conditional on national investment in education, and governments have widely adopted their generally accepted recommendation to tighten social benefits to family involvement in children's education. Even more, closer methods of international coordination introduce new institutional designs of regional education policy frameworks in Europe (e.g., the Education and Training 2020 Strategy), Latin America (e.g., the 2021 Ibero American Educational Goals) and in other regions of the world.

This chapter will discuss the importance of policy transfer in education with regard to two intermediate countries in the world ranking defined by the Human Development Index, Brazil and the Philippines. Even though both of them underwent a significant phase of democratisation in the late eighties, their position in this ranking has flipped during the last decades. Brazil suffered from a worse situation than the Philippines in the mid twentieth century, but the former has experienced quicker and more persistent progress afterwards. This trend posits intriguing and disturbing questions inasmuch as the main international agencies have been intervening systematically in the latter since the end of World War II. Actually, a tentative comparative account of their respective histories concerning education policy and cooperation for international development suggests that different ways of external influence, among many other factors, have contributed to these disparate trends. While Brazilian governments and civil society have actively engaged in varied forms of both collaboration and conflict with international agencies such as UNESCO and the World Bank, and have actively engaged with undergoing processes of international educational planning in Latin America, the Philippines has basically enacted educational reforms according to the conditions required by the World Bank and the Asian Development Bank in exchange for their financial collaboration.

THE POLITICAL ECONOMY OF EDUCATION POLICY TRANSFER: TWO CASE STUDIES

Education for All (EFA) has been a very ambitious experience of educational planning on the global scale. Promoted by a consortium of international donors, coordinated by UNESCO, and supported by other agencies such as UNICEF and the World Bank, it has pushed for international aid and policy reform targeted to universalise access to education as well as to strengthen quality in the functioning of educational institutions. The inception of this grand initiative has to do with the high expectations put on the international order that was to overcome Cold War tensions in the early nineties, when the initial period of EFA started. Although by 2000 multi-lateral reviews openly revealed that the balance of the prior decade had been extremely poor, the consortium decided to launch a second, longer phase in order to make significant progress in fifteen years' time. Recent monitoring reports notice that this second edition was successful in attracting funding and imprinting a positive trend on indicators in the beginning, but later on neither budgeting nor effective advancement have been sound enough (EFA Global Monitoring Report, 2014). Remarkably, an exploration of the interplay of divergent political interests, which were pursued by means of uneven power resources at the national and global scales (Verger, Novelli, & Altinyielke, 2012), may suggest crucial insights on the inconsistency and contradictions of the initial political will. This analysis of education is inspired in a wide-ranging approach to politics and economics which is often labelled as political economy.

An overview of the indicators of Brazil and the Philippines in Google Public Data Explorer tells the same story repeatedly. Brazil was in a worse position by the seventies and eighties but significantly outperformed the Philippines after the launch of EFA. For instance, table 1 summarises the trend of a variable which is particularly sensitive to the situation of intermediate countries like Brazil and the Philippines. Table 1 provides an estimate of the expected years of schooling of children and their average probability to access education and remain in the system during the compulsory years. In 1980 Brazil scored slightly below the high human development countries whereas the Philippines scored slightly above. Over time Brazilian children gained 3.2 years, thus becoming a country of high human development in education, but the expected years of schooling for Filipino children remained at the same level. Although none of them could attain 16.3 years, unlike very high human development countries, disparate progress is apparent when comparing these two countries.

Table 1. Expected years of schooling (of children)

	Very high human development countries	High human development countries	Brazil	Philippines
1980	13.2	10.3	9.9	10.4
1990	14	11.2	12.2	10.7
2000	15.4	12.3	14.2	11.4
2005	15.8	13.1	14.2	11.6
2006	15.9	13.3	14.2	11.5
2007	16	13.3	14.2	11.5
2008	16.1	13.6	14.2	11.7
2009	16.2	13.8	14.2	11.7
2010	16.3	13.9	14.2	11.7
2011	16.3	13.9	14.2	11.7
2012	16.3	13.9	14.2	11.7

Source: UNDP (2014)

In the following sections a correlation between external influence on education policy, on the one hand, and endogenous transformations impinging on development, on the other hand, will be observed in Brazil and the Philippines. The objective of this exercise is basically to highlight the complex phenomena that have been playing a role in the stretch and the impact of EFA.

These cases are viewed as systems in methodological terms (Steiner-Khamsi, 2012, p. 12). That is to say, when looking at development it is not sensible to reduce countries to the role of single units for measure. Statistical measures have to do so in order to produce comparative figures, but this operation can neither delete nor capture two features of the social structuring of a country. First, countries are bounded systems because they include an array of social phenomena that interact with one another. The very limit of these systems has to be carefully documented in each case. Thus, in Brazil in 1988 Education for All coincided with democratisation and regional cooperation in the making of the Southern Common Market, MERCOSUL. In the Philippines, EFA also arrived immediately after democratisation in 1986 as well as an increasing push for regional collaboration in the Asian Pacific Economic Cooperation. However, boundaries have not been constructed in exactly the same way in both cases, since regional cooperation is significantly stronger and more significant in Latin America.

Second, human agency does not reproduce the same pattern everywhere but produces varying webs of causes in different countries. In this vein, while political actors have built a complex, multi- level coalition gathering sub-national and national governments, international agencies and social movements intervening in education in Brazil, in the Philippines the crucial steps in educational policy-making have depended on the interaction between international donors who implemented their projects and the national government. This is not the only factor of the diverging trends in educational development, nor can international agencies be blamed as the sole responsible agents for this disparate political conjunctures, but the observation of recursive causal links between the building of a coalition addressing different layers of governance and the correlative progress in schooling and international tests of learning certainly points at a critical event in Brazil. In other words, an excessive confidence in the method of conditioned coordination normally adopted in the Philippines should be carefully revised from several angles, at least those addressing global issues on development, nation-building and the capacities of the civil society.

POLICY TRANSFER AND INSTITUTIONAL BOUNDARIES WITHIN THE STATE

A number of writers are accumulating evidence of the strategic inspiration of the international circulation of educational policies, the variegation of transfer processes and their impact on the structure of states (Dale, 1999; Steiner- Khamsi, 2004, 2010, 2012). Definitely, the most salient finding of these studies states that policy-makers make use of foreign policies regardless of any evidence on their effectiveness. Their frequent claims about the alleged empirical reasons that underpin their priorities are largely rhetoric, both because conclusive data are not available and because their reasoning is more concerned with endorsing recommendations than testing causal beliefs. Whatever the intrinsic qualities of a given best practice, the contextual political interplay sets the main reason for decision-makers to adopt it (Steiner-Khamsi, 2012). A rigorous analysis of the drivers of educational development cannot rely on establishing a list of policies that work. Rather, a more advisable approach consists of spelling out the interests and strategies of the agents who participated in the social transformations that eventually fostered or hindered the attainment of EFA goals.

Some typologies have distinguished economic and political types of policy diffusion (Dobbin et al., 2007) and educational policy transfer (Dale, 1999; Steiner-Khamsi, 2010). The former one induces governments to adopt policies as a condition to receive international funding. For instance, when attempting to solve the debt crisis of the eighties and nineties, the World Bank asked many governments to concentrate their scarce resources on funding primary education. This was a mandatory condition these governments had to fulfil if they were to become eligible for a loan. The latter type consists of international agencies and think tanks actively disseminating their recommendations so that policy frameworks are defined internationally. Thus, governments are likely to draw on these policy frameworks in order to look for available solutions to their most imminent problems. The very diffusion of EFA has followed this pattern in most countries.

When they investigate this topic, researchers normally observe some significant impacts on the structure of states. The specialised literature has noticed that international policy regimes reinforce the executive branch of government, and has realised that transnational networks of officials and consultants are increasingly influential in such terrains as the military, trade or central banking (Jayasuriya, 2008; Sassen, 2006). Unsurprisingly, analogous changes in the boundaries of the educational sector and the appearance of professional networks have been documented in education policy-making (Robertson, 2011; Steiner- Khamsi, 2010).

A comparative analysis of EFA plans in Brazil and the Philippines (and elsewhere) has to inquire whether the main policies have been borrowed and transferred, and if they have, whether financial conditions or discursive elaboration have been at stake. Such an analysis also has to argue for the influence of these external forces vis-a-vis the endogenous forces of the 'developmental state'. This concept indicates that the stability of bureaucratic planning by means of regular procedures, the intensity of nation- building after de- colonisation and anti-Communist dictatorships backed by the US, and the systemic reaction of Asian small nations to vulnerability and insecurity have dramatically contributed to human development. Although neither of our two countries is a pure illustration of this process, unlike the Asian Tigers, some symptoms of the developmental state can be identified in their recent history (Castells, 1998; Evans, 1992; Doner et al., 2005; Filgueira, 2009; Kang, 2002).

This analysis has to show which specific actors decided to stand for an international recommendation and actively attempted to put pressure on governments to follow it, or tried to convince national leaders and national public opinion that their proposal was particularly rewarding. In Brazil, UNESCO, UNICEF, the Ibero American States Organisation (OEI), the Federal Government, the national coalition of the Global Campaign for Education and the business-friendly All for Education (Todos pela Educaçao) coalition have been playing this role during the most recent decades (Rambla, 2012). In the Philippines, the World Bank and the Asian Development Bank have been deeply involved in designing the institutional scaffolding of the country's education system (Reyes, 2009).

The exploration of connections between types of policy transfer and transformations of the state invites us to be aware of institutional boundary-making. Currently, this research topic is motivating the main critiques to the assumption that education systems are mostly national and have a clearly defined institutional boundary (Dale & Robertson, 2007). Not only is evidence of supra-national influences accumulating but diverging boundaries are also being observed between education, economic and social policy. For example, when the World Bank recommended that governments concentrate on primary education, they were reducing the institutional domain of public education by subordinating decisions to financial stability. Similarly, when this donor decided to ask its beneficiaries to tighten social benefits to family commitment with children's school attendance, it blurred the distinction between education and social policy. The finding that these boundaries are often being displaced is well-known in policy studies (Sassen, 2006), particularly in education policy studies (Robertson, 2011).

Thus, if policy borrowing and transfer impinge on state structures by determining the institutional limits of education, different types of transfer may provoke contrasting effects on these boundaries. Crucial to the comparative appraisal of Education for All in Brazil and the Philippines is the observation that external influence on the education policies of these countries arrived by different types of policy transfer and imprinted quite different boundaries on the education sector. In Brazil, the ideas actively promoted by UNESCO were widely accepted in order to design and implement National Education Plans, as required by the 1988 Constitution. Besides prioritising certain issues, these ideas also favoured the alignment of education with the health system in the vein of cooperative federalism (Arretche, 2010). Conversely, in the Philippines the World Bank, the Asian Development Bank and other international donors have been pushing for programmes that build managerial capacity and expand private education, which have been mostly implemented with their financial support. The outcome has been a plethora of 'projectized reforms' whose durability depends on the availability of external funding and whose general coherence is extremely problematic (Maca & Morris, 2012).

The former correlation between foreign influence and domestic institutional arrangements retrieves the logics of explanation based on mechanisms. Instead of a general law binding the same types of transfer with the same institutional differentiation everywhere, my point is that diverse types of transfer may fashion particular institutional boundaries in particular contexts. Certainly, here this approach remains sketchy because it is only pointing at a likely regularity that still has to be defined in a more formal way and researched in a larger sample of contexts. Mechanisms are structures of causes that may be observed repeatedly to the extent they are activated by social agency in specific conditions. However, social methodologists have proposed some ways of using this intellectual tool to conceptualise and scrutinise social processes (Elster, 2007; Tilly, 1984, 2001). If their action is finally identified in both progress and setbacks of educational development, future policy designs may take them into account in order to foster well-grounded positive synergies as often as possible.

EFA PLANNING AND POLICY TRANSFER IN BRAZIL

Brazil has shown significant improvement in the main EFA goals. A dramatic rise of enrolment in primary and secondary education has reduced the number of out-of-school children. Although the proportion of over-age enrolment due to grade repetition is noticeable, the trend has decreased since 2000. Shortcomings in academic performance are huge, not least because more than half of the studying populations cannot attain the basic competencies. However, both national (INEP, 2012) and international (OECD, 2013) examinations show significant advancement, particularly in the reduction of this very high proportion of low-performers. Nevertheless, despite these symptoms of progress, it is unlikely that Brazil will finally meet the EFA goals by 2015, since early childhood care and education is clearly insufficient, a small share of children are still excluded from primary education, initiatives targeted at providing life-skills to young people after compulsory school leaving age remain underdeveloped, and adult literacy is advancing very slowly (UNESCO Institute for Statistics, 2014a). For the last years UNESCO (2008) has not dropped a disappointing question mark about the capacity of the country to achieve the goals.

The Brazilian Federation has included education among the basic rights enshrined by its 1988 Constitution, and has experimented with an array of solutions to implement the corresponding policies. Mostly, the Constitution requires the government to implement a National Educational Plan each decade. In the nineties the Right-wing Cardoso Administration introduced a very restrictive definition of basic education in the 2001–2011 National Educational Plan—including exclusively the commitment to universal primary enrolment. This reform had to comply with the requirements of a Structural Adjustment Programme run by the International Financial Institutions, mostly the World Bank. But simultaneously, a coalition of teacher unions and social movements looked for the support of other international agencies such as UNESCO and EFA in order to vindicate a more ambitious understanding of education. This coalition became the national branch of the Global Campaign of Education when this transnational movement was launched so as to monitor the effective progress of the second edition of EFA, and put pressure so that governments and international organisations would commit to the principles of this initiative.

Over time, three policy innovations have widened the objective, gradually displacing this narrow understanding toward a wider one. Firstly, in 1996 the Cardoso Administration established a Federal fund to compensate for budget shortcomings affecting primary education in the poorer municipalities and states of the Brazilian Federation, where these three levels of government are responsible for education. This fund conditioned subsidies to an effective commitment of sub-national authorities to invest all the necessary resources so that primary enrolment increased in either their region or their locality. In 2006 the Left-wing Lula Administration expanded the reach of the Federal fund so that it provided support to lower-secondary education too (Frigoto & Ciavatta, 2003; Ramos & Giorgi, 2011).

Secondly, in the late nineties a handful of municipalities and states started to deliver a social benefit to mothers whose income did not attain the poverty level, conditional on an actual, regular school attendance and vaccination of their offspring. Afterwards, these conditional cash transfers were scaled up to configure the Federal *Bolsa Familia* (i.e. family allowance) programme. Many evaluations have noticed its positive effects on enrolment and the decline of child labour (Farrington & Slater, 2006).

Finally, in 2007 the second Lula Administration launched a Plan for the Development of Education (PDE) that integrated a variety of former initiatives. PDE conveyed a strong commitment to extend educational progress beyond the objectives of the national plan that had been approved six years before. A large consultation process was also initiated so that the design of the national plan for the next decade was discussed at the local and state levels. In the end, a final, nationwide conference was held in Brasilia in 2010 (CONAE, 2010). The resulting design sets objectives affecting early child education and training, upper secondary education, vocational education and training, and higher education. Their attainment is continuously monitored by means of the Index of the Development of Basic Education, which looks at the rates of enrolment and the average scores in standard tests (INEP, 2012). Provincial and municipal governments are also designing, implementing and evaluating their plans for the development of education. Despite terminological variation due to contrasting ideological inspirations, the bulk of their objectives are aligned with the Federal plan. Active participation of the civil society has supported these initiatives in many municipalities (Sarmiento, 2005; Ramos & Giorgi, 2011).

The evolution of educational policy-making in Brazil strongly suggests that the Federal government has acquired a sound political capability consisting of coalition building at the scales of sub-national, Federal and international governance. In fact, the progressive extension of the objectives of plans has intermingled with the making of this coalition. Firstly, the inclusion of lower secondary education in the Federal fund was a vindication of the main teachers' union and the national branch of the Global Campaign for Education (GCE). Secondly, the creation of the Bolsa Familia social benefit recognised the policy innovation carried out by many municipal governments (most of them headed by Lula's political party) and also responded to a demand of these two advocacy groups. And thirdly, besides the teachers' union, the national branch of the GCE, and local and regional governments, a variety of political players was invited to the consultation of the new plan designed and discussed between 2007 and 2010. Remarkably, the business-friendly All for Education network joined the general consensus at that moment. This network is led by a group of corporations, and stands for improving enrolment and performance by carefully monitoring the effectiveness of schools and establishing public- private partnerships between schools and business. Although the teachers' union complains about the participation of All for Education, so far both of them are included in the same general consensus.

In a similar vein to the union, the Brazilian GCE has succeeded in convincing the government to underpin public education with a sophisticated index of parity. It has commissioned research in order to estimate a cost-related index of quality in education (CAQi) that has been formally approved for the government as an official tool for budgeting. This index not only takes into account the basic demographic data but also special psychological and physical needs as well as the socio-cultural needs of Afro-Brazilian, indigenous and rural populations (Eickleberg, 2012).

Both the government and these civil society organisations claim that educational planning is inspired in both Education for All and the Ibero American Educational Goals (Ministerio da Educaçao, 2008; CONAE, 2010). Although UNESCO is not convinced that EFA goals will be met, the official confidence in following the guidelines of this international agency was pervasive in the interviews I conducted and the meetings I attended during research on the topic between 2009 and 2011 (Rambla, 2012). Moreover, the government, UNESCO and the national office of the Ibero American States Organisation (OEI, a commonwealth of countries supported by Spain and Portugal) agreed that the same philosophy guided the Ibero American Educational Goals, which are to be achieved by 2021 (OEI, 2010).

Education is a cornerstone of the public self-image of Brazil. Since the Federal definition of the country distributes institutional responsibility between local, regional and Federal authorities, such policies as common funds, a scheme of cash transfers conditional on school attendance, and strategic planning with public data openly reporting on all the administrative units have become a guarantee of nation- building (CONAE, 2010). Political consensus is far from stable, and the political conjuncture is rapidly changing compared to the time of my interviews, but the general reliance on the potential of this approach has not been eroded. On the contrary, widespread doubts on the availability of resources to implement it effectively are triggering mobilisation. In a nutshell, experts in the multi-level government conclude that the country is elaborating its own model of 'cooperative federalism', which has also been systematically applied to other policy areas as the public health system (Arretche, 2010).

EFA PLANNING AND POLICY TRANSFER IN THE PHILIPPINES

One must be more sceptical regarding the statistical trends which are underway in the Philippines than the common perceptions of Brazil. The first section of this chapter already mentioned that the bulk of UNDP indicators rendered stagnant and insufficient patterns. Actually, the number of out-of-school children and adolescents as well as the volume of youth and adult illiterate populations has failed to follow a consistent declining trend since 2000 (UNESCO Institute for Statistics, 2014b). Problems with early childhood education, gender disparities and provision of life-skills also remain overwhelming in some regions (Maca & Morris, 2012).

Certainly, this is not the consequence of political inaction, because a whole set of reforms has been put in place since the peaceful democratic revolution that expelled Ferdinand and Imelda Marcos in 1986. In order to guarantee free public education, in 1989 the first democratic administration introduced the Government Assistance to Students and Teachers in Private Education (GASTPE) so that private schools also contributed to educational expansion. In the nineties the structure of the ministry of education was reformed to stress a clear distinction between the mission of basic education and responsibilities in the areas of vocational, technical and higher education. In 2001 the Governance of the Basic Education Act created the current Department of Education (DepEd) and introduced school-based management by strengthening the role of school leadership. These reforms were expected to overhaul the system by importing innovations of new public management.

The Filipino EFA Plan was drafted and sanctioned soon after these reforms (Republic of the Philippines, 2005). This plan expects to make every school better, expand early education, transform Alternative Learning Systems, involve teachers in continuous practical improvement, and adopt a 12-year cycle of basic education which was finally approved in 2012. Thus, it selects some of the global EFA goals as the national priorities, but does not make explicit reference to out-of-school children and progress between school years.

Later on GASTPE acquired a crucial role in the system. Initially, it was a public initiative aimed at "decongesting" public schools by delivering scholarships to some students from vulnerable socio-economic backgrounds so that they could attend private schools. In 1998 it integrated the financial schemes run by the Fund for Assistance to Private Education (FAPE), a private, non-profit organization which was paradoxically chaired by the minister of education (World Bank, 2011a, 2011b; Asian Development Bank, 2010, 2011). The Asian Development Bank is also providing extra funding to the extent that it understands GASTPE as a critical instrument to implement a 12-year cycle of basic education on the grounds of innovative financial schemes that afford the construction of the necessary infrastructure by using public-private partnerships (Asian Development Bank, 2011: 1).

Thus, GASTPE is not a standard programme relying on controlled school choice but a singular combination of parental choice and positive discrimination. Officially, its main goals align with the EFA plan in at least three ways. Firstly, this type of assistance aims at complementing over-crowed public schools with a new network of private dependent educational institutions. Secondly, GASTPE indirectly wants to contribute to the expansion of public education because it assumes that private education saves substantial resources that can be invested in the neediest areas of the country. And finally, this programme aspires to attract the support of varied private agents to the construction of a longer basic education.

Although it was not fully implemented until 2001, school-based management had been widely discussed in the Philippines during the nineties. So, it did not take long to start new local programmes that contributed to this decentralization in the areas of parental involvement in school funding and pre-school day-care programmes

(Guzman, 2007). Therefore, this reform directly contributed to the goals for school improvement and early childhood education as stated in the country's EFA plan.

Altogether with Australian Aid, DepEd decided to take advantage of this reform so as to pilot a strategy to cope with corruption, a problem deeply ingrained in the Filipino educational system. Their cooperation produced the Programme on Basic Education (PROBE) benefiting about 76,000 educators and approximately 3.7 million school-aged children in the region of Mindanao, one of the poorest in the country and ravaged by civil war for a long time. This initiative also endeavoured to counteract the main focus of corruption, which was detected in certain linkages between principals and local and regional authorities of DepEd, as well as in the selection of staff who could take courses abroad. By stating clear rules and procedures, the programme not only yielded a higher performance of PROBE students (compared to non-PROBE ones) but also defined a visible set of primary tasks that were much easier to monitor (Reyes, 2009).

The World Bank is also assisting the Philippines to attain EFA goals by contributing to finance a conditional cash transfer scheme, run by the Social Welfare and Development Reform Project. The Pantawid Pamilya programme delivers social benefits to poor households who are able to prove their offspring attend school and have regular health checks. Starting in 2009, this benefit will at least be in place until 2015. The programme has been effective in targeting the needy, preventing infiltration of middle-class groups, and delivering basic services to its beneficiaries compared to non-recipients (Fernández & Rosechin, 2011). Due to the similar size of Pantawid Pamilya and some Latin American conditional cash transfers, that have been successful in crucial anti-poverty benchmarks, the World Bank expects a significant, positive impact of its current contribution with $100M. Collaborating with Australian Aid, it has commissioned an evaluation that has seen a real impact. The evaluators also propose the programme as a best practice for other similar initiatives to imitate (Fernández & Rosechin, 2011).

The Filipino branch of the Global Campaign of Education (GCE) has also joined forces with the official institutions to bolster EFA goals in the country. Compared to other GCE branches, it has gathered the support of a variety of small civil society organizations in most islands and regions; further, its internal cohesion is also reinforced by a fluent relationship with the teacher unions. It has managed to induce the government to adopt the Alternative Budgeting Initiative, which takes into account a variety of social conditions of students. The Filipino branch of the GCE has also convinced the government to pass an act to improve teachers' professional status, and the public opinion to be aware of the problems related to the difficulties of Education for All (Hoop, 2012).

Thus, the participation of the civil society has been relevant to underpin advancement toward the EFA goals with sounder budget criteria and better labour conditions for teachers. These contributions have also highlighted the positive feedback that all the former initiatives are producing. For instance, civil society input emphasizes that GASTPE needs the sort of transparency promoted by PROBE. Teachers' conditions are also added to better socio-economic conditions of the poorest families who receive the grants of Pantawid Pamilya. And progress in both parental and teachers' living standards is likely to favour more robust school- and local-based management. International organisations also prove their interest in setting more transparent rules of the game by supporting GASTPE, PROBE and Pantawid Pamilya. They have proposed lines of reform to strengthen the accountability of private schools, curb corruption at the local level and provide social benefits according to objective criteria. But the social portrait of the Philippines is not convincing commentators of the ultimate positive impact of all these initiatives; on the contrary, there is a wide academic consensus that development is failing in the country. Apparently, the emergence of an institutional regime featured by 'projectized reforms' is blamed for this failure (Maca & Morris, 2012). Governments have been looking for the advice of international agencies so often that they have not been able to articulate their policies within a coherent and stable framework.

In sum, commentators search for the reasons of these shortcomings in the absence of key features that define the neighbouring 'developmental states'. First, they highlight that the relationship between business and government has been volatile, with different economic elites hoarding the bulk of resources depending on the political regime (Kang, 2002). Second, they notice that private corporations have gained such a broad autonomy in school management, the production of textbooks and quality assurance that they easily overlook the public good in favour of their private returns. And finally, they argue that national identity is so weak in the Philippines, where most respondents answer public opinion polls saying they would rather have US citizenship and live abroad, that the mutual reinforcing connection of the school curriculum and the sense of belonging repeatedly observed in Korea, Singapore or Taiwan is not taking place at all (Maca & Morris, 2012).

BRAZIL, THE PHILIPPINES AND TWO DIFFERENT WORLD REGIONS

The connection between foreign influence and domestic institutional transformations of educational systems that the former two sections describe must be interpreted with regard to concurring changes in governance in the respective world regions. Innovation in regional governance strongly reverberates in the key role of the Ibero American States Organisation in Brazil and the Asian Development Bank in the Philippines. In fact, countries are not isolated case studies but components of geographic constellations entailing relationships in culture, environmental challenges, geopolitical conflicts, public policy and other issues (Tilly, 1984). When some of them engage in innovative cooperation, their neighbours are logically affected in some ways. If the interaction between governments, business and civil society undergoes important changes in a country, it is likely that these actors will extend the range of these actions to its neighbours too (Jayasuria, 2008).

The contrasting role of the World Bank provides a telling illustration. Why was the Bank approach downplayed in Brazil whereas it kept its momentum in the Philippines? When this international financial institution endorsed Structural Adjustment Programmes throughout the world, indebted governments needed external loans desperately at the same time as they were reforming their economic regimes and their population was suffering increasing deprivation. This is no longer the case with middle-income countries like Brazil and the Philippines in the past few years. Their currency supply is large right now, and the links of their economic cycle with Western countries have been loosened during the series of recessions that started in 2008. However, although the economic situation of the two countries has been improving recently for the last decades, Brazil is significantly more reluctant to collaborate with the World Bank than the Philippines. These diverging attitudes respond to the varying strength of social movements and civil society organisations in the respective world regions. Remarkably, opposition to 'neoliberal' policies such as Structural Adjustment Programmes has become the leit motiv of Latin America's civil society. Not only a variety of social movements opposed these policies at the time of their implementation (Frigotto & Ciavatta, 2003), but in the years around the millennium these movements also wove a region-wide alliance to campaign against the Free Trade Area of the Americas, which was also blamed for conveying 'neoliberal' objectives (Saforcada & Vassiliades, 2011). And they succeeded in halting free trade agreements at the regional level. Since their victory was also associated with electoral victories of Left-wing governments in Argentina, Bolivia, Brazil, Ecuador, Venezuela and Uruguay, the Bank has become a symbolic reminder of the adversaries of those movements and these new leaders, and the political cost of sharing its perspective on anything has dramatically increased for most parties.

The position of the Philippines in the Asia- Pacific region has also contributed to the reception of external influences by the decision-makers involved in education in the country. Shortly after the democratic transition the World Bank issued an emphatic recommendation to experiment with private education by setting GATSPE. Reformers could expect to counteract the excessive power of authorities during the dictatorship by broadening the scope of stakeholders. A diversity of providers could settle a system of checks- and- balances that prevented schools from the corruption of those very authorities.

Thus, a nationally centred account of this reform makes sense at first sight. However, the importance of geography becomes apparent once the international diffusion of recommendations favourable to school quasi-markets is noticed. This approach gained momentum by means of complex international projections that mostly involved the US and the UK (Steiner- Khamsi, 2012), but also some Pacific countries such as Chile and New Zealand (Elacqua et al., 2006; Thrupp, 2007). The Philippines borrowed a policy of incentives to private dependent schools at the same time as they were being promoted in Chile, and competition between public schools was being stressed in New Zealand at an even higher degree than in Atlantic Anglo-Saxon countries.

FINAL REMARKS ON EDUCATION FOR ALL AND POLICY TRANSFER

When an international conference takes stock of Education for All in 2015, the general conclusions will hardly be satisfactory. Although progress was significant in the first years of the programme, afterwards both funding and empirical trends have lagged behind the yearly growth that was necessary for achieving the targets (EFA Global Monitoring Report, 2014). In this context Brazil and the Philippines will present important policy endeavours to foster educational development, and maybe some positive improvements (mostly in Brazil), but an undeniable sense of frustration will pervade any comparison of the actual trends with the official goals.

The overview of these two case studies suggests a number of reflections on Education for All and policy transfer. To start with, it is obvious that initially the focus of public interest was too much restricted to enrolment in compulsory education, with early childhood education, literacy, life-skills and the possible difficulties with gender parity in some minority groups being largely overlooked. Although it is inevitable that concerns should be raised over the wide scope of these goals, their strong implications for human rights do not allow the debate on this consideration to be closed.

My specific discussion wants to add a couple of further comments to the general overview. To start with, it is plausible to open a new debate on the contribution of institutional boundaries to educational development. Both in Brazil and the Philippines governments, civil societies and international agencies have assumed that multiple actions deployed at different levels of government on primary and secondary education, social policy and (mostly in the Philippines) the private sector were likely to yield new progress by activating complex synergies. Although this general statement is coherent in logical terms, the paucity of the empirical effects of education reforms in Brazil and the Philippines invites us to define more qualified hypotheses about the components of these complex synergies, and then to think what programmes could eventually trigger them in a more precise way. At least, the difficulty in improving achievement of the most vulnerable children should be addressed in both cases with this precision, but it is noticeable than the connection between social policy and performance (besides enrolment) would be revised, and that the promise of a private contribution is not warranted in the Philippines.

Finally, the correlation between education policy transfer and the institutional boundaries of education cannot be overlooked. Despite common shortcomings, Brazil has recorded a sounder improvement than the Philippines. A comparative reading of the specialised literature on both countries suggests that the building of a multi-level coalition of social movements, governments and international organisations has played a positive role in their relative advancement of the country towards Education for All. Although they are not the only driver of progress, these coalitions have certainly been crucial for widening the initial goals and exploring new designs which were tailored to cater to the worst-off. Apart from the network of multi-lateral alliances in Brazil, a similar process may be observed in the Philippines, where the national branch of the Global Campaign of Education has also collaborated with the government to move policy in new directions. However, the difficulty to overcome the negative consequences of 'projectized reforms' is bigger in this country. In fact, my comparison with Brazil suggests that a wider public debate and a wider policy framework might contribute to tackle this problem in an even more satisfactory way than the recent innovations that resulted from closer collaboration of the government with the civil society.

NOTE

[1] This chapter is an outcome of Project "Education for All in Latin America", funded by the Ministry of Science- Spain (ref EDU2008-00816) between 2009 and 2011, and Project "New Education Policies and Partnerships for EFA in The Philippines: Building a research and teaching line", funded by the Spain Aid Agency (ref AP/035711/11). A first version was presented at the XV Comparative Education World Congress, Buenos Aires, 24–28 June 2013.

REFERENCES

Arretche, M. (2010). Federalismo e Igualdade Territorial: Uma Contradição em Termos? *DADOS – Revista de Ciências Sociais, 53*(3), 587–620.
Asian Development Bank. (2010). *Education by 2020. A sector operations plan*. Metro Manila: Asian Development Bank.
Asian Development Bank. (2011). Republic of the Philippines: Education improvement sector development program. *ADB Concept Paper* (Project Number: 45089), 1–29.
Castells, M. (1998). *The information age: Economy, society and culture*. New York, NY: Blackwell.
Conferência Nacional de Educação – CONAE. (2010). *Construindo o Sistema Nacional Articulado de Educação: O Plano Nacional de Educação, uas Diretrizes e Estratégias de Ação*. Brasilia: Ministério da Educaçao.
Dale, R. (1999). Specifying globalisation effects on national policy: Focus on the mechanisms. *Journal of Education Policy, 14*(1), 1–17.
Dale, R., & Robertson, S. (2007). Beyond methodological 'Isms' in comparative education in an era of globalisation. In A. Kazamias & R. Cowan (Eds.), *Handbook on comparative education* (pp. 1113–1128). Netherlands: Springer.
Dobbin, F., Simmons, B., & Garret, G. (2007). The global diffusion of public policies: Social construction, coercion, competition, or learning? *Annual Review of Sociology, 33*, 449–472.
Doner, R., Ritchie, B. K., & Slater, D. (2005). Systemic vulnerability and the origins of developmental states: Northeast and Southeast Asia in comparative perspective. *International Organization, 59*(2), 327–381.
EFA Global Monitoring Report Team. (2014). *Teaching and learning: achieving quality for all*. Paris: UNESCO.
Eickelberg, A. (2012). Framing, fighting and coalitional building: The learnings and teachings of the brazilian campaign for the right to education. In A. Verger & M. Novelli (Eds.), *Campaigning for «Education for All». Histories, strategies and outcomes of transnational advocacy coalitions in education* (pp. 101–119). Rotterdam, The Netherlands: Sense Publishers.
Elacqua, G., Schneider, M., & Buckley, J. (2006). School choice in Chile: Is it class or the classroom? *Journal of Policy Analysis and Management, 26*(3), 577–601.
Elster, J. (2007). *Explaining social behavior. More nuts and bolts for the social sciences*. Cambridge, UK: Cambridge University Press.
Evans, P. (1992). The state as problem and solution: Predation, embedded autonomy and structural change. In *Sociology of development*. Aldershot, UK: An Elgar Reference Collection.

Farrington, J. J., & Slater, R. (2006). Cash transfers: Panacea for poverty reduction or money down the drain? *Development Policy Review, 24*(5), 499–511.

Fernandez, L., & Rosechin, O. (2011). Overview of the Philippines' conditional cash transfer program: The Pantawid Pamilyang Pilipino Program (Pantawid Pamilya). *WB-AusAID Philippine Social Protection Note, 2*(May), 1–12.

Filgueira, F. (2009). *El desarrollo maniatado en América Latina : estados superficiales y desigualdades profundas*. Buenos Aires: Consejo Latinoamericano de Ciencias Sociales.

Frigotto, G., & Ciavatta, M. (2003). Educação básica no Brasil na década de 1990: subordinação ativa e consentida à lógica do mercado. *Educaçao e Sociedade, 24*(82), 93–130.

Guzman, A. B. de. (2007). Chronicling decentralization initiatives in the Philippine basic education sector. *International Journal of Educational Development, 27*, 613–624.

Hoop, J. (2012). People power for education: Civil society participation in the Philippine educational politics. In A. Verger & M. Novelli (Eds.), *Campaigning for «Education for All». Histories, strategies and outcomes of transnational advocacy coalitions in education* (pp. 31–50). Rotterdam, The Netherlands: Sense Publishers.

INEP. (2012). (s.d.). IDEB – Resultados e Metas. Retrieved from http://ideb.inep.gov.br/

Jayasuriya, J. (2008). Regionalising the state: Political topography of regulatory regionalism. *Contemporary Politics, 14*(1), 21–35.

Kang, D. C. (2002). *Crony capitalism. Corruption and development in South Korea and the Philippines*. Cambridge, UK: Cambridge University Press.

Maca, M., & Morris, P. (2012). The Philippines, the East Asian 'developmental states' and education: A comparative analysis of why the Philippines failed to develop. *Compare: A Journal of Comparative and International Education, 42*(3), 461–484.

Ministerio de Educaçao BR. (2008). *O Plano de Desenvolvimento da Educaçao: Razoes, Princípios e Programas*. Brasilia: Ministério da Educaçao.

OECD. (2013). Brazil country note. En *Programme for International Student Assessment. Results from PISA 2012 (OECD)*. Paris: OECD.

OEI (Organización de Estados Iberoamericanos). (2010). *Metas Educativas 2021: la educación que queremos para la generación de los bicentenarios* (Documento final). Madrid: OEI y CEPAL.

Rambla, X. (2012). 'Soft power', educational governance and political consensus in Brazil. *International Studies in Sociology of Education, 22*(3), 191–212.

Ramos, R. C., & Giorgi, C. A. (2011). Do Fundef ao Fundeb: avaliando o passado para pensar o futuro: um estudo de caso no município de Pirapozinho-SP. *Ensaio: Avaliação e Políticas Públicas em Educação, 19*(72), 623–650.

Republic of the Philippines. (2005). *Functionally Literate Filipinos: An educated nation. National action plan to achieve education for all by the year 2015*. Metro Manila: Republic of the Philippines.

Reyes, V. Ch. Jr. (2009). Systemic corruption and the programme on basic education in the Philippine Department of Education. *Journal of Developing Societies, 25*(4), 481–510.

Robertson, S. (2011). The new spatial politics of (re)bordering and (re)ordering the state-education-citizen relation. *International Review of Education, 57*, 277–297.

Saforcada, F., & Vassiliades, A. (2011). Las leyes de educación en los comienzos del siglo XXI: del neoliberalismo al Post-Consenso de Washington en América del Sur. *Educaçao e Sociedade, 32*(115), 287–304.

Sarmiento, D. C. (2005). Criação dos sistemas municipais de ensino. *Educaçao e Sociedade, 26*(93), 1363–1390.

Sassen, S. (2006). *Territory, authority, rights. From medieval to global assemblages*. Princeton, NJ: Princeton University Press.

Steiner-Khamsi, G. (2004). Blazing a trail for policy theory and practice. In G. Steiner-Khamsi (Ed.), *The global politics of educational borrowing and lending* (pp. 201–220). New York, NY & London: Teachers College Press.

Steiner-Khamsi, G. (2010). The politics and economics of comparison. *Comparative Education Review, 54*(3), 323–342.

Steiner-Khamsi, G. (2012). Understanding policy borrowing and lending. Building comparative policy studies. In G. Steiner-Khamsi & F. Waldow (Eds.), *Policy borrowing and lending in education* (pp. 3–18). London & New York, NY: Routledge.

Thrupp, M. (2007). School admissions and the segregation of school intakes in New Zealand cities. *Urban Studies, 44*, 1393–1404.

Tilly, C. (1984). *Big structures, large processes, huge comparisons.* New York, NY: The Russell Sage Foundation.

Tilly, C. (2001). Mechanisms in political processes. *Annual Review of Political Science,* (4), 21–41.

UNESCO. (2008). *Educaçao para Todos em 2015. Alcançaremos a meta?* Brasilia: Representaçao da UNESCO no Brasil.

UNESCO Institute for Statistics. (2014a). Literacy in Brazil. *En Country Profiles* (UNESCO). Toronto: UNESCO. Retrieved from www.uis.unesco.org

UNESCO Institute for Statistics. (2014b). Education and literacy in the Philippines. In UNESCO (Ed.), *Country profiles.* Toronto: UNESCO.

United Nations Development Programme (UNDP). (2014). *Human development report data.* Washington, DC: UNDP. Retrieved from www.undp.org

Verger, A., Novelli, M., & Altinyelken, H. K. (2012). *Global education policy and international development.* London: Bloomsbury.

World Bank. (2011a). *Learning for All: Investing in people's knowledge and skills to promote development.* Washington, DC: The World Bank Group.

World Bank. (2011b). *Philippines. Private provision, public purpose. A review of the government's education service contracting program.* Washington, DC: The World Bank.

Xavier Rambla
Department of Sociology
Universitat Autònoma de Barcelona

PART II

THE PROBLEMATIC EFFECTS OF GLOBALIZATION ON EDUCATION

NICHOLAS SUN-KEUNG PANG

5. HOW HIGHER EDUCATION SYSTEMS IN ASIA-PACIFIC RESPOND TO THE CHALLENGES POSED BY GLOBALIZATION

INTRODUCTION

The potential effects of globalization on education are many and far-reaching due to education's scale and nature. This chapter aims to investigate how globalization has been affecting higher education and how higher education has been responding to the challenges that have arisen from globalization. It first outlines what is meant by globalization, the impacts on education, and principal changes which have come about. More specifically, there are reviews of development of higher education in the Asia-Pacific region and how higher education in mainland China, Hong Kong, Taiwan, South Korea, Japan, Singapore and Vietnam have been responding to globalization. When educational systems in the Asia-Pacific region are open to globalization, their traditional cultures and values of collectivism, humanism, self-cultivation, trust, compassion, grace, and honesty in educational governance, administration, management and leadership have changed into those neo-liberal values of contract, market, choice, competition, efficiency, flexibility, managerialism, and accountability.

THE PHENOMENON OF GLOBALIZATION

The Advent of Globalization

Globalization is not a new process. Bates (2002) comments that migration of ideas, artifacts and people has been a constant part of human history but that what appears to be new is the pace with which such migrations are now accomplished and the relative weakness of the barriers constructed by nation states in order to maintain their social, political and cultural integrity in the face of such migration. Although current concepts of globalization are still blurred and hard to define, they are generally accepted as relating to the global reach of processes of exchange of goods, the formation of gigantic multinational or transnational enterprises, and the virtual abolition of time because of the instantaneous nature of communication all over the world (Capella, 2000). Carnoy (1999) argues that globalization means more competition, which means that a nation's investment, production, and innovation are not limited by national borders. Globalization has become possible only because of the technological infrastructure provided by telecommunications, information systems, microelectronic equipment, and computer-controlled transportation systems.

There is no universally accepted conceptualization of globalization. Globalization has many faces, thus different theorists view globalization differently. Held (1991, p. 9) defines globalization as "the intensification of worldwide social relations which link distant localities in such a way that local happenings are shaped by events occurring many miles away and vice versa." Pieterse (1995, p. 45) speaks of globalization in terms of "the ideas that the world is becoming more uniform and standardized, through technological, commercial and cultural synchronization emanating from the West, and that globalization is tied up with modernity." Parker (1997, p. 484) views globalization as "a growing sense that events occurring throughout the world are converging rapidly to shape a single, integrated world where economic, social, cultural, technological, business, and other influences cross traditional borders and boundaries such as nations, national cultures, time, space, and industries with increasing ease." Capling et al. (1998, p. 5) argue that, "globalization refers to the emergence of a global economy which is characterized by uncontrollable market forces and new economic actors such as transnational corporations, international banks, and other financial institutions." Blackmore (2000, p. 133) described it as "increased economic, cultural, environmental, and social interdependencies and new transnational financial and political formations, with both homogenizing and differentiating tendencies."

Globalization is a product of the emergence of a global economy. The process of globalization is seen as blurring national boundaries, shifting solidarities within and between nation-states, and deeply affecting the constitution of national and interest group identities (Morrow & Torres, 2000). The term "globalization" is generally used to refer to a complicated set of economic, political, and cultural factors. As a result of expanding world trade, nations and individuals experience greater economic and political interdependence (Wells et al., 1998). New communication technologies that facilitate expanded world trade as well as cultural interaction are considered the determinants that lead to the emergence of globalization. It is widely believed that globalization is transforming the political, economic and cultural lives of people all around the world, whether in the developed countries or developing ones, and that globalization is driving a revolution in the organization of work, the production of goods and services, relations among nations, and even local culture.

The Impact of Globalization on Education

The potential effects of globalization on education are many and far-reaching, due to its scale and nature. Because the main bases of globalization are knowledge intensive information and innovation, globalization should have a profound impact on education (Carnoy, 2002). Almost everywhere in the world, educational systems are now under pressure to produce individuals for global competition, individuals who can themselves compete for their own positions in the global context, and who can legitimate the state and strengthen its global competitiveness (Daun, 2002).

Economic and technological globalization is challenging the nation-state in different ways. Countries differ in their response to the processes of globalization according to their size, economic and technological level, economic position in world markets, cultural composition, relationships between the state and economy (Green, 1997; Daun, 2002). Carnoy (2002) argues that analyzing how nation-states respond to globalization is crucial to the understanding of the effects of globalization on education. He posits that the approach a nation-state takes in education reform, their educational response to globalization, depends on three key factors: their real financial situation, their interpretation of that situation, and their ideological position regarding the role of the public sector in education. These three factors are expressed through the methods that a nation-state has adopted for the structural adjustment of its economy to the new globalized environment (Mok & Welch, 2003).

Globalization is having a profound effect on education at many different levels. That education has been a national priority in many countries is largely understood in terms of national economic survival in a fiercely competitive world. It is commonly recognized that the production economy is being rapidly overtaken by the knowledge economy. Many countries have taken action to enhance their competitive edge through the development of the knowledge-producing institutions and industries. The development of the knowledge economy through the enhancement of skills and abilities, that is, improved human capital, has become an important agenda in many countries' educational policy (Bates, 2002). Globalization will have even greater effects on education in the future. Because global financial flows are so great, governments rely increasingly on foreign capital to finance economic growth. One way to attract finance capital is to provide a ready supply of skilled labor by increasing the overall level of education in the labor force.

Global competition results in an overall demand for higher skills. Daun (2002) and Suárez-Orozco (2007) argue that global competition leads to an increasing demand for higher skills in the population as a whole, and lifelong learning for all. Global competition also leads to a techno-economic shift. Such a shift results in unemployment in the short term but to a higher standard of living and higher employment in the long term. As the arrival of a global society will also herald that of a knowledge society, the role of education is to enhance a nation's productivity and competitiveness in the global environment. Bates (2002, p. 139) foresees that the challenges ahead for most education systems and their success in global competition will depend on (i) whether they can determine the skills and attitudes required by the young and by lifelong learners, (ii) the construction of an appropriate global curriculum, (iii) the development of an appropriate technologically mediated pedagogy, (iv) the specification of the universal standards by which performance can be evaluated, and (v) the management of the system through which these achievements can be realized.

Globalization and Educational Change

Globalization has brought a paradigm shift in educational policies and administration in many countries (Reid, Gill, & Sears, 2010). Under the impacts of globalization, Mulford (2002) observes that the old-fashioned values of wisdom, trust, empathy, compassion, grace, and honesty in managing education have changed into those so-called values of contracts, markets, choice, and competition in educational administration. At present, school administrators are probing more into the instrumental skills of efficiency, accountability and planning than the skills of collaboration and reciprocity. School education nowadays puts more stress on the short term, the symbolic and expediency, having the answers and sameness, than those of the past, which focused on the long term, the real and substantive goals and objectives, discretion and reserving judgment, and character.

In the competitive global economy and environment, nation-states have no choice but to adjust themselves in order to be more efficient, productive, and flexible. To enhance a nation's productivity and competitiveness in the global situation, decentralization and the creation of a "market" in education have been the two major strategies employed to restructure education (Lingard, 2000; Mok & Welch, 2003). Decentralization and corporate managerialism have been used by most governments to increase labour flexibility and create more autonomous educational institutions while catering for the demand for more choice and diversity in education (Blackmore, 2000; Novelli & Ferus-Comelo, 2010). The emergence of education markets has also been central to education reform for globalization in many states. Carnoy (2002) argues that if education is restructured on market principles and based upon competitive market relations where individual choice is facilitated, education will become more efficient.

While it is true that many educational developments are due to globalization, the dynamics, complexity, and mechanism of such impacts are still not fully grasped. Carnoy (1999, pp. 15–17) analyzes how globalization has been affecting education systems, directly and indirectly, and summarizes that globalization has recently brought the following major educational changes:

1. Globalization has had an impact on the organization of work and on the work people do. Usually this work demands a high level of skill.
2. Such demands push governments to expand their higher education, and to increase the number of secondary-school graduates prepared to attend post-secondary education.
3. Most governments are under greater pressure to increase spending on education to produce a more educated labour force.
4. The quality of education is increasingly being compared internationally. The TIMSS and PISA studies are cases in point.
5. There have been greater emphases on mathematics and science curricula, English as a foreign language and communication skills, in school education.
6. Use of information technology such as the use of the Internet and computer assisted instruction are becoming more common in the classroom.

In the following sections, the impact of globalization on higher education in the Asia-Pacific region will be discussed more specifically and in greater details.

THE IMPACT OF GLOBALIZATION ON EDUCATION IN ASIA-PACIFIC COUNTRIES

In studying the responses to globalization in educational reforms in the Asia-Pacific countries, Currie (1998) identified a few interesting trends, which include: (i) a shift from elite to mass education, (ii) the privatization of education, (iii) the practice of corporate managerialism in education governance and (iv) the spread of transnational education. These trends necessarily confront the traditional values and culture in the practice of educational governance and management (AACSB International, 2011). The Sinic societies around the Asia-Pacific region, for example, mainland China, Hong Kong, Taiwan, South Korea, Japan, Singapore and Vietnam, where Confucianism has prevailed for thousands of years, are more vulnerable to the impacts of globalization (Pang, 2006). One of the major reasons globalization is being condemned is that it seems to undermine traditional values and cultures in these Sinic societies. When globalization is in conflict with personal egos and traditional values, it calls into question the concept of cultural identity. Today, globalized identity has been defined in terms of the way that global markets value an individual's traits and behaviour.

Restructuring Higher Education in the Era of Globalization

There have been a variety of important social, cultural, economic, and political forces that link to the global development of higher education. Schugurensky (2003) identified (i) the globalization of the economy, (ii) the 'commodification' of knowledge, and (iii) the retrenchment of the welfare state as three important forces, among others, for the changes in higher education. Globalization leads to the emergence of a knowledge economy, in which the importance of information technology and knowledge management is coming to outweigh that of capital and labour. Globalization also leads to the intensification of the transnational flows of information, commodities, and capital around the globe. That, in turn, renders both production and dissemination of knowledge increasingly commoditized. In parallel with the onset of globalization, more and more welfare states have adopted a neoliberal ideology geared to promoting economic international competitiveness through cutbacks in social expenditure, economic deregulation, decreased capital taxes, privatization and labour 'flexibilization'. All these forces are implicit in a restructuring of higher education systems worldwide (Peters et al., 2000; Welch & Mok, 2003).

The impacts of these forces on the change to higher education are manifest in the drastic restructuring of higher education systems, in which values, such as accountability, competitiveness, devolution, value for money, cost effectiveness, corporate management, quality assurance, performance indicators, and privatization are emphasized (Mok & Lee, 2002; Ngok & Kwong, 2003). Though nations vary widely in their social, political, cultural and economic characteristics, what is striking is the great similarity in the unprecedented scope and depth of restructuring taking place. In general, most of these changes are expressions of a greater influence of the market and the government over the university system. At the core of these changes is a redefinition of the relationships among the university, the state, and the market (Schugurensky, 2003).

There has been a shift from elite to mass higher education globally, driven by the fact that in a knowledge-based economy, the payroll cost to higher levels of education is rising worldwide. This is a result of the shift from economic production to knowledge-intensive services and manufacturing. Rising relative incomes for more highly educated labour increases the demand for university education, pushing governments to expand their higher education (Carnoy, 2002; Maringe & Foskett, 2010).

In the face of limited resources and the rapid expansion of higher education, governments have been forced towards the privatization of higher education and corporatization of public universities. Privatization is another global trend in higher education, which means a reduction in the level of state provision, and correspondingly, the encouragement of the expansion of private provision (Lee, 2000). The underlying ideology of privatization is based on the belief that the public sector is ineffective, inefficient, and inflexible, while the private sector is deemed more effective, efficient, and responsive to the rapid changes that are needed in the globalizing world.

By corporatization, public universities are run like business corporations. The adoption of business-like approaches will result in financial cost savings; increased administrative efficiencies; and retention of academic staff through the offering of competitive market remunerations (Lee, 2000). Such a global change reflects the fact that higher education institutions are increasingly required to secure additional funds from external sources and to reduce dependence on the government (Ngok & Kwong, 2003).

A unique feature of the rapid expansion of private higher education is the emergence of offshore programmes that are offered by foreign universities. The emergence of foreign-linked programmes reflects a growing trend of transnational education, which means that there is a growing volume of higher education being delivered across national boundaries. Education has become increasingly affected by commoditization. In the global context, the boundaries of how, where, and under whose authority education is carried out and certified are becoming less clear as universities internationalize their campuses, curricula, and teaching staff (Lee, 2000).

There are some backwash effects created from these global currents of restructuring of higher education due to globalization. First, a rapid expansion in higher education may inevitably lead to a fall in the average academic standard and performance of graduates. It is likely that the definition and establishment of quality will become the prerogative of management rather than academic professionals. When universities become more corporatized, they will be linked more to the market and less to the pursuit of truth. Intellectuals will become less the guardians of the search for truth, and administrators will assume a dominant role (Stromquist & Monkman, 2000). In this regard, norms that have traditionally been part of university life may be questioned. Stromquist and Monkman (2000) and Zajda (2010) warned that when guided by a climate of knowledge as production, the university may become indifferent to subjects dealing with ethics, social justice, and critical studies.

In coping with the challenges posed by globalization, Governments in the Asia-Pacific region have no choice but to restructure the governance and management structure in their higher education systems. The following movements are cases identified in the Asia-Pacific societies.

China. Higher education in China has played an important role in the building of the economy, scientific progress and social development by increasing the pool of advanced talent and experts necessary to achieve socialist modernization. The overall objectives of higher education reform in mainland China are to smooth the relationships among government, society, and higher education institutions (HEIs), setting up and perfecting a new system in which the state is responsible for the overall planning and macro management while the HEIs follow the laws but enjoy the autonomy to provide education according to needs of the society.

The recent reforms of higher education in mainland China consist of five parts: education provision, institutional management, scale of investment, recruitment and job-placement, and inner-institute management, of which institutional management reform is of most importance and greatest difficulty (MOE of the People's Republic of China, 2014). Regarding the management system reform, the relationships among universities, government and society have been gradually smoothed out by using tactics such as joint establishment, adjustment, cooperation and merger. A two-level education provision system has taken shape in which central government and local government take up different responsibilities to provide education with the former being responsible for the overall planning and management. The result of this was the elimination of duplication and overlapping effort. At the same time, the government streamlined their administration and delegated more power to the HEIs, bestowing on them greater autonomy to provide education for the society within the laws. With the introduction of the socialist market economy and the growing demand for qualified manpower, China has been focusing on establishing a viable system of human resources development. After about two decades of restructuring and transforming under the impact of globalization, the unified, centralized, closed, and static higher education system of China is becoming more diversified, decentralized, open, and dynamic. All these changes have exposed higher education in China to increasing international exchange and cooperation, as well as wider use of modern educational technology. The two most successful projects in the recent reforms of HEIs have been: The '211 Project' from 1996 to 2000, which was designed to foster 100 world-class universities in the 21st century, and the '985 Project' of May 1998, that provided utmost support to China's top ten universities.

Such projects have allowed mainland China to identify a small group of universities to be resourced as the flagships of China'a higher education sector and to enable them in due course to compete internationally and be measured alongside the best universities in North America and Europe. Along with the further opening of the Chinese higher education sector following China's accession to the World Trade Organization in 2001, international competition and pressure has been intensified and further restructuring and transformation have been introduced.

Hong Kong. In 1989, the Hong Kong Government adopted a policy of dramatic expansion of its higher education system in order to double the first year university enrolments from 9% of the age group in 1989/90 to 18% by 1994/95. It was believed that amongst the reasons for such a rapid expansion was the demand for a highly qualified workforce and the loss of well trained graduates through emigration prior to 1997 due to the political uncertainty. Hong Kong was able to establish seven universities and two degree awarding institutions and one tertiary level teacher education institution along with one private post-secondary college. In 2001, the Hong Kong Government declared a strategic intent to increase the enrollment rate to 60% of secondary school leavers for the relevant age group by the year 2010, as part of the ambitious reform proposed by the Education Commission. The Sutherland Report issued in 2002 called for a restructuring of the governance and management framework in Hong Kong's higher education system, under which it would acquire comparable strength and flexibility in the governance and management of its higher education institutions so that the achievements in teaching and research can provide the most beneficial service to the wider community (University Grants Committee, 2002). For higher education in Hong Kong to be internationally competitive, the Sutherland Report affirmed that the core functions of teaching and research are the drivers of economic opportunity in providing the type of educated workforce which is the pre-condition of a successful knowledge economy.

Taiwan. In the case of Taiwan, the restructuring of higher education aims at pursuing excellence in universities to raise their competitiveness in the era of globalization (MoE of Republic of China (Taiwan), 2014a,b). Some of these strategies include:

- revising the University Act to raise universities' self-government and operating efficiency;
- expanding the R&D Master's Degree Program for Industry to increase the capacity of training professionals;
- establishing a university evaluation system to ensure teaching quality;
- encouraging internationalization of universities and colleges by enrolling more foreign students;
- promoting consolidation of resources between universities to lift competitiveness;
- implementing the Program to Develop First-Class Universities and Top-Notch Research Centers to raise Taiwan 's international competitiveness.

South Korea. The cultivation of human resources has more importance for Korea, because of its lack of natural resources. In order to cope with the challenges posed by globalization, Korea has established development strategies that put the utmost emphasis on nurturing top-notch human resources (MEST, 2014). The then Korean Education Ministry (now, Ministry of Education, Science and Technology) announced a University Restructuring Plan in August 2004 to address the problem of human resources and raise the competitive edge of higher education. The strategies included: (i) reorganizing the governance system of national universities through decentralization; (ii) offering stronger support for leading universities to enhance their competitiveness; (iii) establishing a University Information Disclosure System to facilitate information flow and to enhance competition among universities; and (iv) establishing a Higher Education Evaluation System in the sense of quality assurance (Park, 2005).

Japan. Japan, as one of the fully developed countries in Asia, has been suffering for a long time from economic recession, at least since the early 1990s. From that time, there have been series of political, economic, and social reforms aimed at reviving the whole country. A large-scale educational reform was initiated in 2005, when the Ministry of Education, Culture, Sports, Science and Technology (MEXT) published a "White Paper on Education, Culture, Sports, Science and Technology". The White Paper provided an introduction to recent trends and efforts being made by MEXT in a variety of sectors. In response to the rapid change in global environment and socio-economy, including progress of globalization, the White Paper aims to realize an education and culture-oriented nation, and a nation based on creativity in science and technology, ensuring that Japan can sustain its development into the future in the era of globalization. It stipulates an Action Plan for restructuring the Japanese higher education system in response to rapid global changes such as economic and market growth caused by rapid technological developments, population flow on a global scale, and the advent of the IT society. Proposals for medium- to long-term future models of higher education as a whole, "Modality of Higher Education Institutions," and "Roles of Society toward the Development of Higher Education," as well as policies to be embraced for these models (MEXT, 2005; 2014) are also in the White Paper. Attempts that have been made to implement these in the higher educational system since the year of 2005 include: (i) offering academic degrees to junior college graduates, (ii) restructuring of university faculty organizations by establishing associate professors and assistant professors, (iii) revising methods for calculating colleges of technology credits, and (iv) granting graduate school entrance qualifications to people who have completed a four-year program in a professional training college (MEXT, 2005; 2014). Based on the National Council on Educational Reform final report, the then Minister, Nobutaka Machimura, presented in detail, major policies, tasks, and timetables concerning the roadmap for future higher educational reform, in which priority would be given to the following policies: (i) promoting acceptance of adult students in Universities; (ii) building a new system to secure the quality of Universities; and (iii) further reinforcing the training of professionals with advanced specialized skills in graduate schools, aiming to maintain Japan's competitiveness in the global economy.

Singapore. Perhaps to an even greater extent than Korea and Japan, the government of Singapore frequently refers to the population as its only natural resource and describes education in the vocabulary of resource development. In facing the changes due to globalization, in 1997 the Ministry of Education announced the vision "Thinking Schools, Learning Nation," which describes a nation of thinking and committed citizens capable of meeting the challenges of the future, and an education system geared to the needs of the 21st century. Thinking schools are learning organizations, which will constantly challenge assumptions, and seek better ways of doing things through participation, creativity and innovation. A learning nation is one that envisions a national culture and social environment that promotes lifelong learning in her people. The capacity of Singaporeans to continually learn will determine the collective tolerance for change in the era of globalization (MoE of Singapore, 2014).

Vietnam. Globalization is arguably a large part of the reason for Vietnam adopting an open door policy and participating in international co-operation activities. The open door policy will create more opportunities for Vietnam to approach and benefit from advanced scientific and technological achievements and management experience from the more developed economies. This will mutually assist and strengthen dialogue and international co-operation in solving global and regional problems. In the Education Development Strategy from 2001 to 2010 (MoE of Vietnam, 2008), the goals of higher education in Vietnam have been clearly set out as:

- to provide high quality human resources in line with becoming part of the global economy;
- to enhance the competitiveness of Vietnam in its international economic relationships;
- to facilitate the expansion of post secondary education through diversification of educational programs
- to increase the appropriateness of the training and to meet the development needs of society.

CONCLUSION

Though there is still no universally accepted conceptualization of globalization, what we call "globalization" has brought numerous and profound changes to the economic, social, cultural and political life of nations as well as changes in education. Globalization seems to be leading to some homogenizing tendencies, but it is also opening a space for new identities and contesting established values and norms (Stromquist & Monkman, 2000). The global flow of information and culture as well as the rapid spread of new technologies has enormous consequence for education. Globalization might entail the imposition of the concepts of competition, market, choice, decentralization and privatization on education, that is, the further infiltration by business forces into education. It might also lead to increased commoditization of education and making quality education only accessible to elite elements of society who can afford it (Kellner, 2000).

Globalization has brought a paradigm shift in educational governance, administration and leadership in some Asia-Pacific countries. Under the impacts of globalization, people in the Asia-Pacific region are confronted with sets of conflicting values and dilemmas in the choice between tradition and modern values brought by globalization. People are facing the challenges of choosing the proper values and ethics in determining their thinking and actions in a highly competitive world. People in the Asia-Pacific region are challenged with these impacts when their societies are open to globalization and when their traditional cultures and values meet with new ideologies brought along with globalization. The traditional ethics and values of hierarchical relationships, collectivism, trust, empathy, compassion, grace, and honesty in educational governance and management have changed into the so-called "new" values of contract, market, choice, competition, efficiency, flexibility, productivity and accountability.

The globalization of education might locate the Anglo-Saxon culture in a privileged position in the world as a whole. It is evident that in many places, globalization has led to greater economic and social inequality; and that educational access, whilst expanded, has also become more unequal in quality. Greater decentralization and privatization of education has generally not increased equality in educational services, but rather lead to more inequality (Carnoy, 2002).

There is also a question of whether globalization is a "good thing." Is globalization beneficial to economic growth, equality, and justice, or is it harmful? (Zajda, 2010) Has globalization led to development or division in education, and to what extent? (Welch & Mok, 2003) The question whether globalization in its various manifestations, is bad or good for education, remains largely unanswered. There exist dichotomous accounts of globalization in the literature, for example, (i) the relations between the global and the local; (ii) between globalization viewed as a trend toward homogenization around Western norms and culture and globalization viewed as an era of increased contact between diverse cultures, leading to an increase in hybridization and novelty; and (iii) between the material and rhetorical effects of globalization (Burbules & Torres, 2000; Suárez-Orozco & Qin-Hilliard, 2004). Further research into these controversial issues should be carried out, as long as globalization continues to affect education (Roth & Gur-Ze'ev, 2007; Popkewitz & Rizvi, 2009). The challenge ahead for research on globalization in Education is not only whether progress is being made, but whether it is being made quickly enough.

REFERENCES

AACSB International. (2011). *Globalization of management education: Changing international structures, adaptive strategies, and the impact on institutions* (Report of the AACSB International Globalization of Management Education Task Force). Bingley, UK: Emerald Group Publishing.
Bates, R. (2002). Administering the global trap: The roles of educational leaders. *Educational Management & Administration, 30*(2), 139–156.
Blackmore, J. (2000). Globalization, a useful concept for feminists rethinking theory and strategies in education. In N. C. Burbules & C. A. Torres (Eds.), *Globalization and education, critical perspectives* (pp. 133–155). London: Routledge.
Burbules, N. C., & Torres, C. A. (2000). An introduction to globalization and education. In N. C. Burbules & C. A. Torres (Eds.), *Globalization and education: Critical perspectives* (pp. 1–26). London: Routledge.
Capella, J. R. (2000). Globalization, a fading citizenship. In N. C. Burbules & C. A. Torres (Eds.), *Globalization and education: Critical perspectives* (pp. 227–251). London: Routledge.
Capling, A., Considine, M., & Crozier, M. (1998). *Australian politics in the global era*. Melbourne: Addison-Wesley.
Carnoy, M. (1999). *Globalization and educational reform, what planners need to know*. UNESCO, Paris: International Institute for Educational Planning.
Carnoy, M. (2002). Foreword. In H. Daun (Ed.), *Educational restructuring in the context of globalization and national policy*. New York, NY: Routledge Falmer.
Currie, J. (1998). Globalization practices and the professoriate in Anglo-Pacific and North American universities. *Comparative Education Review, 42*(1), 15–29.
Daun, H. (Ed.). (2002). *Educational restructuring in the context of globalization and national policy*. New York, NY: Routledge Falmer.
Green, A. (1997). *Education, globalization and the nation state*. London: Macmillan Press.
Held, D. (Ed.). (1991). *Political theory today*. Standford, CA: Standford University Press.
Kellner, D. (2000). Globalization and new social movements: Lessons for critical theory and pedagogy. In N. C. Burbules & C. A. Torres (Eds.), *Globalization and education, critical perspectives* (pp. 299–321). London: Routledge.
Lee, M. N. N. (2000). The impacts of globalization on education in Malaysia. In N. P. Stromquist & K. Monkman (Eds.), *Globalization and education: Integration and contestation across cultures* (pp. 315–332). Lanham, MD: Rowman & Littlefield.
Lingard, B. (2000). It is and it isn't: Vernacular globalization, educational policy, and restructuring. In N. C. Burbules & C. A. Torres (Eds.), *Globalization and education, critical perspectives* (pp. 79–108). London: Routledge.
Maringe, F., & Foskett, N. (Eds.). (2010). *Globalization and internationalization in higher education: Theoretical, strategic and management perspectives*. London: Continuum.
Ministry of Education and Training (MoET) of Vietnam. (2008). *Education in Vietnam*. Retrieved September 04, 2014, from http://www.moet.gov.vn/
Ministry of Education, Culture, Sports, Science and Technology (MEXT) of Japan. (2005). *White paper on education, culture, sports, science and technology*. Japan, Tokyo: MEXT.
Ministry of Education, Culture, Sports, Science and Technology (MEXT) of Japan. (2014). *Policies in higher education*. Retrieved September 10, 2014, from http://www.mext.go.jp/english/highered/index.htm
Ministry of Education (MoE) of Republic of China (Taiwan). (2014a). *Summary of what the ministry of education has achieved in 2000–2008*. Retrieved July 15, 2014, from http://english.moe.gov.tw/ct.asp?xItem=9355&ctNode=783&mp=1
Ministry of Education (MoE) of Republic of China (Taiwan). (2014b). *White paper on university education policy*. Retrieved September 28, 2014, from http://english.moe.gov.tw/lp.asp?CtNode=11411&CtUnit=1332&BaseDSD=16&mp=1&nowPage=2&pagesize=15
Ministry of Education (MoE) of Singapore. (2014). *Post-secondary education*. Retrieved August 15, 2014, from http://www.moe.gov.sg/education/post-secondary/

Ministry of Education (MoE) of the People Republic of China. (2014). *Higher education in China.* Retrieved September 28, 2014, from http://www.moe.edu.cn/publicfiles/business/htmlfiles/moe/s4971/index.html

Ministry of Education, Science and Technology (MEST) of Korea. (2014). *Higher education in the Republic of Korea.* Retrieved September 15, 2014, from http://english.moe.go.kr/web/1710/en/board/enlist.do?bbsId=258

Mok, J. K. H., & Lee, H. H. (2002). A reflection on quality assurance in Hong Kong's higher education. In J. K. H. Mok & D. K. K. Chan (Eds.), *Globalization and education: The quest for quality education in Hong Kong* (pp. 213–240). Hong Kong: Hong Kong University Press.

Mok, J. K. H., & Welch, A. (2003). Globalization, structural adjustment and educational reform. In J. K. H. Mok & A. Welch (Eds.), *Globalization and educational restructuring in the Asia Pacific Region* (pp. 1–31). New York, NY: Palgrave Macmillan.

Morrow, R. A., & Torres C. A. (2000). The state, globalization and education policy. In N. C. Burbules & C. A. Torres (Eds.), *Globalization and education: Critical perspectives* (pp. 27–56). London: Routledge.

Mulford, B. (2002). The global challenge: A matter of balance. *Educational Management & Administration, 30*(2), 123–138.

Ngok, K. L., & Kwong, J. (2003). Globalization and educational restructuring in China. In J. K. H. Mok & A. Welch (Eds.), *Globalization and educational restructuring in the Asia Pacific region* (pp. 160–188). New York, NY: Palgrave Macmillan.

Novelli, M., & Ferus-Comelo, A. (Eds.). (2010). *Globalization, knowledge and labour: Education for solidarity within spaces of resistance.* London: Routledge.

Pang, N. S. K. (Ed.). (2006). *Globalization: Educational research, change and reforms.* Hong Kong: The Chinese University Press.

Park, K. J. (2005, July 5). *Policies and strategies to meet the challenges of internationalization of higher education.* Paper presented at the World Conference on Higher Education in Asia and the Pacific, Seoul, South Korea.

Parker, B. (1997). Evolution and revolution: From international business to globalization. In S. R. Clegg, C. Hardy, & W. R. Nord (Eds.), *Handbook of organization studies* (pp. 484–506). London: Sage Publications.

Peters, M., Marshall, J., & Fitzsimons, P. (2000). Managerialism and educational policy in a global context: Foucault, neoliberalism, and the doctrine of self-management. In N. C. Burbules & C. A. Torres (Eds.), *Globalization and education: Critical perspectives* (pp. 109–132). London: Routledge.

Pieterse, J. N. (1995). Globalization as hybridization. In M. Featherstone, S. Lash, & R. Robertson (Eds.), *Global modernities* (pp. 45–68). London: Sage.

Popkewitz, T. S., & Rizvi, F. (Eds.). (2009). *Globalization and the study of education.* Malden, MA: Blackwell Publishing.

Reid, A., Gill, J., & Sears, A. (Eds.). (2010). *Globalization, the nation-state and the citizen: Dilemmas and directions for civics and citizenship education.* New York, NY: Routledge.

Roth, K., & Gur-Ze'ev. I. (Eds.). (2007). *Education in the era of globalization.* Dordrecht: Springer.

Schugurensky, D. (2003). Higher education restructuring in the era of globalization: Toward a heteronomous model? In R. F. Arnove & C. A. Torres (Eds.), *Comparative education: The dialectic of the global and the local* (pp. 292–312). Lanham: Rowman & Littlefield.

Stromquist, N. P., & Monkman, K. (2000). Defining globalization and assessing its implications on knowledge and education. In N. P. Stromquist & K. Monkman (Eds.), *Globalization and education: Integration and contestation across cultures* (pp. 3–26). Lanham, MD: Rowman & Littlefield.

Suárez-Orozco, M. M. (Ed.). (2007). *Learning in the global era: International perspectives on globalization and education.* Berkeley, CA: University of California Press.

Suárez-Orozco, M. M., & Qin-Hilliard, D. B. (Eds.). (2004). *Globalization: Culture and education for a new millennium.* Berkeley, CA: University of California Press.

University Grants Committee. (2002). *Higher education in Hong Kong: The Sutherland report.* Hong Kong: University Grants Committee.

Welch, A., & Mok, J. K. H. (2003). Conclusion: Deep development or deep division? In J. K. H. Mok & A. Welch (Eds.), *Globalization and educational restructuring in the Asia Pacific region* (pp. 333–356). New York, NY: Palgrave Macmillan.
Wells, A. S., Carnochan, S., Slayton, J., Allen, R. L., & Vasudeva, A. (1998). Globalization and educational change. In A. Hargreaves, A. Lieberman, M. Fullan, & D. Hopkins (Eds.), *International handbook of educational change* (pp. 322–348). Dordrecht: Kluwer Academic.
Zajda, J. (Ed.). (2010). *Globalization, education and social justice*. Dordrecht, The Netherlands: Springer.

Nicholas Sun-keung Pang
Department of Educational Administration and Policy
The Chinese University of Hong Kong

CARLOS ORNELAS

6. THE TORTUOUS PATH OF EDUCATIONAL DECENTRALIZATION IN MEXICO

INTRODUCTION

Let me start by explaining why I characterize the 1992 Mexican decentralization of basic education as the victim of a "tortuous path." We have a saying in Spanish: *Árbol que nace torcido jamás su tronco endereza.* "The tree that is born crooked never straightens its trunk." I argue that the metaphor is apt in explaining the trajectory of the strategy of decentralization Mexico adopted in the early 1990s.

On May 18, 1992, the head of the Federal Department of Public Education (SEP), the general secretary of the National Teachers Union (SNTE), and the governors of the 31 states signed the National Agreement to Modernize Basic Education (referred to hereafter as the Agreement). The central government transferred the administration of more than half a million teaching posts in institutions of basic education and teachers' training colleges to the states. The states also acquired ancillary powers, including authority to handle labor relations, manage more than one hundred thousand school buildings, and oversee millions of other assets. The transfer of authority also entailed shifting control of the financial resources used to pay teachers and administrators as well as control of further funds intended to improve the quality of education (Moctezuma Barragán, 1994). Within a few days, the federal government organized this momentous series of resource transfers to the states. Amazed by the extent and speed of the transition, Mark Hanson has dubbed this decentralizing period in May of 1992 the *Blitzkrieg* (Hanson, 2000)

The Agreement had three explicit goals: to increase the quality of education, to make the system more equitable, and to enhance the popular respect accorded to the teachers' guild. Proponents of the Agreement also argued that vesting authority in the states would render the education system's management more effective, since authority would be located nearer to where the problems would arise (SEP, 1992). The system thereby made way for significant variations in governing bodies' decision-making processes, and thus started Mexico down the path for institutional change (Crawford & Ostrom, 1995).

Contemporary government authorities regarded the Agreement as the Salinas administration's most ambitious attempt to modernize the education system. It was more than a mere decentralization—it was commonly believed to usher in a new era of educational federalism in Mexico (Mancera & García, 2000).

After 22 years of this educational federalism, the Peña Nieto Administration decided to recentralize the education workers' payroll as well as to reclaim authority over the recruitment and promotion of teachers and administrators. The President, supported by the leaders of the main opposition political parties, made public an initiative to amend the Constitution and to enact two new laws to achieve those ends. The Peña Nieto administration thus began to radically alter the educational division of labor between state and federal government devised in 1992 (Ramírez Raymundo, 2013). Peña Nieto fast-tracked the initiative.

This institutional change directly opposed the strategy of decentralization. However, it may, like its ideological opposite, be doomed from the start. I argue that the move to recentralize, like the 1992 initiative to decentralize, unwittingly incentivizes counterproductive behavior from governments and unions alike.

This chapter seeks to answer three research questions: What went wrong in the decentralization of education? Why is a PRI government reversing the accomplishment of another PRI administration, the earlier of which was very proud of the move to decentralize? Were there technical problems in the states' exercise of authority, or did the reversal transpire because the SNTE leadership realized it would have more power in the context of a centralized bureaucracy?

I advance two primary claims. First, I argue that the 1992 *federalization of education* was another form—though a more subtle form—of centralism. Despite how it was marketed to the public, it granted very little actionable authority to the states' governors. Instead, it concentrated control over key decisions—the decisions that denoted real power—in centralized institutions. Second, I argue that the governors fell prey to the powerful SNTE machinery, though they also mismanaged the scarce resources they were afforded for funding education in their territories.

In order to understand the complexities of Mexico's move to decentralize its education system, it is necessary to grasp the internal conflict that haunts its infrastructure. Mexico's system of education simultaneously abides by two authoritative structures that have engaged in constant conflict throughout the nation's history. The research literature refers to these structures as the *formal and informal* rules (North, 1990).

The formal system constitutes rules and policies that map the legal layout of the education system. Changes that are codified in law or policy reconfigure how the formal system is legally obligated to operate. However, Mexican legislators' real intent in reconfiguring the formal structure has often been to change the tacit, informal rules.

The informal structure of Mexican education has pulled teachers and administrators like a swift undercurrent; it determines much of what transpires at every level of the education system, from the schoolhouse door to the office of the Secretary of Public Education. The tacit system is characterized by corrupt policies, control by union bosses, deceptive data, and nepotistic hiring. For example, it has been the unspoken expectation that retiring Mexican teachers bequeath their posts to their descendants or sell it to the highest bidder. Unsurprisingly, this kind of under-the-table activity has hugely impinged on the efficacy of the decentralized system.

I will address the tension between these two systems through their manifestations in political conflict, and will then analyze possibilities for institutional change.

BACKGROUND: CENTRALISM AS VOCATION

Article 40 of the Constitution establishes that Mexico is a representative, secular, democratic, and federal republic. Nevertheless, the Executive branch has emerged as the dominant political power over the course of the country's history. The head of the Executive has all the privileges a president would enjoy in a pure presidential regime (Carpizo, 1978).

Moreover, the Mexican revolution institutionalized a corporatist system in which the President controls organized labor, *campesinos,* and groups of merchants, industrialists, and professionals via the Institutional Revolutionary Party (PRI) (Aziz Nassif, 1989; Córdova, 1973). Society was to be highly structured; the President was designated as the ultimate arbiter of all social and political conflicts (Cosío Villegas, 1974; Krauze, 1997).

Nevertheless, in the 1990s, the political tides were shifting and the landscape was growing increasingly democratic. The PRI began to lose its hegemonic control in 1997, when for the first time in more than six decades it failed to secure an absolute majority in Congress. Opposition parties had also been winning state governments since 1989. The major shift came in 2000, when Vicente Fox, the candidate of the right wing National Action Party (PAN), won the Mexican presidency. When the PAN administration took office, the informal rules of government changed drastically. Governors ceased to serve merely as subordinates of the President; they achieved high levels of autonomy from central national powers.

The public largely expected that the new government would be more democratic and would crack down on public corruption. However, the new rulers let numerous opportunities for meaningful reform pass by and the PAN governments failed most egregiously in the management of education (Loyo, 2013; Raphael, 2007). Presidents Fox (2000–2006) and Calderón (2006–2012) did not use their power to dismantle the corporatist pact between the government and the labor unions. In fact, they did the opposite: SNTE and its leadership acquired even more power under the new governments.

Although dissident teachers led uprisings in several states organized by the National Coordinator of Education Workers (CNTE), both Presidents Salinas (1988–1994) and Zedillo (1994–2000) used their informal powers to silence those uprisings and to protect the majority of SNTE that was aligned with PRI politics. Both PAN presidents, Fox and Calderón, failed to rebalance educational power; they bargained with SNTE leaders and granted them numerous concessions, including many powerful administrative posts (Ornelas, 2010; Raphael, 2007). Those concessions, rather than mollifying the SNTE, served as incentives for SNTE section bosses to push for further demands.

Apparently, Peña Nieto was hesitant to bargain from a position of weakness. Therefore, he pushed for an education reform that would put an end to educational federalism and reestablish centralism.

THE FATE OF THE DECENTRALIZATION POLICY

In order to make sense of what happened in the process of decentralizing basic education and teachers' colleges (which are called "normal schools" in Mexico), I will offer a brief background in the changes to both the formal and informal rules. I maintain that the new educational federalism was a smokescreen that hid an insidious version of centralism. In other papers, I have shown that Mexico's basic education system is founded on corporatist (and corrupt) relations between the state and SNTE (Ornelas, 1995, 2002).

The Salinas administration leveraged the Agreement to pursue changes in the formal rules of governance in basic education. In November 1992, president Salinas sent Congress an initiative to amend Article 3 of the Constitution. This reform made junior high school (*secundaria*) compulsory and set the stage for centralism via the underlying structure of the education system. Compulsory education was to be controlled by the central administration but operated by the states. Fraction III of Article 3 stated, "[T]he Federal Executive will determine the plans and curricula of preschool, primary, secondary, and teacher education throughout the Republic" (Poder Ejecutivo Federal, 1993). Before this amendment, SEP only had jurisdiction over the federal system. Now it was to have authority over the states, which each used to have their own system.

The General Act of Education of July 1993, which replaced the 1973 federal law, made still more explicit the centralism that undergirded the formal rules. Under the new institutional model, the Federal Department of Education had the power to "determine," "norm," "regulate," "evaluate," and "ascertain general guidelines." It also required local governments to earmark resources for education despite the fact that the Constitution makes clear that each state congress has the sovereign right to fix the public expenses for schools within its jurisdiction. The states, according to this new federalism, will "provide educational services," "adjust calendars to local needs," and "are to be responsible for labor relations with SNTE." They were not to interfere with the education system's nationally determined structure. These were the silently federalist features of the nominally decentralized education arrangement, as shown in Table 1.

In brief, then, SEP continued to control the major policy decisions while the states were delegated the responsibility for carrying out tasks within centralized government guidelines. The move marked a decentralization of management functions, but a centralization of decision-making authority. The institutional changes that constituted the decentralization of education never attempted to dismantle the corporatist pact between the state and SNTE.

Table 1. Jurisdiction over basic public education

Federal government	State governments	Shared jurisdiction
1. To determine for the whole nation the basic education and teacher training curricula. 2. To establish the national school calendar. 3. To elaborate and update the free textbooks. 4. To authorize the use of any other book for basic education. 5. To prepare general guidelines for the use of teaching materials. 6. To regulate the system of education, in-service training and professional upgrading of teachers. 7. To fix the pedagogical requisites of curricula for private preschools. 8. To regulate a national system of credits and educational equivalents. 9. To have a national register of educational institutions. 10. To design guidelines for the Councils of Social Participation. 11. To realize planning, programming and evaluation of the national system of education. 12. To coordinate cultural relations with other countries. 13. To coordinate all the necessary measures to guarantee the national character of basic education and teacher training institutions.	1. To provide basic education and teacher training services. 2. To propose to SEP the regional curricular contents for basic education and teacher training. 3. To adjust, if necessary, the school calendar to local needs. 4. To provide in-service training for teachers according to SEP determinations. 5. To accept degrees of other states according to SEP regulations. 6. To supply, reject or revoke authorization to the private sector to create and operate basic education and teacher training services.	1. To promote and provide educational services according to national and regional needs. 2. To determine and formulate curriculum content different from column 1, # 1. 3. To acknowledge studies done outside the country according to the guidelines of SEP. 4. To approve, reject or revoke the recognition of private educational institutions different from basic education and teacher training. 5. To publish books or other materials beyond the official ones. 6. To provide library services to assist the national education system, with educational innovation and scientific, humanistic and technological research. 7. To promote educational research. 8. To encourage the development of technical education and technological research. 9. To promote cultural and physical activities. 10. To oversee the enforcement of the General Education Law.

Source: *Ley General de Educación*, Articles 12, 13, and 14

The system's corporatist traits were guaranteed by two additional stipulations. First, SNTE national leadership negotiated with the state governments and persuaded them to accept the Regulation of General Conditions in the Workplace for SEP as the formal guideline for labor relations. Moreover, SNTE's National Executive Committee (NEC) was to be the sole author of this regulation (Rodríguez, 1999). Second, the signatories of the Agreement resolved that from 1994 on there would be two types of labor negotiations: one between the federal government and the NEC (of SNTE), and the other between each local section and its respective state government. The latter type of negotiation became a pressure point routinely exploited by SNTE bosses, and they chose to attack the weak link in the chain even more aggressively when the PRI lost the presidency. Thus, the splitting of labor negotiations paved the way for corruption.

To organize the relocation of resources related to basic education and teacher training, the federal government made treaties with each state via the Treasury Department. However, the formulas for fund allocation reproduced the old inequitable norms, dashing public hopes for a more equitable distribution of funds straight out of the gate (Latapí Sarre & Ulloa-Herrero, 2000). In 1998, the Federal Congress amended the Fiscal Coordination Law to create the Fund for Basic and Normal Education (FAEB). The new formulas for resource allocation were similar to the old ones, but public funds had been growing since 1997 due to the lucrative export of oil. Thus, the federal funds transferred to the states for their local education systems also rose (Trujillo, 2013). The resultant bounty created an incentive for local sections of SNTE to increase their demands and for state governors to request more funds for education.

The growing political diversity in Congress led to modifications of the informal rules of the game. Since 1998, every year had seen bitter debates surrounding the federal education budget. The governors asked the representatives of their states—regardless of their political party—to push for more resources. (The representatives who were SNTE members proved to be the most aggressive in demanding fiscal increases for education.) In 1998, Congress made changes to the Executive proposal for the federal budget, but it benefited only certain players; more than 90% of the increase was allocated to salaries and fringe benefits (Ornelas, 2010, pp. 190–192; Trujillo, 2013).

The government proposed changes to the prescriptions of FAEB in 2007 to make the distribution more equitable and to encourage states to invest more resources into education (especially those states that had historically allocated less than their neighbors). The new formulas seemed like a good idea on paper, but they problematically upset the traditional distribution of government wealth. Some states received more resources and others received less. The changes did not address the inequality of the system, but rather succeeded only in exacerbating some states' education problems (Trujillo, 2013).

Research done in ten states showed that governors felt empowered neither to challenge SNTE leaders nor to take control of the education system that was nominally in their hands. This was due in part to one of the unwritten rules that regulated power and labor relations between the state governments and SNTE. Although the governors were permitted to designate the head of the Department of Education, it was understood that the delegate was to be a member of SNTE. Thus, SNTE cadres colonized the decentralized system and portions of the SEP central offices (Ornelas, 2012).

The colonization of the governance of education had been in progress since the late 1950s, but it accelerated after the enactment of the Agreement and boomed during the PAN governments. During 2006–2012, President Calderón ceded control of basic education to Elba Esther Gordillo, the powerful leader of SNTE. She appointed her son-in-law head of the most powerful branch of the Department of Education. President Calderón also gave Gordillo another important position in the federal bureaucracy—allegedly as payment for the support she had lent him in the 2006 elections (Raphael, 2007). As of December 2012, the Secretaries of Education in 20 states were faithful SNTE cadres whom Gordillo had personally installed through negotiations with state governors (Melgar, 2012).

Thus, Union members controlled local bargains between the government and SNTE for salary increases and fringe benefits on both sides of the table. The goal of SNTE leaders was to achieve more power for themselves. The salary increases legitimated SNTE leadership with rank-and-file teachers. However, the payroll was growing, and the funds from FAEB were insufficient to cover the increased demand. Many states were on the verge of bankruptcy (Trujillo, 2013).

After two decades of decentralization, the number of teaching and administrative posts grew at rates that dramatically exceeded the rate of growth of enrollment in basic education, but quality and equity of education were motionless. According to a variety of evaluations, the quality of education did not improve (INEE, 2014). The decentralization of education had not made a substantial impact on the unjust patterns of the system; neither had the compensatory programs enforced from 1993 to 2006 proven to have favorable effects (Bracho, 2008; Ornelas, 2001). The presence of institutional change was obvious after 1992; there were substantial modifications to governing bodies' decision-making processes. Educational federalism, whether or not it was merely symbolic, was accepted as a common-sense solution. However, the shifts in the administration of basic education from the central government to the states incentivized SNTE branches to pursue their own objectives. The informal rules often trumped their legal counterparts. It seems reasonable that the Peña Nieto administration diagnosed the decentralization of education as socially—and perhaps, even more importantly, politically—counterproductive. Thus, it was clear to him and to his advisors that education had to be recentralized.

THE PEÑA NIETO REFORM

In his inaugural speech on December 1, 2012, President Peña Nieto said, "There will be clear and precise rules for everyone who wants to enter as, remain in the position of, or be promoted as a teacher, principal, or supervisor, based on her/his work and merit." He was responding to a problem that germinated and grew because local governments were unable to control booming teachers' college enrollment levels, despite the fact that it was obvious that enrollment in basic education would be stabilized by the mid-1990's and thus that the supply of teachers would outstrip the demand for them. When there was a surfeit of teachers and few teaching posts available, the practice of bequeathing and selling teaching chairs began.

The situation resulted from a long history of corruption. Since the mid-1950's, when an interest group came to power within the SNTE, most teachers had been forced to pay for their initial post, and then to pay again to acquire an urban placement or to be installed as a school principal. Though it wasn't a legal requirement, it was a practical fact that labor bosses recruited and placed the public teaching force. At the time, this was not seen as a terrible problem, since the public school system was growing and many more teachers were needed—graduates of teachers' colleges were guaranteed a job as soon as they finished their coursework. Even in those rare cases in which teachers and aspiring teachers sought to uncover corruption, it was—and still is—very difficult to make one's case successfully because of the biased forces that control the SNTE (Muñoz Armenta, 2008).

In 1984, the government launched a reform to re-categorize the teachers' colleges as college-level professional schools; before that the courses of studies were of only seven years after primary education. Therefore, enrollment numbers diminished for a few years. The National Pedagogical University branches created programs to upgrade teaching credentials for teachers who already held positions. An uptick in enrollment in teachers' colleges persisted throughout the next 20 years, and some new normal schools were founded to meet the demand. One of the reasons for this increase was that teachers were no longer underpaid.

The federal government honored its commitment to increase teacher salaries and other benefits, as outlined in the Agreement. The standard monthly salary of a starting teacher in the Mexico City area, for instance, rose 56% in real value from December 1988 to December 1992. It decreased 8% before December 1997 due to the economic crisis of 1995, when the GNP fell almost 7%. Nevertheless, since 1993, teachers had been extended another benefit: a system of incentives (*Carrera Magisterial,* or CM) with the specific aim of creating a performance-based meritocracy with a formalized promotion structure (SEP, 1999).

The new incentive system was designed to reward those teachers who fit five criteria: those who (1) had professional qualifications, (2) demonstrated superior classroom performance, (3) attended in-service training courses or acquired other diplomas, (4) maintained good relationships with other teachers, parents, and students, and (5) had seniority. The material rewards attached to these criteria were (and still are) significant, ranging from 27% to 224% of teachers' basic salary, and the benefits accrue for retirement. There are five benefit levels, labeled A through E. In addition, teachers were granted bonuses for Christmas and Teachers' Day and were guaranteed paid vacations. On average, teachers made more than 450 days' worth of salary per year in exchange for 200 days of work (four hours a day) in front of a class. Their role and routines were the same as they were before decentralization, but they were receiving enhanced remuneration. By the end of the last century, around 65% of all teachers were receiving this remarkable bonus (Ornelas, 2002).

The forces that had colonized the education system nevertheless distorted this system, which aspired to reward merit. The government agreed that parity committees, or SEP-SNTE groups, would manage the incentive schema, both at the national and state levels. Soon it became clear that SNTE leaders and SNTE cadres masquerading as public servants were running those groups. Moreover, the fourth criterion (that a teacher maintain good relationships with other teachers, parents, and students) represented 28% of the overall measure of teacher success, and the teacher's colleagues and school principal measured it. This peer review was flawed: in the first three years of the CM implementation, every teacher who participated in an evaluation obtained the maximum of 28 points. SEP reacted to this rating inflation and introduced a *corrective factor*, deciding not to consider that criterion. CM was reformed in 1998 and again in 2011 (Flores Sánchez, 2012).

Research done on that schema at different points in time consistently showed that corruption dominated its internal workings. For instance, all of the members of NEC and the leaders of SNTE sections were automatically assigned to receive additional pay for merit, even though none of them were actually working at schools. Additionally, reports showed that CM rewarded not the best teachers but rather those who proved loyal to SNTE. It was also shown that many *flyers* (personnel who do not work but who nevertheless remain on the payroll) were assimilated into and rewarded by the Schema (Flores Sánchez, 2012; Ornelas, 2002; Santibáñez et al., 2006).

The combination of these three factors—a great number of teachers' college graduates with few teaching posts to accommodate them, the bequest and sale of teaching posts, and corruption funneled through the CM—gradually altered the institutional structure of the basic education system. At the beginning of the twentieth-first century, the first public evaluations (including TIMSS and PISA) showed that Mexican graduates of basic education performed poorly in comparison to other OECD countries. The press blamed teachers and systemic imperfections for the dispiriting results. President Vicente Fox's solution was to accept the suggestion proffered by the leader of SNTE, and thus yet another pact was signed in August 2002: the Social Commitment for Quality Education.

The government and SNTE agreed that entry into teaching and promotion to positions of headmaster and supervisor should be judged and awarded based on meritocratic, open competition. They also agreed that new evaluation mechanisms must be established to reward teachers—that is, that the government should modify CM. However, in fact the Social Commitment for Quality Education was a symbolic pact designed to satisfy the press. True, the National Institute for the Evaluation of Education (INEE) was created on the day the agreement was reached to ameliorate the failing evaluation system, but it was installed under the Executive branch, and the secretary of Public Education was the head of its governing body. The bequest and sale of teaching posts continued. Apparently, the informal rules were untouchable (Jordan, 2004).

President Calderón wanted to stop the corrupt practice. He agreed to tackle it via another pact with SNTE. He ordered his Secretary of Public Education to sign the Alliance for the Quality of Education (ACE) to reach a settlement with the powerful labor boss Elba Esther Gordillo. Gordillo was a politico of questionable ethics—a "Jimmy Hoffa with a skirt," as she was termed by Delal Bear, the head of the Mexico Center at Georgetown University (Cordoba, 2003). Again, the agreement's primary objective was to establish fair and meritocratic competition as the arbiter of access to the teaching profession as well to higher posts like school principal and district supervisor.

The government held open competitions from 2008 through 2012, but only for newly created teaching posts. Those posts vacated by retiring teachers—the majority of available posts—were bequeathed or sold (Ornelas, 2012). There was no incentive for any of the parties involved to alter their unethical practices. If a radical reshaping were enforced, SNTE leadership would lose a great deal of its internal power, and the government would risk losing a powerful ally. ACE, in short, defrauded the public. Whatever earnest intentions of institutional change underlay the agreement, they bowed to the informal rules and power relations. The basic structure of the hiring system in education remained intact (Fuentes Molinar, 2013; Ornelas, 2012).

When Peña Nieto was president elect and had not yet entered office, he refused to receive Gordillo. It seems that he was already working with the leaders of PAN and the left-wing Party of the Democratic Revolution (PRD) to draft the Pact for Mexico; they agreed that the reform of education would be the first initiative in a larger package of structural reforms. The education system's wrongs were the most egregious and conspicuous, and Gordillo was widely discredited (and she had wronged the leaders of the three major parties, to boot). Consequently, once again, the government resolved to rewrite the rules of the game.

The signatories of the Pact for Mexico decided to begin their ambitious reform with an amendment to the Constitution. Their diagnosis was simple: the Agreement had made SEP into an archipelago, just as the Secretary of Public Education had said. Moreover, the government had lost control of the education system because the governors had proven to be uninterested in educational issues. Declaring that it had the cure for the ailing education system, the PRI government moved to recentralize.

BACK TO THE BEGINNING

Some technical and institutional problems arose in the states because of the Agreement. New state-decentralized institutions were established to manage the transferred personnel and assets, and the administration of the payroll during the first few years proved challenging. However, the main blind spot of the decentralization model was its neglect of the centrality of power relations to Mexico's system of education. Both the national leaders and the local bosses of SNTE immediately colonized everything related to basic education, and they put the management of CM in a headlock.

The Agreement invested no power in the state governors. In reaction to the legislation, PAN state governors in Baja California, Chihuahua, and Nuevo León attempted to recover control of education, but their efforts were stymied by strikes and teacher mobilization. The SNTE leaders contended that the governors had appointed high-level functionaries without bargaining with them or that the officials the governors had appointed were not teachers. One might rightly suspect that the SNTE's actual objection was that the state governments had not installed SNTE cadres in the roles in question (Reyes Santos, 2008).

At the local level, the complicated interactions between the players gave rise to unwritten constraints on the governors. Besides having no legal power over the system of education, the governors had no incentive to face up to SNTE. Their reason for quiescence was simple. As former Secretaries of Education in four states and two ex-governors told me, "If the federal government gives important posts to SNTE and the President invests the SNTE boss with the authority of a Minister of Education, what can we do?" (Ornelas, 2010).

What's more, the bilateral bargaining over salaries and fringe benefits gave more power to local bosses. There was a national pact to increase the income of the teaching force across the board, followed by state-by-state bargaining processes. This benefited local interests. Bit by bit, the local leaders were taking control of the funds transferred from FAEB. They asked the governors for more teaching posts (despite the fact that enrollment was decreasing), more personnel commissioned for Union business, funds for building and remodeling Union offices and teachers' sporting clubs, and a host of resources for Teachers' Day, including cars, gasoline, and money for presents and parties (Muñoz Armenta, 2008). The governors had to choose between surrendering the resources or facing labor problems. FAEB turned into a bottomless pit of demands for money from the local governments.

Across the nation, the payroll was growing rapidly; in some states, like Michoacán, it grew at the rate of about 10% per year from 1993–1999 (Barba, 2000). In addition, payroll wasn't the only expense. The Superior Audit Office of the Federal Congress documented that state governments were using FAEB funds for purposes other than education.

Moreover, civil social organizations were entering into the debates surrounding education. At the outset, the organizations were asking for accountability, improved test scores, and a better distribution of funds. However, both SEP and SNTE ignored those requests. These groups had no authority according to the corporatist pact, so the system bypassed them. When PAN won the Presidency, these organizations revamped their claims, now asking for the *third chair*. A number of social organizations were agitating at both the state and national scale. The most aggressive among these agitators, Mexicanos Primero (Mexicans First), was and is competently led, well funded by private enterprises, and linked to Televisa, the largest Mexican TV network. Mexicanos Primero has its own publication, funds critical studies of the education system, and provides a daily news service that reports on education and links to a huge number of other online news networks.

Since 2006, this NGO has sought to represent the demands of scholars and journalists and has championed a national campaign for transparency. Mexicanos Primero asks for a census of schools, teachers, and students in order to establish an accurate database that will replace the faulty data sets the states have used to hide corruption through arrangements with SNTE. In 2007, some of the NGO's efforts bore fruit. The Federal Congress ordered SEP to collect data from the states and to make that data accessible to the public. Most states ignored the SEP request; others gave only portions of the requested information; and still others have gone to court with the claim that the command from the Federal Congress was not a legal mandate.

The interventions made in the Pact for Mexico identified clear areas for improvement and proposed to radically change the conditions for entering into the teaching profession. Its designers recognized that the bequest of teaching posts was besmirching Mexico's reputation. The Pact also sought to provide constitutional autonomy to the National Institute for the Evaluation of Education—thus establishing its credibility—and to take back control (*rectoría*) of education.

Beginning in December 2012, the new government muscled its way through a huge change in the education system's formal rules. The presidential initiative included amendments to Articles 3 and 73 of the Constitution. Once those alterations were approved, the government sought to institute two new laws and reforms to the General Education Act. Ignoring the massive protests led by dissident teachers taking place on the streets outside, legislators issued a new set of laws to regulate the teaching profession and labor relations in September 2013. This most recent intervention was the Act for INEE.

The state governors provided the key incentive to President Peña Nieto to move toward recentralization. In August 2013, in a meeting of the National Board of Governors (Conago) in Mazatlán, Peña Nieto asked the state governors to endorse his package of structural reforms, especially his reform of education, which was under discussion in the Federal Congress. The governors had no incentive to support reforms that would write them out of the educational equation. Nobody invited them to sign the Pact for Mexico or to partake in the legal changes. However, the governors in Mexico never say no to the President. In keeping with this tradition, they acceded to the reform, but they also requested more funds for FAEB. The President responded soon thereafter with a supplementary legal initiative to reform the Fiscal Coordination Act, which was hastily approved by Congress (Poder Ejecutivo Federal, 2014). In January 2015, the federal government took control of the teachers' payroll through the Fund for Teachers Payroll and Operative Expenditure (FONE).

CONCLUSION

Education is contested territory worldwide. Whenever and wherever an educational reform is undertaken, it raises hopes and inspires powerful opposition (Carnoy & Samoff, 1990; Gorski, 2014). Machiavelli foretold that the prince who endeavors to change the order of things in his kingdom must contend with the opposition of those whose goods may be negatively affected. Neither can he rely too heavily on his supporters. He finds "only lukewarm defenders in all those who would profit from the new order" (Machiavelli, 2003, p. 25).

After the initial wave of enthusiasm that the Pact for Mexico inspired among liberal groups, the Peña Nieto educational reform garnered only tepid public supporters. Its detractors were far more visible and vocal. The federal government dealt with public opposition in two ways. First, it imposed its will on the majority of SNTE. Then it bribed the more radical opponents to cease their hostilities by granting them special privileges in under-the-table negotiations.

Even before the changes were announced, Gordillo, "lifetime" president of SNTE, was preparing her political counterattack. She may have expected to enjoy the same close relationship with Peña Nieto that she had maintained with past presidents of Mexico; she had been in direct contact with Peña Nieto's predecessors. However, president elect Peña Nieto did not receive her and sent signals that she was not slated to occupy any important post in the federal administration. Later, when the presidential initiative on education was made public, Gordillo launched her campaign against it, claiming that it would affect the "stability" of teachers' jobs. She announced a national crusade for the "dignity of teachers." She was jailed on February 26, 2013, the same day that the constitutional amendments were published in the official newspaper of the federal government. The accusations against Gordillo of fraud and money laundering were seemingly well substantiated. The next day, Gordillo's second-in-command was appointed president of SNTE, apparently on the instructions of the Department of Government or Segob (Del Valle, 2013).

The imprisonment of Gordillo motivated the dissident teachers to adopt a more radical response to Peña Nieto's reforms. I have documented elsewhere the movements they spearheaded in 2013 and in the beginning of 2014 (Ornelas, 2014). They challenged the government with wildcat strikes, seizing highways and public offices in Oaxaca, Guerrero, and Michoacán. They fomented vehicular chaos in Mexico City. High Segob officials received leaders of CNTE and, seeking relief from their destructive tactics, agreed that CNTE would be exempted from some of the laws' "teeth." The radicalized dissenters thus managed to win a compromise through applying significant pressure to the government. It seems that the President begged the dissidents to accept the reforms and offered to provide them with special privileges and benefits in exchange. This government concession incentivized radical strategies; the President taught CNTE that by using extreme and disruptive tactics they could successfully shake down the government for whatever they want.

Nevertheless, the reform is far from establishing a clear legacy of institutional change. The recentralization suffers from many institutional defects. First, it further alienates the local governments from education. They have no incentive at all to support the reform (Fernández Martínez, 2014) but they *do* have an interest in maintaining good relations with the local bosses of SNTE, because they are electoral allies. Second, the centralized management of the payroll is problematic. Nineteen out of 31 Mexican states each have a unique local system that accommodates local traditions and cultural particularities, and therefore each state provides different fringe benefits and ensures particular labor conditions. The General Act, by contrast, homogenizes the payroll, and there is as of yet no indication of how the government will answer to local differences. Third, CNTE has been incentivized to keep the federal government under siege; its leaders have established a bargaining routine with the Segob. Dissident teachers will continue to rally and strike, collecting their payments all the while.

The formal rules of the centralist reform have been established, and those rules envision a model that may well be an improvement on Mexico's current education system. However, the president's resolve appears weak, and he has dealt ineffectively with violent and vocal opponents. Peña Nieto has few strong supporters, and, worst of all, he is unwisely allowing SNTE to survive. The secretary of Public Education criticizes the state governors for their handling of local education, but the federal government has set a bad example. Segob makes under-the-table arrangements with CNTE in direct violation of the law, and SEP gives SNTE a monopoly on teachers' representation and grants it a privileged status as an established institution. The main enemies of all of Mexico's education reforms have been the corporatist unions, and this reform is no exception.

If institutional change shapes how societies evolve—and thus is the key to understanding historical change, as North (1990) argues—the move toward centralism bodes ill for Mexico. This sapling is growing as crooked as its elder, the decentralizing reform of the 1992 Agreement.

ACKNOWLEDGEMENTS

I presented a first draft of this chapter at the 2015 Comparative and International Education Society Conference in Washington, DC. My friends and colleagues Bob Arnove and Mark Hanson contributed valuable criticisms and suggestions. I could not make all the changes they suggested, but I deeply appreciate their comments. I also value the editing assistance of Annie Atura.

REFERENCES

Aziz Nassif, A. (1989). *El Estado mexicano y la CTM*. México: Ediciones de la Casa Chata.
Barba, B. (2000). *La federalización educativa. una valoración externa desde la experiencia de los estados*. México: SEP.

Bracho, T. (2008). *Programa de acciones complementarias para abatir el rezago educativo: informe final de la evaluación*. México: SEP-Flacso.
Carnoy, M., & Samoff, J. (1990). *Education and social transformation in the third world*. Princeton, NJ: Princeton University Press.
Carpizo, J. (1978). *El presidencialismo mexicano*. Mexico City: Siglo XXI Editores.
Cordoba, J. D. (2003, July 30). Gordillo, Top Union Boss and, She Says, No 'Angel' Ascends in the Congress. *Wall Street Journal*.
Córdova, A. (1973). *La ideología de la Revolución mexicana: la formación del nuevo régimen*. México: Era.
Cosío Villegas, D. (1974). *El estilo personal de gobernar*. México: Cuadernos de Joaquín Mortiz.
Crawford, S. E. S., & Ostrom, E. (1995). A grammar of institutions. *American Political Science Review, 89*(3), 582–600.
Del Valle, S. (2013, November 7). Ablanda SNTE a Gobernación. *Reforma*.
Fernández Martínez, M. A. (2014). Los desafíos de la implementación de la reforma educativa y la perspectiva estatal. In Instituto Mexicano para la Competitividad A.C. (Ed.), *Las reformas y los estados: la responsabilidad de las entidades en el éxito de los cambios estructurales* (pp. 31–45). México: IMCO.
Flores Sánchez, R. (2012). *La carrera magisterial como instrumento para mejorar la calidad de la educación* (Honor thesis in Política y Gestión Social). Universidad Autónoma Metropolitana, México.
Fuentes Molinar, O. (2013). Las tareas del maestro y los desafíos de la evaluación docente. In R. Ramírez Raymundo (Ed.), *La reforma constitucional en materia educativa* (pp. 17–34). México: Senado de la República.
Gorski, P. C. (2014). Poverty, economic inequality, and the impossible promise of school reform. In P. C. G. K. Zenkov (Ed.), *The big lies of school reform: Finding better solutions for the future of public education* (Kindle edition). New York, NY: Routledge.
Hanson, M. E. (2000). Educational decentralization around the Pacific Rim: Editorial. *Journal of Educational Administration, 38*(5), 406–411.
INEE. (2014). *Panorama educativo de México*. México: Instituto Nacional para la Evaluación de la Educación.
Jordan, M. (2004, 14 de julio). A union's grip stifles learning; teaching posts inherited, sold in Mexico's public schools. *The Washington Post*.
Krauze, E. (1997). *La presidencia imperial: ascenso y caída del sistema político mexicano (1940–1996)*. México: Tusquets Editores.
Latapí Sarre, P., & Ulloa-Herrero, M. (2000). *El financiamiento de la educación básica en el marco del federalismo*. México: Fondo de Cultura Económica.
Loyo, A. (2013). *La reforma educativa en curso*. Paper presented at the Dipomado de Análisis Político Estratégico, Centro de Investigación y Docencia Económicas.
Machiavelli, N. (2003; original en 1503). *The prince and other writings* (W. A. Rebhorn, Trans.). New York, NY: Barnes and Noble Classics.
Mancera, C., & García, L. V. (2000). Oportunidades y retos del federalismo educativo: el camino recorrido: 1995–2000. In Secretaría de Educación Pública (Ed.), *Memoria del quehacer educativo 1995–2000* (Vol. I, pp. 45–83). México: SEP.
Melgar, I. (2012, December 15). Elba acotada: ¿una ilusión? *Excélsior*.
Moctezuma Barragán, E. (1994). *La educación pública frente a las nuevas realidades*. México: Fondo de Cultura Económica.
Muñoz Armenta, A. (2008). Escenarios e identidades del SNTE. *Revista Mexicana de Investigación Educativa, XIII*(37), 377–417.
North, D. C. (1990). *Institutions, institutional change and economic performace*. Cambridge: Cambridge University Press.
Ornelas, C. (1995). *El sistema educativo mexicano. la transición de fin de siglo* (2nd ed, 2013). México: Fondo de Cultura Económica.
Ornelas, C. (2001). Equidad: educación comunitaria y programas compensatorios. In C. Ornelas (Ed.), *Investigación y política educativas: ensayos en honor de Pablo Latapí* (pp. 135–185). México: AulaXXI/Santillana/México.

Ornelas, C. (2002). Incentivos a los maestros: la paradoja mexicana. In C. Ornelas (Ed.), *Valores, calidad y educación* (pp. 137–161). Mexico: Santillana 7AulaXXI.
Ornelas, C. (2010). *Política, poder y pupitres: crítica al nuevo federalismo educativo* (2nd ed.). México: Siglo XXI Editores.
Ornelas, C. (2012). *Educación colonización y rebeldía: la herencia del pacto Calderón-Gordillo*. México: Siglo XXI Editores.
Ornelas, C. (2014). La oposición a las reformas. In G. Guevara Niebla & E. Backoff Escudero (Eds.), *Las transformaciones del sistema educativo en México, 2013–2018* (pp. 360–375). México: Fondo de Cultura Económica.
Poder Ejecutivo Federal. (1993, 5 de marzo). *Decreto que declara raformados los artículos 3 y 31 de los Estados Unidos Mexicanos*. Diario Oficial de la Federación.
Poder Ejecutivo Federal. (2014, August 11). Ley de Coordinación Fiscal. Diario Oficial de la Federación.
Ramírez Raymundo, R. (Ed.). (2013). *La reforma constitucional en materia educativa: alcances y desafíos*. México: Senado de la República Instituto Belisario Dominguez.
Raphael, R. (2007). *Los socios de Elba Esther*. México: Planeta.
Reyes Santos, M. (2008). Descentralización educativa y actores locales. *Revista Mexicana de Investigación Educativa, XIII*(37), 471–494.
Rodríguez, R. (1999). Modernización y cambio institucional de la educación en Nuevo León. In V. A. Espinosa Valle (Ed.), *Modernización educativa en el norte de México* (pp. 15–78). Tijuana: El Colegio de la Frontera Norte.
Santibáñez, L., Martínez, J. F., Datar, A., McEwan, P. J., Messan-Setodji, C., & Dávila, R. B. (2006). *Haciendo camino: análisis del sistema de evaluación y del impacto del programa de estímulos docentes Carrera magisterial en México*. Santa Monica, CA: The Rand Corporation.
SEP. (1992). *Acuerdo nacional para la modernización de la educación básica*. México: Secretaría de Educación Pública.
SEP. (1999). *Profile of education in Mexico*. México: Secretaría de Educación Pública.
Trujillo, J. R. (2013). *El FAEB: ¿Asignación equitativa?* Jalapa: Secretaría de Educación del Estado de Veracruz.

Carlos Ornelas
Universidad Autónoma Metropolitana (UAM)
Xochimilco Campus, Mexico City

ANGÉLICA BUENDÍA ESPINOSA

7. PRIVATIZATION AND MARKETING OF HIGHER EDUCATION IN MEXICO

Contributions to a Debate

INTRODUCTION

Interest in studying private systems of higher education has its origins primarily in the processes of expansion and transformation that various nations have undergone in recent years. Among these processes, diversity has become a characteristic trait reflected in systems' internal composition and high complexity. The differentiation of the public and private sectors has had great impact on the development of systems of higher education at the international level. The expansion of private sectors is associated with the public policies of a neoliberal nature that have been promoted in most nations with regard to higher education. An additional factor is the debate surrounding the marketing of educational services, within the framework of the General Agreement on Tariffs and Trade (GATT), whose consequences are reflected in the diversification of the suppliers of education and in the emergence of a type of suppliers directed to the market, for profit (Buendía, 2011; Levy, 2009).

Private higher education has dominated systems like those of Japan, South Korea, Taiwan, and the Philippines; it is the fastest growing sector in many countries of Central and Eastern Europe, as well as in the nations of the former Soviet Union. In Latin American, on the other hand, post-secondary education has shown a considerable shift from public to private institutions, even in nations traditionally characterized by their development of dominant public sectors with peripheral private sectors (Geiger, 1986), such as Mexico and Argentina. At least one-half of the university students in Brazil, Colombia, Peru, and Venezuela attend private universities (Altbach, 2002).

In Mexico, the state's role as the leader of public policy has determined the sector's configuration. The passage of time has accented the problems of regulation, control, and deficient quality in many private institutions of higher education: a result of laxity and in some case, of improper practices in the application of regulating instruments, with a persistent absence of a regulatory perspective and a permissive framework, resulting in uncontrolled growth (Levy, 1995; Kent, 1995; Kent & Ramírez, 2002). The market has been given an active role as the principal regulating agent in the supply of educational services, a reaffirmation of the idea that the state has not developed an active role in the governance of private universities.

This chapter is divided into four sections. The first addresses the historical evolution of the configuration of the private sector in Mexico, in four stages: emergence (1935–1959); expansion and deregulation (1960–2000), which can be divided into two periods (1960–1980 and 1982–2000); a market stage (2000–2006); and lastly, the stage of uncontrolled stabilization since 2007. The second section of the chapter discusses if Mexico has a market or non-market model of higher education, according to the model proposed by Brown (2011a). The third section analyzes one of the most relevant matters in the study of private higher education in Mexico: quality. The chapter's final section includes final remarks and pending matters in the study of this sector.

CONFIGURATION OF AN UNPLANNED BUT NECESSARY SECTOR

The current configuration of Mexico's system of higher education is characterized by the complexity of its academic functions and by the diversity of institutions and the education offered. This arrangement originated in the economic, political, and social transformations that occurred after World War II. The massification[1] of higher education around the globe represented a transformation process that moved from the formation of national political and social elites, to the democratization and promotion of massive access to tertiary education; the purpose was to contribute to remedying the major problems of social and economic inequality among individuals and strengthen nations' economic and social growth.

The expansion of enrollment brought major transformations in the configuration and coordination of the national system of higher education.[2] A process of diversification accompanied the process of expansion. The situation in the 1990s was different not only because of the dimension of its components, but also because of its internal composition and its high degree of complexity, which translated into the coexistence of widely different institutions of higher education, both public and private. In addition, while the supply of education in the phase previous to expansion was relatively homogeneous, broad diversification occurred in terms of academic and professional fields, types of institution, levels, and duration of studies.

Although institutions dedicated to the education of the elites have existed since colonial times, the institutionalization of the system of higher education had its beginnings in the recognition of Universidad Nacional Autónoma de México (UNAM) as a university in 1910. At that time, the current system of higher education began to be constituted, with an historical evolution that can be summarized in the following stages: emergence (1910–1950), unregulated expansion (1950–1989), and modernization (1989–2000) (Gil, 1992, 1994; Ibarra, 2001).

In the context of the nation's political transition of 2000, with the change in the ruling party from the Partido Revolucionario Institucional (PRI) [Institutional Revolutionary Party] to the Partido Action Nacional (PAN) [National Action Party], a fourth stage in the evolution of Mexico's higher education began. We could call this stage the *rationalization of the system and its institutions,* using a basis of policies that since 1989 has operated along the lines of transversal evaluation/quality/financing/ organizational change; but with different systems of intervention and effects for the public and private sectors. Only the private sector will be analyzed here.

In 1960, the number of students enrolled in Mexico's higher education totaled 76,269. The most intense period of growth was between 1970 and 1980. In 1970, total enrollment was 208,944 students, representing an increase of 273.9% over ten years; in 1980, the school population in higher education reached 731,147 students, equivalent to an increase of 349.9% in one decade. In contrast, during the decade from 1990 to 2000, enrollment increased by only 507,217 students, equivalent to 68%. During the first decade of the new century, the percentage of growth remained constant.

Although historically a large proportion of the enrollment in higher education has been in public institutions, during the so-called phase of expansion the private sector was much more dynamic. The five to ten private institutions of higher education that existed in Mexico in 1950 had increased to 1,253 by the 2000–2001 school year.[3] In 1980, the students served by that educational sector totaled 98,840—a number that practically doubled in ten years, since by 1990, the students served by private institutions of higher education totaled 187,819. One decade later, in 2003, the private system served 620,533 students, and 33.2% of the nation's undergraduate students were enrolled in a private institution (ANUIES, 2003); the trend persisted until 2014, when private institutions of higher education served 1,128,592 undergraduate students (Figure 1).

Although this sector can be explained as a function of the public sector's trajectory, its roots are different. Four stages can be identified in the chronology of the Mexican private sector: emergence (1935–1959); expansion and deregulation (1960–2000),

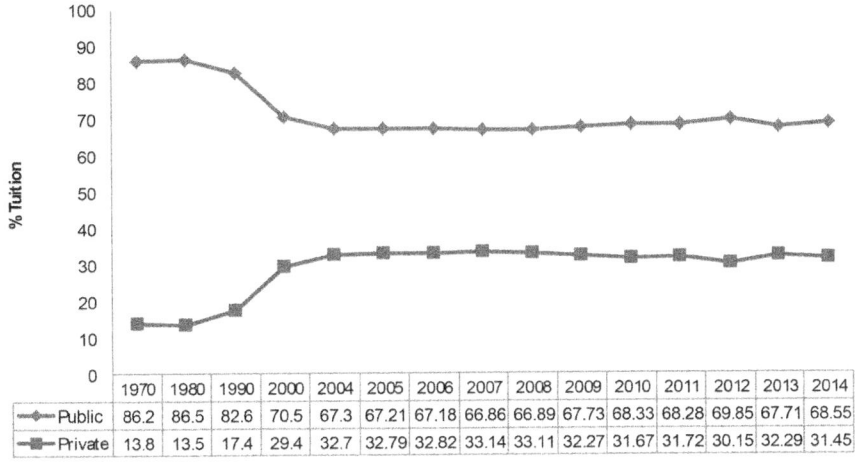

Figure 1. Undergraduate enrollment by sector (1970–2014).
Source: Based on National Association of Universities and
Institutions of Higher Education (ANUIES, 2014)

which in turn is divided into two periods (from 1960 to 1980 and from 1982 to 2000); a third stage of the market (2000–2006); and most recently, the uncontrolled stage of stabilization that started in 2007.

Emergence (1935–1959)

In the 1930s and the 1940s, the first institutions of private education were established in Mexico. Three factors were key in their emergence: social class, religion, and economy. Social conservatism operated as a determining element in the development of Mexico's system of private education, to the degree that socioeconomic status and prestige declined in the rapidly growing public sector; a middle class capable of paying for private higher education was expanding thanks to the nation's steady economic progress. The conflicts between the Catholic Church and the government from 1926 to 1929, partially overcome in the 1940s, as well as the politicization of public universities, especially the UNAM, also influenced the creation of private universities with a religious nature (Levy, 1995).

In addition to social and political conservatism, the economic factor contributed to the creation of private universities. Industry required human resources with specific profiles, especially in administration, in response to company needs and independent from the political position of public universities.

During that period, the first seven private institutions were created in Mexico. The Universidad Autónoma de Guadalajara (UAG) was founded in 1935, in the context of intense political and ideological debate in the field of higher education, between a liberal conception of universities (characterized by freedom in the classroom and institutional autonomy) and the revolutionary conception that the followers of Cárdenas (1934–1940) promoted in Mexico, in which universities were required to be at the service of the aims of the Mexican Revolution (Levy, 1995; Acosta, 2000). UAG was the product of an internal conflict in the Universidad Estatal de Guadalajara: one sector of the institution was not in agreement with the revolutionary orientation and decided to institute a private autonomous university with a religious and conservative nature.

In January of 1940, the Universidad de las Américas was created in Mexico City, the first private institution of higher education in the nation's capital. It was "founded by a small group of students" as the Mexico City College (MCC), obtaining accreditation from the Southern Association of Colleges and Schools (SACS) (ANUIES, 2000, p. 74).

In 1943, the Instituto Tecnológico de Estudios Superiores de Monterrey (ITESM) was formed, with a clear tendency to train expert professionals in managing the economy and business, and the exclusion of a religious orientation in its model; its presence responded to the demands of one of the nation's most important industrial cities. ITESM adopted the models of the Massachusetts Institute of Technology (MIT) and the University of California, basing its development on the primary source of its financing: Grupo Monterrey.

That same year, the Jesuits founded the Universidad Iberoamericana (UIA), with a marked religious identity. Its creation should be analyzed against the background of the prolonged and occasionally violent conflict between the state and Church. Both UIA and UAG were conceived in part as educational options versus the politicization of UNAM. Since its appearance, UIA has been characterized as a university of Christian inspiration yet not a confessional university (Meneses, 1993); in other words, "although it assumes adhesion to a doctrine, it does not imply that the university depends on this confession" (Meneses, 1993:5). During the 1960s, UIA joined the progressive current which, along with numerous Latin American churches and Catholic universities, pushed disenchanted religious and financial groups toward the Universidad Anáhuac (Levy, 2005, p. 250).

In 1957, the Instituto Tecnológico y de Estudios Superiores de Occidente (ITESO) was constituted with support from the Company of Jesus; today it is part of the UIA-ITESO system and shares the same religious tendency.

The Instituto Tecnológico Autónomo de México (ITAM) was created in 1946, also with evident emphasis on economics and administrative areas of study. It was founded by Asociación Mexicana de Cultura, A.C., a group of bankers, industrial leaders, and businessmen.[4]

Table 1. Private institutions of higher education (1935–1959)

Year	Institution	Location
1935	Universidad Autónoma de Guadalajara	Guadalajara, Jalisco
1940	Universidad de las Américas	Mexico City
1943	Instituto Tecnológico de Estudios Superiores de Monterrey	Monterrey, Nuevo León
1946	Instituto Tecnológico Autónomo de México	Mexico City
1943	Universidad Iberoamericana	Mexico City
1947	Universidad de las Américas, Puebla	Cholula, Puebla
1957	Instituto Tecnológico de Estudios Superiores de Occidente	Guadalajara, Jalisco

Source: ANUIES, 2001

Phase of Expansion and Deregulation (1960–2000)

In the 1960s, Mexico's university system experienced profound change that translated into unregulated expansion. While the subsystem of public higher education was characterized by reactive government leadership, permeated by the political logic of an authoritarian and populist administration (Ibarra, 2001), the private sector remained outside of any regulated framework that would integrate it into the system. In general, the educational policy of the time revealed the absence of a normative framework that would permit regulating the private sector, which began to be formed as an ever more disjointed set of different institutions.

The expansion of the private sector in this period occurred in two periods: first from 1960 to 1980, part of a series of events that occurred in public higher education—events that oriented the growth of the private sector, propelled by Mexican business leaders. In 1964, the Confederación de Cámaras Industriales (CONCAMIN) issued the "Carta Económica Mexicana", which in a brief reference to education sustained that education was "essential for economic development" and promoted a climate of freedom that would allow business leaders to exercise the right and the obligation to participate in education. With the political movement of 1968 and the politicization of public universities, business leaders' distrust of public education increased, the main cause for their support for the creation of private institutions to educate their children, as well as the technical and administrative teams for their companies (Tirado, 1999; Puga, 1999).

During this period, thirteen private institutions of higher education appeared in the nation's major cities: Mexico City, Monterrey, and Guadalajara, as well as in Puebla, Veracruz, and Hermosillo. The chronology is detailed in the following table.

Table 2. Private institutions of higher education (1960–1982)

Year	Institution	Location
1960	Universidad del Valle de México	Mexico City
1961	Universidad del Valle de Atemajac	Guadalajara, Jalisco
1962	Universidad La Salle	Mexico City
1966	Universidad Tecnológica de México	Mexico City
1967	Universidad Panamericana	Mexico City
1969	Universidad de Monterrey	Monterrey, Nuevo León.
1969	Universidad Regiomontana	Monterrey, Nuevo León
1969	Universidad Cristóbal Colón	Veracruz, Veracruz
1970	Centro de Estudios Universitarios	Monterrey, Nuevo León
1973	Universidad Popular Autónoma del Estado de Puebla	Puebla, Puebla
1976	Universidad Intercontinental	Mexico City
1976	Universidad Valle del Bravo	Reynosa, Tamaulipas
1979	Universidad del Noroeste	Hermosillo, Sonora

Source: ANUIES (2001)

The second period of expansion encompasses the period from 1982 to 2000, when educational policies attempted to reorient the educational system's growth through exercises of planning and evaluating higher education.

The 1980s were characterized, especially in the early years, by extensive managerial mobilization motivated by the economic crisis and the nationalization of the nation's banks. The antigovernment and anti-presidential reaction that polarized business leaders and the government had a large impact on the population. In education, the critical positions of business with regard to public education became harsher. The discourse of business organizations like the Consejo Coordinador Empresarial (CCE) and the Confederación Patronal de la República Mexicana (COPARMEX), criticized public education severely, emphasizing its doctrinaire and ideological nature in opposition to the values and traditions that business expected education to promote (Tirado, 1999).

In the late 1980s and early 1990s, business organizations believed that the topic of education was the most important, "the item of greatest need and priority", as well as Mexico's main obstacle to competing in the international setting. Education, according to business leaders, required modernization. This was reiterated with greater force as President Salinas' modernizing project became a reality, along with the possibility of signing the North American Free Trade Agreement (NAFTA). In this context, FIMPES was formed in 1988, on the initiative of business leaders involved in education, and with the perspective of becoming a line of defense against government impositions, which restricted the freedom of action of individuals in education (Olmos, 2001).

Business leaders' proposals were projected in two directions. On one hand, they addressed educational reforms, primarily Constitutional Article 3, in order to allow religious education and strengthen private education, ending the so-called "defenseless state" of individuals who offered educational services and providing them with legal security. Another proposal was to eliminate official discretion regarding the validity and recognition of studies completed in private institutions, as well as to suppress the regulation of education for rural and urban laborers. On the other hand, education was to move toward international productivity and competitiveness, skills and entrepreneurship in the context of globalization, the objective of the state of wellbeing and modernization. In *Modernización educativa. Propuestas del sector empresarial,* the definition of education alluded to "abilities" and "skills" rather than values (Comisión de Educación del Sector Empresarial (CESE)) [Educational modernization: Proposals from the Business Sector], 1989; quoted by Tirado, 1999).

The educational modernization proposed by the administration of President Salinas de Gortari emerged as the way to make progress in constructing a productive and competitive nation on the international scale. In the setting of higher education, the discourse of modernization took the form of actions directed at improving quality based on evaluation, which permeated the design and implementation of public policy. According to Ibarra (2001), modernization consisted of the definitive re-composition of relations between the government and universities. On the other hand, the modernizing process assumed new rules of the game to favor certain behaviors and discourage others, and to respond to the pressures and demands of the market and politics, according to the strategies or programs negotiated or imposed by the agents of greatest influence (Ibarra, 2001).

Modernization translated into the configuration of various programs and instruments of public policy. The most important included: Sistema Nacional de Planeación Permanente de la Educación Superior (SINAPPES), Coordinación Nacional para la Planeación de la Educación Superior (CONPES), Programa Nacional de Educación Superior (PRONAES), Programa Integral para el Desarrollo de la Educación Superior (PROIDES), Comision Nacional de la Evaluación de la Educación Superior (CONAEVA) y Programa de Modernización Educativa (PME). Such groups were aimed at better coordination and regulation of the system, based on "improving the quality of higher education and forming a system of higher education consisting of institutions of excellence" (Mendoza, 2002). The incorporation of the private sector into these instruments became evident upon the emergence of PROIDES, in 1986.[5]

Subsequently, the Programa para la Modernización de la Educación 1989–1994 (PME) mentioned that private institutions formed part of the system of higher education and that their functioning depended on the legal system of their incorporation into the federation, states, or autonomous public universities (SEP, 1989). In addition, PME established that public and private institutions should support each other in modernizing higher education through evaluation, in order to improve quality.

During this era, the private sector registered surprising expansion, growing from 133 to 1,253 institutions. The heterogeneity of these institutions increased and was reflected in the size of their enrollment, and in their missions, objectives, forms of organization, and position within the educational system. In general, two types of institutions emerged: those with regional or local settings of important growth, with populations of more than three thousand students, an attractive option for the middle sectors of the population able to pay their fees; and very small institutions (numbered in dozens of students) of doubtful academic quality (Mendoza, 2002, p. 335), later called "ugly duckling universities".

This period was also known for the formation of institutional networks with a regional or national impact, like ITESM, UVM, Universidad Tecnológica de México (UNITEC), Universidad La Salle (ULSA), and UIA, among others.

2000–2006 Beyond the Market

Although NAFTA did not include the educational sector in the approved text that came into effect on January 1, 1994, it dedicated two sections to professional services: Chapter 12, "Cross-Border Trade in Services" and Chapter 16, "Temporary Entry for Business Persons". These sections stated the principles, reserves, and commitment to conduct professional activities in the setting of 63 professions (general, scientific, and medical), for which minimum requirements and alternative degrees were established. These initial actions indicated the competition that would be generated among institutions of higher education, which intensified with the General Agreement on

Tariffs and Trade (GATT), signed by 144 countries in the framework of the World Trade Organization (WTO), which included higher education.[6]

The reactions to the effects of GATT on higher education arose in greatest part from the academic media; in principle they disagreed because they were not included from the beginning in the agreement's negotiations, which were directed by individuals responsible for the economy in each nation.[7] In Latin America, the rejection of GATT began in Brazil in the Social Forum of Porto Alegre in February, 2002. The participants proposed a global pact with the purpose of ensuring the consolidation of the principles of action approved at the World Conference on Higher Education, promoted by the United Nations Educational, Scientific and Cultural Organization (UNESCO) in Paris in 1998. As a conclusion of the Third Ibero-American Summit of Rectors of Public Universities, the Letter of Porto Alegre was signed, to inform the university academic community and society in general about the negative consequences of GATT and to request the governments of their respective countries not to sign any commitment in higher education.[8]

Mexico's position toward GATT in regard to education, even since the signing of NAFTA, has been to keep the educational sector open to foreign investment in items stipulated in the agreement: supplying across borders, commercial presence and individuals, as well as consumption abroad. In Mexico, foreign direct investment in educational services from 1994 to 2003 reached a maximum with the sale of UVM in 2000, when direct investment was 16.4487 billion dollars and only 0.2% corresponded to educational services (Rodríguez, 2004).

This means that the sector still has a majority state presence, a very concentrated rate of privatization in higher education, and a limited potential market served by multiple local suppliers. Nonetheless, it is possible to affirm that the case of UVM has been profitable, and that favorable signals have been sent to other investors seeking presence in the Mexican market. Such is the case of Apollo Group Inc., a company dedicated to adult education and the closest competitor of Silvan/Laureate Inc., the entity that made manifest its intent to participate through an alliance with UNITEC, the institution that it acquired in 2007.[9]

Unregulated Stabilization (2007...)

A constant in Mexico has been the absence of government policies to contribute to the orientation of Mexico's private sector, to promote the integration of a system of higher education. In spite of full recognition of the proliferation of private institutions, some of which are referred to as "ugly ducklings", the limited modifications made to the institutional and regulatory framework have had little impact on the sector's expansion.

According to Fielden and Varghese (2009), regulation begins with the decision to allow a private supplier to plan or develop an academic unit, continues with the approval and recognition of its programs, the establishment of fiscal incentives or mechanisms, and ends with the regular monitoring of its forms of operation, based on access to information about its academic and financial performance. Therefore, an unregulated private sector causes the appearance of suppliers of all types, some interested only in using education as a part of business, and with little protection for the student-consumer. The case of Mexico is quite close to this model. Levy (1995; 2006) affirmed that in Mexico, the state has not developed an active role in the governance of private universities. The sole aspect that this relation shows in the constitutional authority of the state is the concession of the official license to private institutions and their programs, reaffirmed by the General Law of Education of 1973 and the modifications of 1993. "Opening a university is as easy as opening a tortilla shop, some observers have affirmed" (Levy, 1995, p. 278).

Nonetheless, since 2007, sector growth has shown clear stabilization that began in 2000 but was accented in the later period. According to Álvarez (2011), this phenomenon is due, on one hand, to the opening of new spaces in the public sector through financing policies for increasing enrollment in existing institutions; and on the other hand, to the creation of new institutions in the framework of a policy of institutional differentiation, diversification of the educational supply, and mechanisms of quality assurance. The new public institutions have been created with federal and state funds and are operated by state governments, constituting a decentralizing policy that has contributed to modifying the local configurations of higher education (Álvarez, 2011, p. 13).

The stabilization of the sector does not translate into a reduction. As Álvarez (2011) indicates, not only because there will be more high school graduates, but also because the public sector, in spite of its efforts, will not be able to reverse the market dynamics that have become fixed in Mexico. Over the short term, the private sector is not expected to contract. According to the projections of the Under Secretariat of Higher Education, undergraduates in private institutions will increase from 813,000 students in 2010 to 1,600,000 students in 2016, accumulated growth of 23.75%: almost the same as the projected growth for the public sector (Table 3).

Table 3. Projections for undergraduate enrollment until 2016*

	2009–2010	2010–2011	2011–2012	2012–2013	2013–2014	2014–2015	2015–2016	Growth 2010–2016
Public	1690,033	1,754,287	1,820,362	1,887,445	1,954,756	2,021,423	2,086,919	23.48
Private	813,105	844,966	877,207	909,991	942,486	974,822	1,006,182	23.75
Total	2,503,138	2,599,253	2,697,569	2,797,436	2,897,242	2,996,245	3,093,101	23.57

Source: Álvarez (2011), based on SEP-UPEPE/DGPyP, at http://www.snie.sep.gob.mx/estadisticas_educativas.html

* Figures estimated by SEP

MARKETS OR NON-MARKETS OF PRIVATE HIGHER EDUCATION IN MEXICO?

Brown (2011a) proposes a set of categories to study the existence of markets or non-markets of higher education. The discussion behind this international phenomenon calls for referring to the marketization of higher education, according to Furedi (2011), as a political/ideological process and an economic phenomenon, in which paradoxically there is no evidence of the triumph of the free market economy; on the contrary, greater state intervention is observed, through the implementation of policies that promote less regulation, as in the case of Mexico.

From the perspective of the economic theory of markets, it is a form of social coordination in which the supply and demand of a certain good or service find their equilibrium through price. It is assumed that consumers select among alternatives that are offered, based on what they consider the ideal option, due to characteristics of price, quality, and availability (Brown, 2011b). Also important is the assumption that since the market provides the best use of society's resources, less state participation means greater efficiency. This is true only if consumers are presumed to have complete information about the various options. Apparently the problem of the market is reduced to rational individual selection and the supremacy of freedom as the main value of society.

In 1962, Friedman proposed the hypothesis that allowing the market to regulate education would result in higher levels of quality and greater "client" satisfaction, so that only schools able to offer good services would remain in the market. In only exceptional cases (education in rural areas), would compensatory mechanisms have to operate to give underprivileged citizens access to equity. The role of the government, according to Friedman (1962), is essential only to determine the "rules of the game" and as a referee in interpreting and implementing the agreed upon rules. The market reduces the possibility of the politicization of agreements and increases the diversity of options, so that individuals have the freedom to select the institution they prefer to attend. The proposal is based on the voucher system and on the privatization of schools to make them more efficient.

Friedman's proposal revolved around elementary education, but what does that freedom mean for higher education? According to Brown (2011a), a market of higher education is presumed to include the concept of freedom for at least two actors: suppliers and consumers. For suppliers, freedom has four aspects: entry in the market, supply of products, available resources, and established prices. Entry in the market of higher education generally responds to two conditions. The first is related to the regulations of the system in question, which in the case of Mexico has functioned not as a "barrier to entry" (Porter, 1985) for new suppliers of educational services, but as a true incentive to carry out a quite lucrative activity. The second condition is related to financial investment, and possibly to the required policy.

In terms of suppliers, the regulatory framework in Mexico allows private suppliers to make their initial investment in higher education in low-cost products. As a result, it is not unusual for academic programs like administration, law, accounting, finance, and some areas of computer science to be found in most private institutions of higher education. Only 1.89% of the enrollment served by the private sector in Mexico is in natural and exact science, while 40.5% corresponds to social and administrative science (Table 4).

This is proof of the freedom to offer certain products at the price most convenient for the supplier, to cover the cost of investment. As a consequence, what we could call "re-investment" or opening new academic programs will depend solely on the owners' decisions, and apparently on the state's supervision and possible legal sanctions consisting of the withdrawal of Official Recognition of Validity of Studies, if necessary. The problem of greatest relevance in this respect is that the regulatory framework is extremely restricted and does not foresee the possibility of orienting the educational supply (Buendía, 2011).[10]

Table 4. Enrolment by area of knowledge (2010–2011)

Area of knowledge	Enrollment	%
Agricultural Science	62,893	2.28%
Health Science	272,730	9.87%
Natural and Exact Science	52,658	1.91%
Social and Administrative Science	1,119,126	40.49%
Education and Humanities	287,993	10.42%
Engineering and Technology	968,392	35.04%
Total	2,763,792	100.00%

Source: Anuario estadístico 2010–2011, ANUIES, 2012

For consumers, the topic of freedom rests on the possibility of selecting the supplier, and at the same time, the product-program. It is assumed that this selection depends on students' access to information about the market characteristics of higher education and the cost of investing in education, with gains that could be measured only over the long term, primarily upon entry in the labor market. Theoretically, the necessary information for students to decide what, where, and how to study takes into account the price, quality, and the availability of programs and institutions (Brown, 2011a). At least in the case of Mexico, such information is lacking, a demonstration that the market does not comply with Brown's proposal. In spite of the efforts made, a solid system of information is not yet available to facilitate and sustain the decisions of students and other actors related to the organization of private higher education.

By following this reality closely, Álvarez (2011) analyzes the systemic differentiation that characterizes the private sector and the consequences for price. The author indicates the wide variability of prices, as well as their polarization, and proposes an interesting exercise involving undergraduate majors in administration, a program that practically all private institutions of higher education offer; he defines three major segments of consumption—elite, intermediate, and low. In 2011, the total cost of the program majors for elite consumption varied between approximately 464,000 pesos and 1,200,000 pesos. For the intermediate group, the cost ranged between 86,000 and 420,000 pesos, and for the low segment, from 1,000 to 96,000 pesos per year (Álvarez, 2011).

In addition to variable prices, the issue of institutional prestige and reputation must be considered. The price will depend on those factors, and not necessarily on the quality of the product offered. As mentioned above, the range of tuition costs in the market of private higher education is very broad, and can even vary for a single product within an institution. The price of the same program, with an identical plan and program of study, offered by a university that has campuses in various states, will be different in the northern, central and/or southern regions. This phenomenon is common in private institutions of higher education that function as networks with multiple campuses, such as Universidad Insurgentes, Instituto Tecnológico de Monterrey, Universidad la Salle, and Universidad del Valle de México (Buendía, 2013). The specifics regarding the programs derive from local conditions related to working conditions, teacher availability and academic background, infrastructure, organization, academic management and the administration of academic units, in addition to other relevant aspects.

In light of this discussion, the characteristics of the market of higher education in Mexico are summarized below (Table 5).

Table 5. Market model of private higher education in Mexico

Market conditions	Definition	Mexico
Institutional Status	Self-government of institutions, independent organizations with a high degree of autonomy to determine prices, programs, number of students to enroll, admissions processes, and scholarships.	Mexican regulations establish minimum requirements for academic programs (Agreement 279 and state agreements). Private institutions of higher education enjoy full freedom to determine the programs they offer, the number of students to enroll, and their admissions processes. Support for students is determined by institutions, except for the percentage of scholarships that the government has established as obligatory (5% of enrollment).

(*Continued*)

Table 5. (Continued)

Market conditions	Definition	Mexico
Competition	Low barriers to entry. High number of suppliers for profit. Financing linked to enrollment. Low degree of innovation in process or product.	Regulation does not limit the entry of new competitors, but only establishes the minimum requirements for new suppliers. The financing of private institutions of higher education is directly related to enrollment and tuition. The academic programs offered tend toward homogenization, since the state does not have the ability to orient the supply of education based on criteria of pertinence. Homogenization leads to standardization and the lack of innovation in academic programs.
Price	Competition in tuition. The costs of programs as well as associated expenses (room and board) are the student's responsibility. Variations in the price of the same program cannot be explained as a function of local factors.	The cost of programs is competition solely for suppliers. Students absorb costs of room and board. Variability in prices is a generalized characteristic and is associated with the prestige and reputation of the institution and program. Quality is an attribute associated with the institution's prestige and reputation.
Information	Students make a rational selection based on information regarding the price, quality, and availability of programs and suppliers.	The system of information behind student decisions is imperfect. "Rational selection" is limited to the selection criteria for most incoming students; predominantly price and geographic location. The criteria of quality are surpassed by price and geographic location.

(Continued)

Table 5. (Continued)

Market conditions	Definition	Mexico
Regulation	Facilitates competition and provides basic protection to consumers. Plays an important role in the supply of information and responds to consumer complaints.	Academic regulation facilitates competition and promotes low barriers to entry. Commercial regulation does not provide basic protection to consumers. Lack of evidence.
Quality	Determined by what the market can offer in terms of price. The evaluation and guarantee of quality are in the hands of the state and the academic sector.	Price and quality are generally associated criteria. The establishment of quality assurance processes through external organizations, in addition to the minimum requirements established by the state. Institutional accreditation of FIMPES. Accreditation of programs of organizations recognized by COPAES. Institutional accreditation and or programs with international agencies.

Source: Based on Brown (2011a)

THE PENDING MATTER: QUALITY

In the design and implementation of policies that orient the private sector of higher education, and given the limitations that characterize current regulation, the state has attempted to reorient the sector by establishing certain mechanisms that seek to incorporate private institutions of higher education into policies of quality assurance. The initial actions in this sense were not a product of the state, but a consequence of the initiative of a group from the private sector, the Federación de Instituciones Mexicanas Particulares de Educación Superior (FIMPES).

The process of institutional accreditation that appeared in 1992 had the main objective of differentiating among the private institutions in the educational market, based on the improvement of their quality (Buendía, 2011; FIMPES, 2005). Subsequently, in 2000, debate between the government and FIMPES [Federation of Mexican Higher Education Institutions] led to Agreement 279 (SEP, 2016), in which the state apparently promised to supervise private institutions of higher education more closely, mainly those of "doubtful academic quality". The state's acceptance of the system of institutional accreditation with results in the category of "lisa y llana" ("absolute") as an instrument of guaranteed quality, through the so-called Administrative Simplification, has been one of the primary measures to protect students; however, the number of institutions participating in this program is extremely limited. Recent data show that of the 106 institutions associated with FIMPES, 80 (75.5%) are accredited and 26 (24.5%) are not. Of those, 46 institutions, equivalent to 57.7%, are evaluated in the category of "lisa y llana" ("absolute"), 31.2% in "sin observaciones" ("without remarks"), 10% "con recomendaciones" ("with recommendations") and 1.2% "con condiciones" ("with conditions") (FIMPES, 2014). Of the total of private institutions of higher education that are members of FIMPES, 34 have received the "Registry of Academic Excellence" granted by SEP (SEP, 2010).

On the other hand, some private institutions of higher education, in a desire to become legitimate, have attempted to gain inclusion in processes of evaluation and accreditation of academic programs carried out by inter-institutional committees for the evaluation of higher education and by organizations recognized by the Consejo para la Acreditación de la Educación Superior (COPAES) [Council of Accreditation of Higher Education]. According to SEP data, in 2010, Mexico had 27,017 academic programs with Recognition of Official Validity (RVOE), including those of a federal, state, and incorporated nature. Of those programs, only 35% had been subject to a process of evaluation and/or accreditation. In addition, it would be necessary to include schools that are lacking RVOE and still offer their academic programs. Little or nothing is known of these institutions.

Another initiative that has been relevant in the area of quality is the Programa de Fomento a la Calidad para las Instituciones Particulares, proposed in 2010 by SEP and the Consejo Nacional de Autoridades Educativas [Program for Promotion of Quality in Private Institutions]. Through this program, the government attempted to develop quality processes in the services of private institutions, offer information to society about these processes, and encourage coordination with local educational authorities through the traditional model of quality assurance that various national and international agencies have followed (SEP CONAEDU, 2010).

It was not until 2012 that SEP launched the program and issued the guidelines that regulate the Programa de Fomento a la Calidad en Instituciones Particulares del Tipo Superior, with federal RVOE. The program included two processes: an obligatory diagnostic evaluation to evaluate the rendering of educational services by institutions that have federal RVOE. The results would allow private institutions to obtain a classification at one of the levels and sub-levels of the criteria designed for this effect; and in second place, the process relative to the formulation of an improvement plan to be implemented within a year's time, based on the results obtained from the evaluation.

The formalization of the process would occur through the signing of a letter of intent; once the corresponding goals were reached, the institutions could reclassify the program (SES, 2012). As evident, like the process of institutional accreditation, the program is related more to institutional legitimacy, recognition, and prestige.

It is also probable that, similar to institutional accreditation and the evaluation and accreditation of academic programs, the program benefits only a few institutions since the mechanisms are not obligatory; at the same time, quality problems remain in another broad sector of institutions. As long as the involved actors do not promote a profound, integral revision of the institutional framework for the private sectors, these programs only legitimize what has already been legitimized, without truly reflecting on the coordination of the sector.

FINAL COMMENTS

The first study of private higher education that I carried out approximately eight years ago allowed me to conclude that the topic was not yet of interest on Mexico's agenda of educational research. And although increasingly more colleagues have become interested in the topic since then, I believe that the work completed to date is not sufficiently vast; and that very probably we are quite far from understanding the sector's complexity and diversity. Setting aside my pessimism in this matter, I hope that this chapter will contribute to an approach that will help us to reevaluate the importance of the object of study.

Another conclusion derived from my analyses from several years ago has remained over the passage of time. The institutional design of the private sector in Mexico continues to be the same: practically nothing has changed. The organization of government agencies and the regulatory framework are still in place, anchored without doubt in routine, rejecting some RVOE, but approving the majority. The law has been of little help in encouraging the contrary. It is also clear in this respect that the differentiation of "for profit" or "nonprofit" institutions, in countries like the United States, is not applicable in Mexico.

The system of private higher education operates as a market model, but it is a market with many problems. Noticeable aspects are the asymmetry of information for consumers and in general for other actors in the organizational field; the low barriers to entry and the constant problem of the quality of programs and institutions. The measures the government has implemented in this sense have generated only a reproductive effect of apparently good or bad quality; the description of "quality suppliers" is reaffirmed for some—those who can adhere to old and new indicators that assume better performance; and the generalized idea persists that other, smaller entities are necessarily bad—simply because they are small.

Regarding the issue of quality, the system of evaluation and accreditation promoted by the state and by the private institutions themselves, is added to attempts to regulate the market of institutions of higher education. However, evident in both cases is a process of reproduction of the behavior that the private sector has shown. The participants in these processes are the private institutions of higher education that have the academic, economic, and managerial capacity to do so, while the large set of dispersed institutions of higher education is still relegated to nonparticipation. It is possible to refer to the typical Matthew effect or the notion that the rich get righer and the poor, poorer.

On the other hand, it is necessary to advance in a regulatory framework with a system of control and rendering of accounts that includes both the academic and economic dimensions. It must surpass the vision of an administrative process and follow an integrated institutional design, and it must reevaluate the deficiencies of the current model and the radical positions generated for some by the so-called privatization of higher education. In this sense, it is necessary to consider that although the state is responsible for the nation's higher education, through educational policies, the participation of individuals is necessary in a scenario where government investment has not and will not be sufficient to satisfy the demand for higher education. The central relevance is that such participation must be mediated by a model of coordination and regulation that cannot be the market model since this model, at least in Mexico, has revealed its shortcomings.

NOTES

[1] The phenomenon of massification has been addressed by other authors, by Trow (1987), Clark (1983) and Neave (2001) in the comparative analysis of the configuration of the system of higher education in various countries. Becher and Kogan (1992) propose that two main dimensions characterize the systems of higher education. The first dimension refers to the access that can configure a system according to an elitist model in contrast to a universal model (Trow, 1974, quoted by Becher & Kogan, 1992). Trow (1974) describes the intermediate situation as higher education of the masses. To define the transition between elite systems and massified systems, these authors used in their research the criteria of a rate of schooling of 15% in the post-secondary age group. This limit, however, should be taken with flexibility, especially in the case of developing nations, since it has been employed to study the phenomenon of massification in countries like the United States and Great Britain. The indicator acquires a different meaning where, for example, literacy rates can be relatively high and extended university enrollment is a completely new and different phenomenon when compared with the previous universalizing of elementary education and the massification of secondary education (Brunner, 1990).

[2] The cycle of expansion and reform of higher education, which intensified in the 1970s, corresponds to the policy of educational change promoted during the administration of President Echeverría, and oriented in higher education through the Sistema de Institutos Tecnológicos Regionales throughout Mexico, as well as in the reform of the plans of study of these institutions and the creation of new majors, new institutions, and the institutional modification of existing universities through agreements among universities, primarily through the Asociación Nacional de Universidades e Instituciones de Educación Superior (ANUIES) as an intermediary between the government and universities. This period marked the creation of the Consejo Nacional de Ciencia y Tecnología, Universidad Autónoma Metropolitana, and UNAM's Escuelas Nacionales de Estudios Profesionales. There was also an attempt to broaden educational services beyond major cities and state capitals, although geographical concentration is still a characteristic of the system. Growth was seen in the educational supply, the distribution by area of knowledge and disciplines, the structure by level, and the distribution by type of financing; in other words, an ongoing process of institutional and academic diversification and differentiation (Ibarra, 2001; Luengo, 2003).

[3] Statistics of higher education published by SEP in 2000–2001, consulted in www.sep.gob.mx.

[4] The main shareholder, Raúl Bailléres, consolidated his business leadership in the 1940s by promoting the purchase of various companies and serving as the president of the Asociación de Banqueros de México (1941–1942). In 1941, he presided over the group of Mexican investors that acquired the majority shares of Cervecería Moctezuma, S.A., which had belonged to foreigners. He also directed the financial group that bought the majority shares of El Palacio de Hierro, S.A. and Manantiales Peñafiel, S.A., and participated in the nationalization of Metalúrgica Mexicana Peñoles, S.A. and Compañía Fresnillo, S.A. (www.itam.mx, consulted in 2007).

5. PRONAES appeared in 1984 under the government discourse of educational revolution and with the central purpose of attaining the institutional reorganization of universities, with the assumptions of rationality in the use of resources and improvement of educational quality. PRONAES was not the product of consensus among the main involved actors (universities and state); rather it appeared as an imposition on the universities, and thus lost legitimacy. Neither was it constituted as a program to include the overall development of higher education, since in reality it involved only state universities, while the autonomous universities continued political negotiations for the assignment of resources, and private universities did not even appear. In 1986, PROIDES appeared as part of a change in state strategy toward universities, which considered the importance of the expansion of the private sector. The program, as a planning instrument, attempted to integrate, coordinate, and regulate the various subsystems that formed part of the system of higher education, but through the participation of the involved actors to avoid losing legitimacy, as had occurred with PRONAES. The program's objectives centered on the reorientation of the supply of education, the linking of higher education to national development, and innovation in the functions developed by institutions.
6. The agreement is the result of negotiations carried out within the Uruguay Round of 1986 to 1994. This became the WTO, concerned with the trade of goods (GATT) as well as services (AGCS). The agreements of the OMC and its predecessor, the General Agreement on Trade in Services (GATS), provide the framework for the international trade of goods and services. Theoretically, the objective of both institutions is to strengthen the world economy through greater stability in trade. The basic principle of the current system of international trade is that exported goods and services should be totally free, except for tariffs (Malo, 2003).
7. Some international organizations have voiced their criticism in various declarations. These include the joint statement signed in September of 2001 by several associations, both American and European: *Association of Universities and Colleges of Canada, American Council on Education, European University Association* y *Council for Higher Education Accreditation* (Garcia Guadilla, 2001, 2003).
8. This letter states that the agreement "seriously injures the policies of equity that are indispensable for social balance, especially for developing nations, necessary for correcting social inequalities, and that they have serious consequences for our cultural identity [...] Contributions are made to all of these aspects by higher education, whose specific mission is defined as a conception of public social good, destined to improve the quality of life of our people. A function that in no case can be complied with if it is transformed into simple merchandise or the object of market speculation, through international marketing [...] The serious problems we must mention include the uniformity of education and the grave injury that it represents for national and community sovereignty", in www.grupomontevideo.edu.uy/documentos/carta dePOA.htm, consulted May, 2011.
9. In general, the forms of transnationalization of higher education in Mexico have been the following: a) foreign universities, b) distance education and e-learning, c) franchises, and d) university alliances of domestic and foreign institutions of higher education (Didou, 2002).
10. In 2006, an interview was conducted with a SEP official, who argued that "in the setting of (private) institutions, it happens like that [...]. We cannot say, 'You know what, it turns out that there are already a lot of doctors, a lot of medical schools.' So what should we do? Well, prohibit the private institutions, 'You know you cannot open medical school or law schools, or accounting schools!' 'Why not?' 'Because the state requires schools of agronomy, of marine biology.' So there would be no democracy. (...) What is required is an integral reform of the regulation of higher education in Mexico to homogenize standards and procedures to grant RVOE at the national level, since these mechanisms are different at the federal and state levels. If we tell them no at the federal level, then they go to the state SEP or to another university ...and in many cases they give them to them ..." (Buendía, 2011).

REFERENCES

Acosta, A. (2000). *Estado, políticas y universidades en un periodo de transición* [State, policies and universities in a transition period]. México: Universidad de Guadalajara y Fondo de Cultura Económica.

Altbach, P. (2002) *Educación superior privada* [Private higher education] México, D.F.: Miguel Ángel Porrúa.
Álvarez, G. (2011). El fin de la bonanza. La educación superior privada en México en la primera década del siglo XXI [The end of the boom. Private higher education in Mexico in the first decade of the XXI century]. *Reencuentro*. Análisis de problemas universitarios, no. 60.
Asociación Nacional de Universidades e Instituciones de Educación Superior. (2014). *Anuario estadístico 2014* [Statistics 2014]. México: ANUIES.
Asociación Nacional de Universidades e Instituciones de Educación Superior. (2001). *Anuario estadístico 2000* [Statistics 2000]. México: ANUIES.
Asociación Nacional de Universidades e Instituciones de Educación Superior. (2001). *Anuario estadístico 2001* [Statistics 2001]. México: ANUIES.
Asociación Nacional de Universidades e Instituciones de Educación Superior. (2001). *Anuario estadístico 2012* [Statistics 2012]. México: ANUIES.
Becher, T., & M. Kogan. (1992). *Process and structure in higher education*. London and Nueva York: Routledge.
Brown, R. (2011a). Markets and non-markets. In Roger Brown (Ed.), *Higher education and the market* (pp. 6–19). New York: Routledge.
Brown, R. (2011b). The impact of markets. In Roger Brown (Ed.), *Higher education and the market* (pp. 20–52). New York: Routledge.
Brunner, J. (1990). *Educación superior en América Latina. Cambios y desafíos*. Chile: Fondo de Cultura Económica.
Buendía, A. (2011). Análisis institucional y educación superior. Aportes teóricos y resultados empíricos [Institutional analysis and higher education. Theoretical contributions and empirical results]. *Perfiles Educativos, XXXIII*(134).
Buendía, A. (2013). De rechazados a estudiantes ¿o clientes? en la educación superior privada [Students rejected or customers? in private higher education]. *Semanario LAISUM*, No. 5, http://www.laisumedu.org/showNota.php?idNota=228087, accessed April 12, 2013.
Clark, B. (1983). *El sistema de educación superior. Una visión comparativa de la organización académica* [The higher education system: Academic organization in cross-national perspective]. México: Nueva Imagen.
Didou, S. (2002). Trasnacionalización de la educación superior y aseguramiento de la calidad en México [Transnationalization of higher education and quality assurance in Mexico]. *Revista de la Educación Superior, XXXI* (4)(124), October/December, 11–23.
Federación de Instituciones Mexicanas Particulares de Educación Superior. (2005). *Manual para la aplicación del sistema de acreditación* [Process for the implementation of the accreditation system]. México: FIMPES.
Federación de Instituciones Mexicanas Particulares de Educación Superior. (2014). *Sistema de información* [Information system]. México: FIMPES, http://www.fimpes.org.mx/index.php/reservorio-electronico, accessesd January 12, 2014.
Fielden, E., & Varghese, H. (2009). Regulatory issues. In Svava Bjarnason, Kai-Ming Cheng, John Fielden, Maria-Jose Lemaitre, Daniel Levy, & N. V. Varghese, *A new dynamic: Private higher education*. Word Conference on Higher Education, UNESCO, Paris.
Friedman, M. (1962). *Libertad de elegir. Hacia un nuevo liberalismo económico* [Freedom to choose. Towards a new economic liberalism]. México: Planeta Agostini.
Furedi, F. (2011). Introduction to the marketization of higher education as the students as consumer. In M. Molesworth, R. Scullion & E. Nixon (Eds.), *The marketization of higher education as the students as consumer* (pp. 1–7). Abingdon: Routledge.
García Guadilla, C. (2001). Lo público y lo privado en la educación superior: algunos elementos para el análisis del caso latinoamericano [Public and private higher education: Some elements for analysis of the Latin American case]. *Revista de la Educación Superior, 30*(3) (119), July–September, 39–55.
García Guadilla, C. (2003). Educación superior y AGCS. Interrogantes para el caso de América Latina [Higher education and GATS. Questions for the case of Latin America]. In Carmen García Guadilla

(Ed.), *El difícil equilibrio: la educación superior como bien público y comercio de servicios* [The difficult balance: Higher education as a public good and services trade] (pp. 109–130). Perú: Universidad de Lima-Columbus (Documentos Columbus sobre la Gestión Universitaria).

Geiger, L. R. (1986). *Private sectors in higher education. Structure, function and change in eight countries.* USA: The University of Michigan Press.

Gil Antón, Manuel, de Garay Sánchez, Adrián, Grediaga Kuri, Rocío, Pérez Franco, Lilia, Ángel Casillas Alvarado, Migule, & Rondero López, Norma. (1992). *Académicos. Un botón de muestra* [Academics. A sample button]. México: UAM-A.

Gil Antón, Manuel, de Garay Sánchez, Adrián, Grediaga Kuri, Rocío, Pérez Franco, Lilia, Ángel Casillas Alvarado, Migule, Rondero López, Norma. (1994). *Los rasgos de la diversidad. Un estudio sobre los académicos mexicanos* [The features of diversity. A study of Mexican academics]. México: UAM-A.

Kent, R. (1995). *Regulación de la educación superior en México* [Regulation of Mexican higher education]. México, D.F.: ANUIES.

Kent, R., & Ramírez, Rosalba. (2002). La educación superior privada en México: crecimiento y diferenciación [Private higher education in Mexico: Growth and differentiation]. In P. Altbach (Ed.), *Educación superior privada* (pp. 123–143). México, D.F.: Miguel Ángel Porrúa.

Ibarra, E. (2001). *La universidad en México hoy: gubernamentalidad y modernización* [University in Mexico today: Gubernamentality and modernization]. UNAM, UAM y Unión de Universidades de América Latina.

Instituto Tecnológico Autónomo de México (ITAM). (2007). wwe.itam.mx

Levy, D. (1995). *La educación superior y el Estado en Latinoamérica. Desafíos privados al predominio público* [Higher education and the state in Latin America: Private challenges to public dominance]. México: Centro de Estudios sobre la Universidad y Miguel Ángel Porrúa, México.

Levy, D. (2006). How private higher education's growth challenges the new institutionalism. In Heinz-Dieter Meyer & Brian Rowan (Eds.), *The new institutionalism in education* (pp. 143–162). New York: State University of New York Press, Albany.

Levy, D. (2009). Growth and typology. In Svava Bjarnason, Kai-Ming Cheng, John Fielden, Maria-Jose Lemaitre, Daniel Levy, & N. V. Varghese, *A new dynamic: Private higher education* (pp. 7–27). Paris: UNESCO.

Luengo, E. (2003). *Tendencias de la educación superior en México: una lectura desde la perspectiva de la complejidad* [Trends in higher education in Mexico: A reading from the perspective of complexity]. Paper presented at the Seminario sobre Reformas de la Educación Superior en América Latina y el Caribe, UNESCO IESAC y ASCUN, Bogotá.

Malo, S. (2003). La comercialización de la educación superior [Comercialization of higher education]. In Carmen García Guadilla Carmen (Ed.), *El difícil equilibrio: la educación superior como bien público y comercio de servicios* [The difficult balance: Higher education as a public good and services trade] (pp. 101–108). Perú: Universidad de Lima-Columbus (Documentos Columbus sobre Gestión Universitaria).

Mendoza, J. (2002). *Transición de la educación superior contemporánea en México: de la planeación al estado evaluador* [Transition of contemporary higher education in Mexico: From planning to evaluator state]. México: CESU & Miguel Ángel Porrúa.

Meneses, E. (1993). El modo específico de ser de la Universidad Iberoamericana [The specific mode of being of the Iberoamerican University]. *Cuadernos de Umbral, XXI*(2), 4–12.

Neave, G. (2001). *Educación superior: historia y política. Estudios comparativos sobre la universidad contemporánea* [Higher education: History and politics. Comparative studies on the contemporary university]. Madrid: Gedisa.

Olmos, L. (2001). Puntos sobresalientes de la educación superior particular en el programa nacional de educación 2001–2006 [Issues of higher education in the national education program 2001–2006]. *Revista de la Educación* Superior, *XXXI*(121), January–March, 93–103.

Porter, M. (1985). *La estrategia competitiva* [Competitive strategic]. México: Editorial Continental.

Puga, C. (1999). Las organizaciones empresariales y la educación para la producción [Business organizations and education for production]. In Aurora Loyo (Ed.), *Los actores sociales y la educación* [Social actors and education] (pp. 137–180). México: Plaza & Valdés Editores y UNAM.

Rodríguez Gómez, R. (2004). Inversión extranjera directa en educación superior. El caso de México [Foreign direct investment in higher education. The case of Mexico]. *Revista de la Educación Superior, XXXIII*(2) (130), April–June, 29–48.

Secretaría de Educación Pública (SEP). (1989). Programa para la modernización educativa (1989–1994) [Educative modernization program (1989–1994)] (pp. 123–143). México: SEP.

Secretaría de Educación Pública (SEP). (2002). Estadísticas de la educación superior publicadas por la SEP en 2000–2001 [Statistics of higher education published by SEP in 2000–2001]. México: SEP.

Secretaría de Educación Pública (SEP) CONAEDU. (2010). *La participación de las instituciones educativas particulares y el sistema educativo nacional* [Participation of private higher institutions and national educative system]. México: SEP-CONAEDU, March.

Secretaría de Educación Pública (SEP). (2016). Acuerdo 279 [Law 279]. Available from http://www.sirvoes.sep.gob.mx/sirvoes/doc_pdf/ACUERDO%20279%20rvoe.pdf, accessed July 4, 2016.

Tirado, R. (1999). La cúpula empresarial en el debate educativo [Business leaders in the educational debate]. In Aurora Loyo (Ed.), *Los actores sociales y la educación* [Social actors and education] (pp. 137–180). México: Plaza & Valdés Editores & UNAM.

Trow, M. (1974). Problems in the transition from elite to mass higher education. In Ocde (comp.), *Policies for higher education. General report on the Conference on Future Structures of Post-Secondary Education* (pp. 51–101). París: OECD.

Trow, M. (1987). The analysis of status. In Burton R. Clark (Ed.), *Perspectives on higher education. Eighth disciplinary and comparative views*. Los Angeles: University of California Press Berkeley.

Angélica Buendía Espinosa
Universidad Autónoma Metropolitana (UAM)
Xochimilco Campus, Mexico City

VANESSA DE OLIVEIRA ANDREOTTI

8. EDUCATION, KNOWLEDGE AND THE RIGHTING OF WRONGS

[T]he world we live in is shaped far less by what we celebrate and mythologize than by the painful events we try to forget.
(Hochschild, 1999, p. 294)

INTRODUCTION

In this chapter, I present three metaphors or narratives that unapologetically raise "a thousand questions" about education and do not provide any clear cut answers. My intention is to raise the stakes in our collective struggle with the joys, challenges and dilemmas involved in enacting education beyond historical patterns that have cultivated unsustainable and harmful forms of collective relationships and have limited human possibilities for imagining (and doing) otherwise. My own focus in this chapter is concerned particularly with the urgency of imagining education in ways that can pluralize possibilities for relationships in the present with a view of pluralizing possibilities for collective futures (Nandy, 2000) that may enable a "non-coercive relationship with the excluded 'Other' of Western humanism" (Gandhi, 1998, p. 39).

I start from the assumption that certain features of modernity and humanism itself, which we often cherish as sacred grounds for our interpretations of social justice, *paradoxically create the conditions of injustice we are trying to address*. This does not mean we should dismiss or abandon these concepts altogether. The idea is to understand their limitations as well as their gifts in order to stretch possibilities for thinking and living together precisely based on the humanist idea that it is our responsibility (especially at the university) to question received wisdom, in this case, the historicity and limitations of democracy, human rights, development individualism, freedom, secularism, etc.): we can 'step up' beyond the simplistic acceptance of given concepts (without throwing them away), and take responsibility to open up new possibilities for the future—this is explored further in the third metaphor (see for example Quijano, 1997; Gandhi, 1998; Mignolo, 2000; Maldonado-Torres, 2004; Souza Santos, 2007; Souza, 2011; Hoofd, 2012).

The body of literature I draw on (postcolonial, decolonial, critical race and indigenous studies) problematises the ethnocentric and hegemonic effects of key Enlightenment principles that are the foundations of modernity, such as rational unanimity in regard to conceptualizations of humanity, human nature, progress, and justice, as well as Cartesian, teleological anthropocentric and dialectical reasoning (see Andreotti, 2011a; Andreotti & Souza, 2011).

I agree with Mignolo's proposition that modernity's "shine" (i.e., its "light" side represented in moral progress, freedom, rights, citizenship, Nation States, Protestant work ethic, property ownership, universal reason, representational democracy, etc.) is only historically possible and presently sustainable through its "shadow" (i.e. its "darker" side of colonialism, continuous exploitation, dispossession, destitution and genocide). The emphasis on modernity's shine depends on a constitutive denial, or an active sanctioned ignorance, of its shadow. Inayatullah and Blaney argue that while the empirical agenda of progressive ethical advance takes precedence in achieving modernity's sparkly goals, the continuous epistemic, cognitive, structural, economic, cultural and military violences necessary for this endeavour are placed securely in the past, as collateral damage, to liberate the future for the shiny heroic entrepreneurship and allegedly un-coercive leadership of those who can head humanity towards its imagined destiny, which becomes a "teleological alibi for death and destruction" (Inayatullah & Blaney, 2012, p. 170).

In proposing a serious engagement with the idea of the two faces of modernity (i.e. its shine and shadow), I acknowledge the difficulties of engaging in polarized orientations that embrace or reject modernity wholesale and dismiss the complexity, provisionality and contingency of different positions. I propose that the grey area in between unexamined embraces or rejections needs much further exploration. In this chapter, however, I focus on positions concerned with the exclusionary effects of "epistemic blindness" (Souza Santos, 2007) caused by the colonization of the imagination through education itself (including its progressive forms).

EDUCATION AND THE EXPANSION OF IMAGINAGION

In order to illustrate such effects, I will invite readers to construct the first metaphor with me: imagine a field of corn, harvest your cobs and peel off the husks. Place your corn cobs in front of you and compare them with the picture at the end of this chapter, page 138 below (Andreotti, 2011a). My argument is that, in the same way that our experiences and imagination have been colonised by one variety of corn cob (i.e. yellow), our over-socialisation in modes of being enchanted by modernity (epitomised in schooling itself) creates a condition of epistemic blindness where we see ourselves as autonomous, individuated and self-sufficient beings inhabiting a knowable and controllable world moving "forward" in a direction that we already know and contribute to (Andreotti, 2011b). From this perspective, we are able to describe the world and define for others the best pathway for their development. This is different from, for example, seeing ourselves as non-individuated, co-dependent in relation to each other and insufficient before a complex, uncertain and plural world moving towards contestable "forwards." This attachment to and investment in individual autonomy/independence, self-sufficiency and a single collective "forward" is precisely what produces the idea of difference as a deficit rather than a necessary productive and creative force as many have suggested before. Audrey Lorde (1979) indicates that in order to address the problems created by this conceptualization of self/other, difference must be seen as something different:

> Difference must be [seen] as a fund of necessary polarities between which our creativity can spark... Only then does the necessity for interdependency become unthreatening. Only within that interdependency of different strengths, acknowledged and equal, can the power to seek new ways of being in the world generate, as well as the courage and sustenance to act *where there are no charters*. Within the interdependence of mutual differences lies that security which enables us to descend into the chaos of knowledge and return with true visions of our future, along with the concomitant power to effect those changes which can bring that future into being. Difference is that raw and powerful connection from which our personal power is forged. (Lorde, 1979)

In translating these insights into educational thinking, I have found Spivak's (2004) work extremely enabling as a pedagogical compass (rather than a map). Her insistence on hyper-self-reflexivity, self-implication, accountable reasoning, and learning to unlearn, to listen and to be taught by the world have expanded possibilities for what I can do/feel and think as a teacher and as a "relation" (Spivak, 2004). Hyper-self-reflexivity involves a constant engagement with three things: (a) the social, cultural and historical conditioning of our thinking and of knowledge/power production; (b) the limits of knowing, of language and of our senses in apprehending reality; and (c) the non-conscious dynamics of affect (the fact that our traumas, fears, desires and attachments affect our decisions in ways that we often cannot identify). Self-implication entails an acute awareness of our complicity in historical and global harm through our inescapable investments in violent systems, such as modernity and capitalism.

In this sense, two of Spivak's ideas in particular have sparked very challenging questions and interesting possibilities: the idea of "*education as an uncoercive rearrangement of desires*" (Spivak, 2004, p. 526) and the idea that this education should aim towards an "*ethical imperative to relate to the Other, before will*" (p. 535). Both ideas acknowledge that the problems of unexamined investments in harmful systems cannot be addressed in education through cognition alone.

Questions that emerged from these two "simple" assertions include: How on earth can one *uncoercively* enable a "*re-arrangement of desires*" that may command an imperative for an ethical responsibility toward the Other, "*before will*"? How can a pedagogy of self-reflexivity, self-implication, dissensus, and discomfort support people to go beyond denial and feelings of shame, guilt, or deceit (Taylor, 2011)? How is an education based on uncoercive rearrangement of desires different from transmissive, "transformative" or "emancipatory" education? How can one ethically and professionally address the hegemony, ethnocentrism, ahistoricism, depoliticization, paternalism, and deficit theorization of difference that abound in

133

educational approaches benevolently concerned with helping, fixing, defending, educating, assimilating, or giving voice to the Other (Andreotti, 2011a)? How could a pedagogy address the arrogance of the "consciousness of superiority lodged in the self" (Spivak, 2004, p. 534), *including my own*? How can we learn from social breakdowns in ways that might open ourselves to ethical obligations (Pinar, 2009; Pitt & Britzman, 2003; Zembylas, 2010) and to being taught by the world (Biesta, 2012)? How can one theorize learners, teaching, and learning in ways that take account of power relations, of the complexity of the construction of the self and of alterity, and of the situatedness and the limits of my own constructions and theorizations?

These questions also raise further issues in relation to knowing and acting in the context of righting wrongs through education. I will explore some of those issues through my second and third metaphors.

EDUCATION AS A VEHICLE FOR SOCIAL TRANSFORMATION

A common "feel good" teaching practice that I have often found in my field of study and work is an activity where a teacher educator gets student teachers to identify what is wrong with the world, what they imagine an ideal world would look like and what people should do to make things right. In most cases student teachers in the contexts I have witnessed come up with ideas related to pollution, homelessness, violence, poverty, destruction and (less often) discrimination as examples of "wrongness". Next, symbols of flowers, clean streets peace, harmony, nuclear families, children and people holding hands for "rightness", and, finally, education (as knowledge transmission) is imagined as a means to get from wrong to right. Invariably, the assumption seems to be that "wrongness" is a result of ignorance or immorality, not of knowledge, and that once people have the right piece of information or have acquired "appropriate" values, their patterns of behaviour and relationships will magically change. In the context of teacher pre-service education or professional development, I have seen this exercise being used to introduce curriculum guidelines that justify or mandate the inclusion of themes like global citizenship, conflict resolution, human rights, peace, or environmental education as part of the curriculum. In a similar way, the assumption on the part of policy makers and teacher educators seems to be that by delivering the right mandate or policy information, teachers and student teachers will immediately change their practices to include the new themes in the curriculum. I have seen many teacher educators frustrated when this does not happen, but assumptions about learning, knowledge, and teaching – and the effectiveness of the methodology used in this exercise – are seldom questioned.

What I would like to suggest is that the righting of wrongs in the world through education, from the perspective I propose today, requires us to think about the connections between "rights" and "wrongs" in a very different way. Perhaps a starting point is a shift in the understanding of knowledge from "knowledge versus ignorance" toward "every knowledge is also an ignorance" (of other knowledges).

The body of literature I draw on affirms that *"wrongs" are caused by knowledge too*. The "every knowledge is an ignorance" approach requires an understanding of how knowledges are produced, how they relate to power and how they may shape subjectivities and relationships in conscious and non-conscious ways. This shift in conceptualization on its own would change the exercise considerably. For example: after identifying "wrongs," participants could be invited to perform an analysis of what (socially, culturally, and historically situated) systems of knowledge/power production produce such wrongs; after identifying "rights" they would be invited to analyse what kinds of systems of knowledge production produce the possibilities for the "rights" they are able to imagine, and what kinds of ignorance could block their imagination to other possible "rights", or make their own knowledge systems complicit in the production of the wrongs they intend to right.

This, in turn, would shift the question of methodology of righting wrongs significantly too: if education is the means to right wrongs, what kind of education could take account of the complexity, multiplicity, complicity, and inequality inherent in the politics of knowledge production (including those happening through education itself)? What kind of education could support us to undo (at a deep psychic level, beyond surface cognition) the legacy of knowledges that make us blindly complicit in perpetuating wrongs? What kind of education could enable the emergence of ethical relationships between those who have historically marginalized and those who have been marginalized, moving beyond guilt, anger, salvationism, triumphalism, paternalism, and self- interest? What kind of education could equip us to work in solidarity with one another in the construction of "yet-to- come" collective futures in ways that do not require enforced or manufactured consensus? What kind of education could help us find comfort and hope in precisely "not having absolute answers" and being frequently challenged in our encounters with difference?

EDUCATION FOR "SAVING CHILDREN"

My third metaphor evokes the image of a river with a strong current. If a group of people saw many young children drowning in this river, their first impulse would probably be to try to save them or to search for help. But what if they looked up the river and saw many boats throwing the children in the water and these boats were multiplying by the minute? How many different tasks would be necessary to stop the boats and prevent this from happening again? I suggest there are at least four tasks: rescuing the children in the water, stopping the boats from throwing the children in the water, going to the villages of the boat crew to understand why this is happening in the first place, and collecting the bodies of those who have died – honoring the dead by remembering them and raising awareness of what happened. In deciding what to do, people would need to remember that some rescuing techniques may not work in the conditions of the river, and that some strategies to stop the boats may invite or fuel even more boats to join the fleet – they may even realize that they are actually in one of the boats, throwing children in the water with one hand and trying to rescue them with the other hand.

Therefore, education should help people in the task of learning to "go up the river" to the roots of the problem so that the emergency strategies down the river can be better informed in the hope that one day no more boats will throw children in the water. Going up the river involves asking essential, difficult and often disturbing begged questions that may implicate rescuers in the reproduction of harm and expose how self-serving practices can be disguised as altruism. Questions such as: How is poverty *created*? How come different lives have different value? What are the relationships between social groups that are over-exploited and social groups that are over-exploiting? How are these relationships maintained? How do people justify inequalities and dominance? What are the roles of schooling in the reproduction and contestation of inequalities in society? When do institutionalized initiatives, such as the human rights declaration or military interventions, become helpful in promoting justice and when do they worsen or create new problems? How would people respond if they realized that bringing justice to others meant going against national or local economic and cultural interests? How are Nation States – and nationalism – implicated in the proliferation of divisions, fragmentations, fundamentalisms and inequalities? How have cherished humanist ideals contributed to the dispossession, destitution, exploitation and extermination of peoples and the destruction of ecological balance?

Through this metaphor, I propose that education is about preparing ourselves and those we work with to enlarge possibilities for thinking and living together in a finite planet that sustains complex, plural, uncertain, inter-dependent and unequal societies. In order to do this, we need an attitude of *sceptical optimism* or *hopeful scepticism* (as opposed to *naïve hope* or *dismissive scepticism*) in order to stretch the legacy of frameworks we have inherited. In simpler language, perhaps we need:

- to understand and learn from repeated historical patterns of mistakes, in order to open the possibilities for new mistakes to be made
- more complex social analyses acknowledging that if we understand the problems and the reasons behind them in simplistic ways, we may do more harm than good
- to recognize how we are implicated or complicit in the problems we are trying to address: how we are all both part of the problem and the solution (in different ways)
- to learn to enlarge our referents for reality and knowledge, acknowledging the gifts and limitations of every knowledge system and moving beyond "*either ors*" towards "*both and mores*"
- to remember that the paralysis and guilt we may feel when we start to engage with the complexity of issues of inequality are just temporary as they may come from our own education/socialization in protected/sheltered environments, which create the desire for things to be simple, easy, happy, ordered and under control.

Hopefully, once we go up the river together we will be able to come down and address the issue of justice as an on-going agonistic conversation that is going to be really difficult, but that we cannot shy away from. Going up the river is necessary for substantially committing this conversation to a form of radical democracy that moves beyond practices embedded in historical patterns of

- Hegemony (justifying superiority and supporting domination)
- Ethnocentrism (projecting one view, one "forward", as universal)
- Ahistoricism (forgetting historical legacies and complicities)
- Depoliticization (disregarding power inequalities and ideological roots of analyses and proposals)
- Salvationism (framing help as the burden of the fittest)
- Un-complicated solutions (offering easy solutions that do not require systemic change)
- Paternalism (seeking affirmation of superiority through the provision of help) (Andreotti, 2012, p. 2).

However, if we take seriously Spivak's (2004) calls for hyper-self-reflexivity and a commitment to the Other "before will", we need to become affectively accountable for the new and old problems our social justice solutions may engender. This for me means changing again the questions we ask, for example:

- How can we address hegemony without creating new hegemonies through our own forms of resistance?
- How can we address ethnocentrism without falling into absolute relativism and forms of essentialism and anti-essentialism that reify elitism?
- How can we address ahistoricism without fixing a single perspective of history to simply reverse hierarchies and without being caught in a self-sustaining narrative of vilification and victimisation?
- How can we address depoliticization without high-jacking political agendas for self-serving ends and without engaging in self- empowering critical exercises of generalisation, homogenisation and dismissal of antagonistic positions?
- How can we address salvationism without crushing generosity and altruism?
- How can we address people's tendency to want simplistic solutions without producing paralysis and hopelessness?
- How can we address paternalism without closing opportunities for short-term redistribution?

The ethical responsibility towards the other "before will" poses a series of intense and tough demands. It requires us to have the courage, strength, confidence *and* humility to rise to the challenges and difficulties that these questions create; it commands that we educate ourselves to become comfortable with the discomfort of the uncertainties inherent in living the plurality of existence; and it calls us to become inspired and excited by the new possibilities opened by unchartered spaces, processes and encounters that do not offer any pre-determined scripts or guarantees. How do we teach for that? And how do we prepare ourselves to teach for that given that we have been over-socialised in forms of education that go exactly in the opposite direction of finding personal comfort and security in certainties (unequivocal fixed knowledge, right/wrong answers), conformity (external validation), subtle deference to institutional authorities, and unexamined ideas of autonomous and independent thinking?

Corn cobs image (first metaphor) kindly offered by Nella de La Fuente

EDUCATION FOR "CULTIVATING HUMANITY"

Sharon Todd (2009) warns us against common sense conceptualizations of humanity as "goodness", something to be cultivated, constructed in contrast with violence (or "evil") conceptualized as "inhuman", something to be eliminated. She argues that such conceptualizations fail to recognize humanity's complexity, pluralism and imperfection and that an education for facing humanity would be more productive in addressing ethical questions related to our collective suffering and connections with each other.

Jacqui Alexander (2005) suggests the idea of dismemberment as an alternative insight on questions of violence and inter-dependence. She states that:

> [S]ince colonisation has produced fragmentation and dismemberment at both the material and psychic levels, there is a yearning for wholeness, often expressed as a yearning to belong, a yearning that is both material and existential, both psychic and physical, and which, when satisfied, can subvert, and ultimately displace the pain of dismemberment. (Alexander, 2005, p. 281)

She suggests that strategies of membership in coalitions, like those of citizenship, community, family, political movement, nationalism and solidarity in identity or ideology, although important, have probably not addressed the source of this yearning (Alexander, 2005). For Alexander, these coalitions have reproduced the very fragmentation and separation that she identifies as the root of the problem. She states that the source of this yearning is a "deep knowing that we are in fact interdependent – neither separate, nor autonomous" (Alexander, 2005, p. 282). She explains:

> As human beings we have a sacred connection to each other, and this is why enforced separations wreak havoc in our Souls. There is a great danger then, in living lives of segregation. Racial segregation. Segregation in politics. Segregated frameworks. Segregated and compartmentalised selves. What we have devised as an oppositional politics has been necessary, but it will never sustain us, for a while it may give us some temporary gains (which become more ephemeral the greater the threat, which is not a reason not to fight), it can never ultimately feed that deep place within us: that space of the erotic, that space of the Soul, that space of the Divine. (Alexander, 2005, p. 282)

Since contemporary theoretical discussions have conceptualized hostility either as a natural human response or an effect of discourse, it may be useful to think about it a little differently. Echoing Alexander's (2005), Todd's (2009), and Duran's (2006) concerns for shifting root metaphors, my last set of questions refers to education as a host and/or a medicine for social diseases:

- *What if* racism, sexism, classicism, nationalism and other forms of toxic, parasitic and highly contagious viral divisions are preventable social diseases?
- *What if* the medicine involves coming to terms with our violent histories, being taught to see through the eyes of others (as impossible as it sounds), and facing humanity (in our own selves first) in all its complexity, affliction and imperfection: agonistically embracing everyone's capacity for love, hatred, compassion, harm, goodwill, envy, joy, anger, oppression, care, selfishness, selflessness, avarice, kindness, enmity, solidarity, malice, benevolence, arrogance, humility, narcissism, altruism, greed, generosity, contempt *and* reverence?
- *What if* our holy texts (both religious, activist and academic), our education (both formal and informal), our politics and agency, and our ways of knowing and being

have carried both the mutant virus that spreads the disease and the medicine that prevents it?
- *What if* learning to distinguish between toxins, viruses and medicines involves disciplining our minds, bodies, psyches, and spirits by confronting our traumas and letting go of fears of scarcity, loneliness, worthlessness and guilt (generated precisely by the imperative for autonomy/independence, self-sufficiency and control)? What if we have to learn to trust each other without guarantees?
- *What if* the motivation to survive alongside each other in our finite planet in dynamic balance (without written agreements, coercive enforcements or assurances) will come precisely through being taught collectively *by the disease itself*?
- *What knowledge would be enough, what education would be appropriate, and what possibilities would be opened, then?*

ACKNOWLEDGEMENTS

A previous version of this chapter was presented in a Featured Presidential Session of the 2013 AERA meeting on April 16 in Vancouver, with Crain Soudien and Sarada Gopalan, entitled: Knowing Enough to Act: The Educational Implications of a Critical Social Justice Approach to Difference. A previous version of this chapter appeared in the open-access journal *Other Education. The Journal of Educational Alternatives*, Vol. 1:1, pp. 19–31 (2012). This version printed with permission of the author.

REFERENCES

Alexander, J. (2005). *Pedagogies of crossing: Meditations on feminism, sexual politics, memory and the sacred*. Durham, NC & London: Duke University.
Andreotti, V. (2011a). *Actionable postcolonial theory in education*. New York, NY: Palgrave Macmillan.
Andreotti, V. (2011b). (Towards) decoloniality and diversality in global citizenship education. *Globalisation, Societies and Education, 9*(3–4), 381–397.
Andreotti, V. (2012). Editor's preface: HEADS UP. *Critical Literacy: Theories and Practices, 6*(1), 1–3.
Andreotti, V., & Souza, L. (Eds.). (2011). *Postcolonial perspectives on global citizenship education*. New York, NY: Routledge.
Biesta, G. (2012). Receiving the gift of teaching: From 'learning from' to 'being taught by.' *Studies in Philosophy and Education, 32*(5), 449–461. doi:10.1007/s11217-012-9312-9
Duran, E. (2006). *Healing the soul wound: Counseling with American Indians and other native peoples*. New York, NY: Teachers College Press.
Gandhi, L. (1998). *Postcolonial theory: A critical introduction*. New York, NY: Columbia University Press.
Hochschild, A. (1999). *King Leopold's ghost: A story of greed, terror, and heroism in Colonial Africa*. New York, NY: Houghton Mifflin.
Hoofd, I. (2012). *Ambiguities of activism: Alter-globalism and the imperatives of speed*. New York, NY: Routledge.
Inayatullah, N., & Blaney, D. (2012). The dark heart of kindness: The social construction of deflection. *International Studies Perspectives, 13*(2), 164–175.

Lorde, A. (1979). *The master's tools will never dismantle the master's house.* Comments at 'the personal and the political' panel, Second Sex conference, USA. Retrieved May 10, 2011, from http://www.historyisaweapon.com/defcon1/lordedismantle.html

Maldonado-Torres, N. (2004). The topology of being and the geopolitics of knowledge: Modernity, empire, coloniality. *City, 8*(1), 29–56.

Mignolo, W. (2000). *Local histories/global designs: Essays on the coloniality of power, subaltern knowledges and border thinking.* Princeton, NJ: Princeton University Press.

Nandy, A. (2000). Recovery of indigenous knowledge and dissenting futures of the university. In S. Inayatullah & J. Gidley (Eds.), *The university in transformation: Global perspectives and the future of the university* (pp. 115–123). Westport, CT: Greenwood Publishing.

Pinar, W. F. (2009). *The worldliness of a cosmopolitan education: Passionate lives in public service.* New York, NY: Routledge.

Pitt, A., & Britzman, D. (2003). Speculations on qualities of difficult knowledge in teaching and learning: an experiment in psychoanalytic research. *International Journal of Qualitative Studies in Education, 16*(6), 755–776.

Quijano, A. (1997). Colonialidad del poder, cultura y conocimiento en América Latina. *Anuario Mariateguiano, 9*(9), 113–122.

Souza, L. (2011). Engaging the global by resituating the local: (Dis)locating the literate global subject and his view from nowhere. In V. Andreotti & L. de Souza (Eds.), *Postcolonial perspectives on global citizenship education* (pp. 68–83). New York, NY: Routledge.

Souza Santos, B. (2007). Beyond abyssal thinking: From global lines to ecologies of knowledges. *Eurozine.* Retrieved February 27, 2012, from http://www.euro zine.com/articles/2007-06-29-santos-en.html

Spivak, G. (2004). Righting wrongs. *The South Atlantic Quarterly, 103*(2/3), 523–581.

Taylor, L. (2011). Beyond paternalism: Global education with preservice teachers as a practice of implication. In V. Andreotti & L. de Souza (Eds.), *Postcolonial perspectives on global citizenship education* (pp. 177–199). New York, NY: Routledge.

Todd, S. (2009). *Toward an imperfect education: Facing humanity, rethinking, cosmopolitanism.* London: Paradigm.

Zembylas, M. (2010). Racialization/ethnicization of school emotional spaces: The politics of resentment. *Race Ethnicity and Education, 13*(2), 253–270.

Vanessa de Oliveira Andreotti
Department of Educational Studies
University of British Columbia

LIST OF CONTRIBUTORS

THE EDITORS

Macleans A. Geo-JaJa is Professor of Economics and Education at Brigham Young University, where he directs the Research Program in Poverty, Development, and Globalization. He received his doctorate in economics from the University of Utah. He has taught at University of Port Harcourt, Nigeria and the University of Utah. He is the recipient of the prestigious Carnegie Foundation Fellowship and the Fulbright Senior Specialist Fellowship. His research interests is on rights in education as an agent of inclusive development, and the effectiveness of rights-capability based approach in nested equity, education poverty and development in post-2015. For the past ten years, in advocating for principled socio-economic change that solidified development with security, he has worked beneath the rhetoric of development to explore necessary hard choices needed. He is an editorial consulting board member of the UNESCO, *International Review of Education Journal* and many others. Geo-JaJa has done on-site research and program work in many countries of the Global North and Global South, and is a consultant to the World Bank, the United Nations Development Program (UNDP), USAID, and the Department for International Development (DFID).
Email: Geo-JaJa @byu.edu

Suzanne Majhanovich is Professor Emerita/Adjunct Research Professor at the Faculty of Education, Western University n London, Ontario, Canada. She is the past Chair of the WCCES Standing Committee for Publications and the former editor of the journal *Canadian and International Education*. With Allan Pitman and Miguel Pereyra she is the co-editor of the Series *A Diversity of Voices* published by Sense. She has served as guest editor of four special issues of the *International Review of Education* related to presentations from the World Congresses of Education held in Havana, Cuba; Sarajevo, Bosnia; Istanbul, Turkey and Buenos Aires, Argentina. Her research interests inclue first and second language acquisition, the teaching of English as a Foreign Language in international contexts, globalization, education restructuring, decentralization and privatization of education. She is the author of numerous articles and books, and most recently has co-edited with Susana Gonçalves *Art and Intercultural Dialogue,* published by Sense (2016).
Email: smajhano@uwo.ca

THE AUTHORS

Vanessa de Oliveira Andreotti is a Canada Research Chair in Race, Inequalities and Global Change at the University of British Columbia. Her scholarship focuses on analyses of historical and systemic patterns of reproduction of inequalities

and how these limit or enable possibilities for collective and global change especially in educational contexts). Her research background is inter-disciplinary and informed by postcolonial, (post)critical decolonial and poststructural theories. Her research focus is on building bridges between contemporary theory and debates around globalization and diversity and pedagogical practices. She is the author of numerous books, chapters and refereed articles, including most recently "Towards Different Conversations about the Internationalization of Higher Education (*Comparative and International Education,* Vol. 45:1, 2016), co-authored with S. Stein, J. Bruce and R. Suša. Originally from Brazil, she has taught at the Universities of Oulu, Finland, Canterbury, Ireland and Nottingham, UK before moving to Canada.
Email: vanessa.andreotti@ubc.ca

Nazia Bano is a 2015 PhD graduate in Educational Studies from the University of Western Ontario. She started her career as a Research Officer in a CIDA funded research based company in Karachi, Pakistan. As a Research Advisor, she worked with youth of tribal communities in Balochistan, Pakistan. She led a development education project of "Formation of School Management Committees in 13 districts of Sindh, Pakistan. Since 2015, she has been working as a Research Associate with local organizations in London, Ontario, Canada. Her research interests include alternative practices of development education in South Asia, youth empowerment in indigenous and immigrant communities, transformative pedagogics, peace education.
Email: nbano@uwo.ca

Angélica Buendía Espinosa is a researcher at the Universidad Autónoma Metropolitana, Unidad Xochimilco. Her lines of research are "Processes of institutionalization and change in higher education", "Institutional analysis of the Mexican university system" and "Study and comparative analysis of public policies in public and private higher education". She is a member of the National System of Researchers and of the Mexican Council for Educational Research, body and currently serves as a member of the Steering Committee, term 2013–2015. Her most recent chapters, articles and books are: "Change or continuity in the Mexican private sector? The case of Laureate – the University of the Valley of Mexico", "Genealogía de la evaluación y acreditación de instituciones en México", "Liderazgo de los rectores frente a la "tercera misión" de la universidad: visiones globales, miradas locales, en colaboración con Rosalba Badillo y Georg Krücken".

Her most recent books are: *La FIMPES y la mejora de la calidad en instituciones privadas. Cambio, prestigio y legitimidad. Tres estudios de caso (1994–2004)* and *Evaluación y acreditación de programas: revisar los discursos, valorar los efectos. El caso de cinco universidades públicas mexicanas.*
Email: a.buendia0531@gmail.com

LIST OF CONTRIBUTORS

Enver Motala is an Adjunct Professor at the Nelson Mandela Metropolitan University, a researcher at the Nelson Mandela Institute for Education and Rural Development, University of Fort Hare, East London and a research associate at the Centre for Education Rights and Transformation at the University of Johannesburg. He was a regional co-ordinator of SACHED Trust, the director of the Macro-Economic Policy Unit and a deputy-director of the Gauteng Department of Education. He is currently a member of the Councils of the University of South Africa (UNISA) and Rhodes University and a member of the editorial board of the Human Sciences Research Council. Motala works on various projects for the Education Policy Consortium (EPC), and co-edited a book *Education, Economy and Society* (UNISA Press, 2014) with Salim Vally. His scholarly interests include education policy and implementation, community education and the relationship between work, education and training.
Email: emotala1@gmail.com

Carlos Ornelas is a professor of Education and Communications at the Universidad Autónoma Metropolitana (UAM) Xochimilco Campus, in Mexico City. His teaching experience includes being a Visiting Professor at Hiroshima University (2014); Visiting Professor of Comparative Education and Transcultural Studies at Teacher College Columbia University (2008–2009); and Visiting Lecturer and Fulbright Scholar at Harvard University Graduate School of Education (1986–1987). He earned a Ph.D. in Education from Stanford University in 1980; and a MA in International Education from Stanford University in 1978.

He is the author of five books as a single author; editor of nine other books; 46 chapters in academic compilations; 33 articles in professional journals (in Spanish, English, and French). Also, he authored 83 reviews, extended essays reviews, and other professional articles. He is also the author of 22 additional unpublished policy and research reports. He writes two columns per week in Excélsior, a Mexican national newspaper.
Email: carlosornelasnavarro@outlook.com

Nicholas Sun-keung Pang is Professor and Chairman of the Department of Educational Administration and Policy at the Chinese University of Hong Kong Shatin, N.T., Hong Kong SAR, China. He is also the Director of the Hong Kong Centre for the Development of Educational Leadership (HKCDEL). Professor Pang specializes in educational administration, management and leadership, as well as school effectiveness and improvement. He is a sought after presenter and keynote speaker, and has published widely, locally and internationally, with five books, as well as numerous book chapters and internationally refereed journal articles. He is Co-author of an academic book entitled *Leadership and Management in Education: Developing Essential Skills and Competencies* (2003); Editor of an academic book entitled *Globalization: Educational Research, Change and Reforms* (2006); and Co-

LIST OF CONTRIBUTORS

Editor of another academic book entitled *East-West Perspectives on Educational Leadership and Policy* (2015).
Email: nskpang@cuhk.edu.hk

Xavier Rambla is Associate Professor of Sociology at the University Autònoma de Barcelona, Spain. He has researched globalization, education and inequalities by leading projects on Education for All in Latin America as well as on education and anti-poverty policies in the Southern Cone, by collaborating on projects in education and social cohesion in Europe and by participating in critical coeducational action research in several regions in Spain. He has been a visiting lecturer in a number of European and Latin American universities. He has authored several books, reports and articles including "La desigualidad que no cesa (2006), The SDGS and inclusive education for all. From Special Education to addressing social inequalities. Briefing Paper, Austrian Foundation for Development Research (OFSE) 14. Open access on OFSE site; and "A Complex web of education borrowing and transfer. Education for All and the Plan for Development of Education in Brazil. *Comparative Education Vol. 50*(4), pp. 417–432.
Email: xrm1966@gmail.com/Xavier.rambla@uab.cat

Salim Vally is the director of the Centre for Education Rights and Transformation, an Associate Professor at the Faculty of Education, University of Johannesburg and a Visiting Professor at the Nelson Mandela Metropolitan University.

Vally was a visiting lecturer at Columbia and York universities. His academic interests include education and social policy as these relate to social class, transformation and social justice; critical and liberatory pedagogies; and extensive involvement in action research and interdisciplinary and comparative approaches to critically examining education policy. Vally co-edited a book *Education, Economy and Society* (UNISA Press, 2014) with Enver Motala.

He serves on the editorial boards of a number of academic journals including *Education as Change*, the *McGill Journal of Education* and the *Journal for Critical Education Policy Studies* and is on the board of various global organisations such as the Right to Education (RTE) and a 'Critical Friend' of Education International (EI).
Email: svally@uj.ac.za

Xinyi Wu is a visiting faculty member at Brigham Young University in Provo, UT. She received her Ph.D. in Comparative and International Development Education from the University of Minnesota-Twin Cities. Her research interests include economics of education, cultural foundations of education, and language and education. She is particularly interested in the issues of ethnicity, ethnic identity, and their relationship with educational equality and quality. She has conducted fieldwork in China, especially on the Chinese Muslim population. She also participated in projects for disadvantaged youth in Africa. Her recent publications include comparative studies

of educational policies for China and Vietnam, Chinese ethnic minority students' access to higher education, and state schooling and religious education in China. She is currently working on a book manuscript on Chinese Muslim students' constructions and negotiations of identities amidst poverty and modernity.
Email: Xinyi_wu@byu.edu

CPSIA information can be obtained
at www.ICGtesting.com
Printed in the USA
BVOW06s2144081116
467303BV00006B/51/P

9 789463 007276